MW01412021

THOMAS A. FINLAY SJ

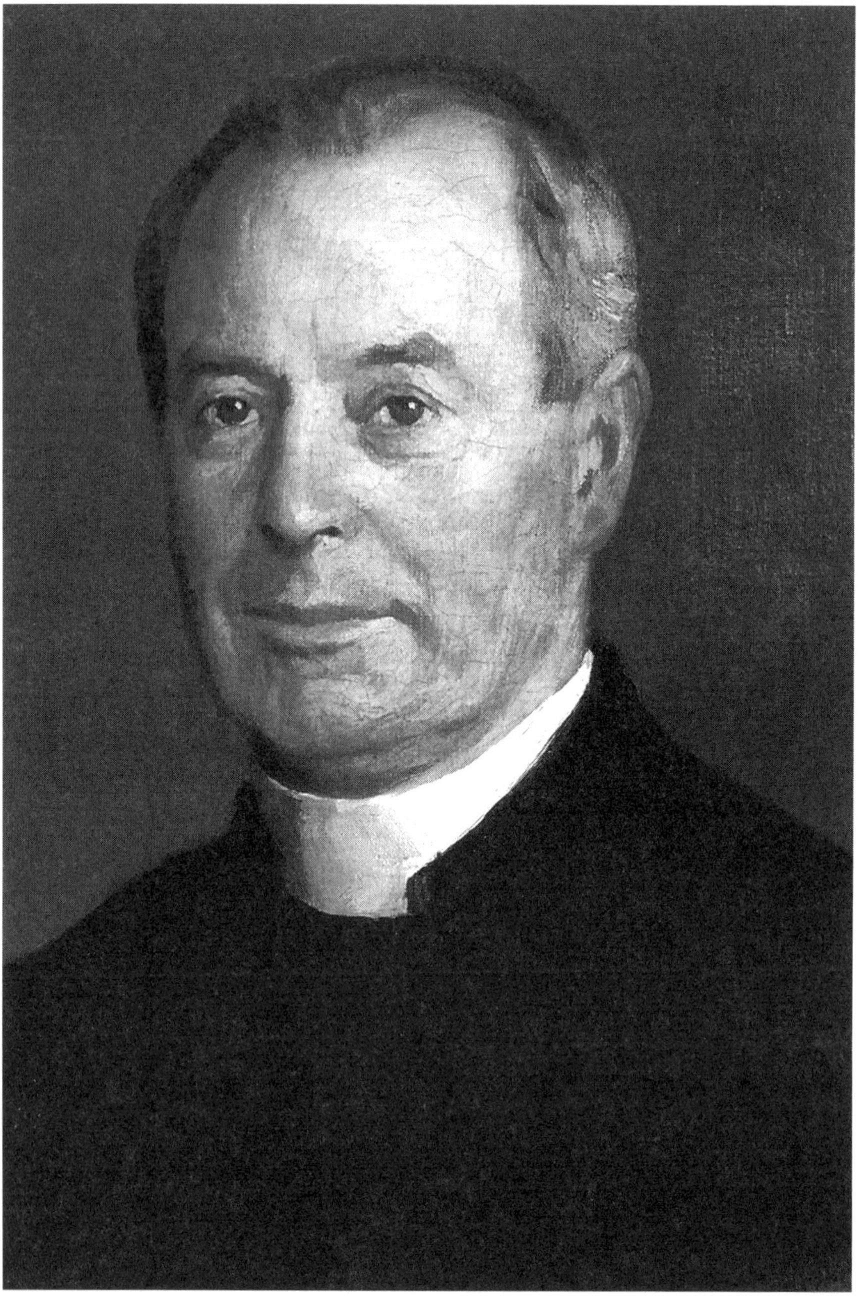

THOMAS A. FINLAY SJ, 1848–1940
Educationalist, Editor, Social Reformer

'Perhaps the most universally respected man in Ireland'
W.E.H. LECKY

THOMAS J. MORRISSEY SJ

FOUR COURTS PRESS

Set in 10.5 pt on 12 pt Bembo for
FOUR COURTS PRESS LTD
7 Malpas Street, Dublin 8, Ireland
e-mail: info@four-courts-press.ie
http://www.four-courts-press.ie
and in North America by
FOUR COURTS PRESS
c/o ISBS, 920 N.E. 58th Avenue, Suite 300, Portland, OR 97213.

© Thomas J. Morrissey SJ 2004

A catalogue record for this title
is available from the British Library.

ISBN 1–85182–827–3

All rights reserved. No part of this publication may be reproduced, stored in or introduced into a retrieval system, or transmitted, in any form or by any means (electronic, mechanical, photocopying, recording or otherwise), without the prior written permission of both the copyright owner and publisher of this book.

Printed in Great Britain
by MPG Books, Bodmin, Cornwall.

'To write about him is like writing about a number of persons rather than a single man'
GEORGE O'BRIEN

'He is pre-eminently the Renaissance man of the Irish Renaissance'
OWEN DUDLEY EDWARDS

Contents

LIST OF ILLUSTRATIONS 8

PREFACE 9

PART ONE
YOUTH AND TEACHING CAREER

1 The years of preparation 13
2 University professor and rector of Belvedere College 18
3 At University College, St Stephen's Green 24
4 Finlay and literature; George Moore and D.P. Moran 34
5 The editor of journals 43
6 Socio-political ambience, 1890–1908 55

PART TWO
THE IRISH CO-OPERATIVE MOVEMENT, 1889–1932

7 The early years of co-operation 77
8 The Recess Committee; growth and difficulties 87
9 Vice-president of IAOS; speeches and the course of the movement 99

PART THREE
THE PRIEST, HIS COMMITMENTS AND FRIENDS; THE FINAL YEARS

10 The priest and preacher 123
11 A range of friends and services; introducing Caravaggio and Paddy the Cope 128
12 The final decades 145

NOTES 154

SOURCES 161

INDEX 165

Illustrations

	Portrait of Fr Thomas A. Finlay (artist unknown)	*frontispiece*
1	An early Foxford Mills school orchestra	63
2	Title page of the 1895 Annual Report of the IAOS	64
3	Preparing the wool at Foxford Mills	65
4	Foxford Mills interior	65
5	Lord Monteagle	66
6	Fr Joseph Darlington SJ	67
7	Dermot O'Brien, *Portrait of R.A. Anderson*	67
8	Thomas Kettle	67
9	Map showing the spread of cooperative societies by the end of 1902	68
10	T.M. Healy	69
11	Douglas Hyde	69
12	Eoin MacNeill	69
13	Fr Edward Coyne SJ, president of the IAOS	69
14	Fr William Delany SJ	70
15	Paddy 'the Cope' Gallagher	71
16	Dermot O'Brien, *Portrait of Sir Horace Plunkett*	72
17	Caravaggio, *The Taking of Christ* (1602)	73
18	University College Dublin at 86 St Stephen's Green	74

CREDITS

Illustrations 1, 3 and 4 are courtesy of Foxford Mills; illustrations 5, 7, 9, 13, 15 and 16 are courtesy of the Irish Cooperative Organisation Society. Illustration 17 is courtesy of the National Gallery of Ireland.

Preface

Tom Finlay has been described as 'pre-eminently the Renaissance man of the Irish Renaissance'. The term 'Renaissance man' is most frequently used to describe a person of many and diverse attainments. In that sense the application to Finlay is very understandable. He was, in turn, professor of Classics, of Philosophy, and of Political Economy. In all he won the admiration of his students, and in the golden age of University College, St Stephen's Green, Dublin, from 1883 to 1909, his influence among them was exceptional, and many of the leaders of the new Irish State, it has been claimed, received from him their high standards of public service. He was a prolific writer on a wide range of subjects, had written a novel as a young man, and was a founder member, with John O'Leary, W.B. Yeats, and Maud Gonne, of the National Literary Society of Ireland. He founded four periodicals, each quite distinct from the other: the *Irish Messenger*, the *Lyceum*, the *New Ireland Review*, the *Irish Homestead*; was co-founder of the *Irish Monthly*; and was involved in the foundation of *Studies*. He contributed to all these, and was editor of the *Lyceum*, the *New Ireland Review*, and the *Irish Homestead*. This last was the organ of the Irish Co-operative Agricultural Organisation Society, of which Finlay was assistant to Horace Plunkett and virtual co-founder with him. They travelled together throughout Ireland, and Finlay's contact with numerous clergy and his known nationalist views paved the way for the acceptance of Plunkett, a landlord, unionist, and Protestant. Finlay's ability, his commitment to the improvement of the lot of farmers, especially small farmers and the poor generally, his humour, independence, and his genius for friendship reached across all barriers of class, culture, gender, and religion or no-religion. Among his close friends were members of Orange lodges, and a lady doctor who presented him with a painting which turned out to be a celebrated Caravaggio. James Connolly paid tribute to Finlay's work and claimed he was the only clergyman from the pope down who understood socialism! In addition, Finlay prepared a whole series of school textbooks and copy-books, was a Commissioner of National Education, chaired the committee on Intermediate Education, was chairman of the trustees of the National Library, and was a member of various Royal Commissions. A founder member of the Central Saving Committee, he was one of the first to be consulted by the new Irish government in 1923 on the establishment of the Irish savings movement. As a priest, moreover, he was greatly in demand as preacher and retreat director among diocesan clergy and religious. Some 300 clergy attended his funeral.

All in all, one might say, an ideal subject for a biography. The problem is, he left scarcely any papers. He had no interest in posthumous reputation, which makes it likely that he personally destroyed all his correspondence. He resisted requests to write his memoirs. The biographer, as a result, is largely dependent on the occasional letters to others which have survived, the observations of those who knew him, his writings, and his public addresses as vice-president of the Irish Co-operative Agricultural Organisation Society over a period of thirty years. In every book by the present author, whether related to education, social reform, or ecclesiastical history, Fr Finlay kept turning up. Hence, this present attempt, however inadequate, to capture something of his career, his influence, and, hopefully, his personality.

It remains to express my thanks to Fr Brendan Woods and the librarian of Miltown Park library, Ms Patricia Quigley; to Malachy McGlynn of Plunkett House, Dublin, for his invaluable assistance with printed material and photographs; to Ms Jillian Harris and Ms Kate Targett of Plunkett House, Oxford, for their assistance in relation to Plunkett's diary and letters; to Fergus O'Donoghue SJ, of the Irish Jesuit Archives, to David Sheehy, archivist of the Dublin Diocesan Archives, and to the courteous staff of the National Library archives and the UCD archives; to Paul Andrews SJ, for reading the manuscript and for his encouragement and support; to Katie Armstrong and especially Gerard Clarke SJ for their interest and work on the cover for the book. Finally, a very special acknowledgment to those who made this publication possible: William Finlay and Judge Thomas A. Finlay, and also John T. Tyrrell, director general of ICOS Ltd.

PART ONE

Youth and teaching career

I

The years of preparation

There has been some confusion about the birthplace of Thomas Aloysius Finlay. He has frequently been described as a Cavan man, but, on his arrival at the Jesuit novitiate on 1 November 1868, he entered Lanesborough, County Roscommon, as his place of birth. The mystery was solved by a reminiscence he liked to retail. His father was an engineer on the Shannon River Works, involved in bridge-building and maintenance in different locations, and Tom Finlay was born on an island just north of Lough Rea, which his father was later to submerge beneath the waters of the Shannon.[1] His father, William Finlay, was a native of Fifeshire in Scotland, a Presbyterian, who later became a Catholic. He married Maria Magan, from County Roscommon, a Catholic, at Lanesborough, on 2 June 1844. They had nine children, four boys and five girls. Two of the girls died young. For many years, as the work on the Shannon came to an end and William Finlay moved to navigation work on the river Erne, it was a struggle to make ends meet. They acquired a public house *cum* grocery in Cavan town. The premises appear to have been largely run by Mrs Finlay, who is remembered as a magnificent manager. Her husband died in 1864 before the family were fully reared. Tom was only sixteen at the time, his sister Margaret only an infant. William's own family in Scotland, however, were well-to-do and happy to help rear the children.

The first child, John, born in 1846, was sent to Scotland, settled there, and never returned to Ireland. Next in line was Thomas (Tom) Finlay, born on 6 July 1848, who acted, in fact, as the eldest of the children, carrying the responsibilities that tend to devolve on the first child in a large family. Of the other surviving children, Peter was born in 1851, Mary in 1852, Annie in 1854, William in 1855, and Margaret in 1863. The three girls joined the Sacred Heart Congregation of religious sisters and worked and died abroad: Mary died in 1913 at Puerto Rico, West Indies; Annie in 1934, in Santiago, Chile; and Margaret in 1936, also in Chile. William inherited the public house and played an active role in county affairs after the 1898 Local Government Act, serving, in turn, as chairman, and then as the first secretary to Cavan County Council. He married Margaret O'Hanlon, whose family owned the Cavan-based *Anglo-Celt* newspaper. They had two children: Eileen, born in 1904, still active at the age of ninety-nine as this book is being written; and Thomas A. Finlay, born in 1893, who was named after his uncle and studied law on his uncle's advice. He was to become a senior counsel and a member of Dáil Éireann.² William Finlay's two brothers, Tom and Peter, joined the Jesuits.

Peter, interestingly, joined first. He was accepted by the order on 2 March 1866, at the age of fifteen years. Tom was a mature eighteen when he entered on 1 November 1866. In that era, boys joining the Jesuits, and girls entering the Sacred Heart Congregation, left home for good, not returning at all in the girls' case, returning only in the case of a death or something very grievous where the Jesuits were concerned. The fact that five religious vocations took root in the Finlay household, and that the young people's mother was prepared to part with them so finally, says a great deal about Maria Finlay. She was not only a practical, organised woman, she was also a strong personality with a deep religious faith.³ Her daughter, Annie, recalled her mother's vigilance lest the Presbyterian influence of her husband's family undermine her children's belief.⁴ As time passed, Maria Finlay became concerned about her son John's religious upbringing, and for many years none of the other children were permitted to go to the Scottish relatives for any length of time. She relented, however, with her final child, Margaret, who was a particular favourite of the Scottish grandparents. Margaret spent long periods with them. When she was five or six years, however, all that changed. Returning to Cavan for what was meant to be a short stay, she was brought to Mass by her mother and startled her with the question – 'Why does the minister put on a dress?' Maria Finlay thought it better to keep the child at home in future.⁵

Something of the atmosphere of the home is indicated in Annie's humorous account of how the children sought to convert their big dog that came from Presbyterian Scotland. They decided to make him observe the Friday abstinence, which was strictly kept in their house. So, on the fixed day, they went to the garden with the dog's portion, which they offered to him while shouting the command – 'Friday! Friday!' The dog snapped at the food, and immediately was scolded for being at fault. The lesson, repeated over weeks, is said to have eventually borne fruit, and the bemused animal never again snapped at the food when he heard the words – 'Friday! Friday!' Another account furnished by Annie, who was bookish and clever and destined to become an educationalist of note, was of how she used to help her brothers in the study of Latin. Faced with translations of Caesar or Sallust, they used to employ their little sister to look up words in a dictionary, offering her sixpence per dozen. She agreed readily, and tenaciously continued the work, even though the sixpences were rarely forthcoming.⁶

Tom Finlay's early educational memories included a hedge-school, probably near Kilmore, County Cavan, which he attended in the early 1850s. The hedge-school experience was short-lived, leaving as its chief memory, it would seem, a master who used to test his pupils by asking them to spell 'anti-trinitarian'.⁷ Not long afterwards, Tom was sent as a boarder to the seminary college of St Augustine, Farnham Street, Cavan, the educational establishment of the diocese of Kilmore before the erection in 1874 of St Patrick's College, Cavan.⁸ His brother, Peter, followed him. Nothing is known of their years at St Augustine's. It may be presumed that both boys gave indications of their later ability.

At home, Tom, who, as the eldest in the family, had been encouraged to look after the other children, was a particular support to his mother. During school vacations, it is probable that he helped in the public house. His later easy relationship with all classes and personalities was moulded in these early years, as was the self-reliance and quiet self-assurance that enabled him to listen to criticism, and even abuse, and to come back in a measured way. In these years, too, was born his ease in women's company. Although there was little contact with the Scottish side of the family, his mother's family, the Magans of Lanesborough and Kilashee, were a constant source of support and friendship. Tom remained friendly with his mother's side of the family all through his life.[9] The mother's sense of loss when both boys joined the Jesuits in the same year must have been intense. It marked a loss also for William. Although he succeeded to the public house and did well financially and socially, he is said to have always regretted not being able to go to university because of having to cater for the family.[10] For him, nevertheless, as for his mother, a religious vocation was seen as a special calling from God, something that would bring blessings on the house, something of which to be proud.

Tom entered the Jesuit novitiate at Miltown Park, Dublin, on 1 November 1866, and took his first vows in the order on 13 November two years later. From Miltown he was despatched to St Acheul, near Amiens, to a house of studies of the French Jesuits. He spent part of 1869 there, and then was sent to the Gregorian University in Rome for further studies. It was a stirring time to be in the ancient city. The first Vatican Council was in progress, and Garibaldi invaded Rome. The latter event caused confusion at the university. Tom Finlay was withdrawn from Italy and sent to Maria Laach in Germany, where he spent 1871–3.[11] Here he observed the new agricultural policy of the Prussian government and the functioning of the Raiffeisen co-operative credit societies,[12] experiences in practical economics that he was later to turn to practical use. From the German Jesuits at Maria Laach he received training in modern scientific methods, which, for a time, made him eager to specialise in biology. His energy and intellectual activity during those years must have been remarkable. In addition to these scientific and agricultural interests, he did notably well in his main studies in philosophy. Ten years later his competence in metaphysics earned him the professorship in the subject at University College, Dublin; and he paid tribute to his time in Germany by translating Albert Stoeckl's *A Handbook of the History of Philosophy*, published in Dublin in 1887 and reprinted in 1903, for the benefit of his students.[13]

From 1873 to 1876 Finlay taught French, German, and other subjects in the Jesuit college at the Crescent, Limerick. In addition, for his last two years he acted as prefect of studies, an unusual responsibility to entrust to a scholastic or student teacher. His interest in writing became apparent in those years. He joined with Fr Mathew Russell, then stationed at the Crescent, in developing a periodical, *Catholic Ireland*, subsequently to be the *Irish Monthly*, which provided an important outlet for emerging writers. Finlay was one of the regular contributors during his Limerick years. In 1873 he had articles published entitled 'Occasional sketches of Irish life: no. 1, The Emigrant' and 'no. 2, The Vagrant', and also 'Catholicity and the spirit of the age'. The following year, he wrote, 'How things are under Bismark'. In 1875 he extended his range. As well as diverse contributions such as 'Memorare: a poem beginning "Gentle Lady who has ever",' and 'The aggressions of science', he embarked on a serial novel which ran from May 1875 to February 1877, and was published in book form in October 1877 as *The Chances of War*. He published under the pseudonym, 'A. Whitelock', an allusion, perhaps, to the Irish of Finlay – the fair-haired one.

Most of Finlay's later characteristics were already in evidence during his early years. His intellectual energy and ability were matched by a strong physique, and a genius for making and keeping friends that was aided by prowess as a conversationalist and by a lively sense of humour. His personality, besides, was marked by a sturdy self-reliance, and by a balance that punctuated intensive work with periods of leisure. In later life, he kept one day a week free for his favourite pastimes of fishing and shooting. As a scholastic he had fewer such opportunities, but he managed to find some openings for them. His high profile as prefect of studies and writer, his popularity with parents and pupils, and especially, no doubt, his self-reliance, provoked criticism from some members of his religious community, who complained to the provincial. The latter, it is alleged, suggested to him that he take care to remain in the legitimate obscurity of a scholastic! In 1877 he was sent to St Beuno's, the English Jesuit theologate, situated in Wales. Shortly afterwards, his historical novel, *The Chances of War*, was published. It was to be republished in Dublin in 1908 and 1911, and was also printed in the United States of America. Later, in 1930, it would be revised and re-edited, under Finlay's own name, with the new title, *With the Army of O'Neill*.

'THE CHANCES OF WAR'

Set in seventeenth-century Ireland, the story moves well despite lengthy passages of historical explanation. It is a romantic tale, displaying insight into characters, historical and fictional, and presenting an imaginative depiction of the background. This last captures something of the majestic power of the Shannon at Limerick before the river was harnessed. Among the real historical figures who featured in the book were the papal nuncio, Rinuccini, and Eoin Rua O'Neill, on the side of the Catholic Confederacy, and on the other side, in the war of the 1640s, the duke of Ormond, General Thomas Preston, and Lord Inchiquin. Lesser-known real figures, such as Fr Mathew O'Hartegan SJ, who had acted for the Confederacy at the court of France, also featured. Ironically, the villain of the novel was a Nicholas Plunkett, an unscrupulous Anglo-Irish gentleman. In later years, one of Finlay's closest friends was to be a member of that historic family, Horace Plunkett. The story ends with a depiction of the siege of Limerick, defended valiantly by Hugh Dubh O'Neill but betrayed by faint-hearted, self-interested burghers, who insist on surrendering. Plunkett, who is presented as encompassing the death of Eoin Rua O'Neill, subsequently meets his own death, as too, with bathos, does Kathleen Dillon, the delicate young sister of the heroine, Mary Dillon. The latter is portrayed as an innocent and loving young woman, who marries the hero, Captain Heber MacDermott, an ardent follower of Eoin Rua. With the exception of the Dillons, the Anglo-Irish gentry are generally presented as devoted to England rather than to Ireland. By and large, *The Chances of War* remains a perceptive period novel. It appears to have appealed to boys and young men and, doubtless, was aimed at such – teaching an appreciation of Irish national history and inculcating high moral manly and womanly virtues.

OTHER WRITINGS AND ORDINATION

While at St Beuno's, Finlay joined the entire Jesuit community in signing his name to a letter to John Henry Newman to congratulate him both on his elevation to the cardinalate and on his seventy-eighth birthday, and to acknowledge that they were all in some way or other indebted to him. Sent on 21 February 1879, it was one of the first of the numerous messages of congratulation received by the new cardinal.

During his four years in Wales, Finlay continued to provide articles for the *Irish Monthly*. They included 'A story told by a Breton grandfather', articles entitled 'Pombal and the Society of Jesus', relating to the expulsion of the Jesuits from Portugal by the government of the Marques de Pombal, 'The centenary of Voltaire', and a review of *Science and Scepticism* by Stephen M. Lanigan. He also had published in Dublin, in 1877, a pamphlet entitled *Rationalism in its two phases of Idealism and Materialism*, based on an address to the Debating Society of the Limerick Literary Institute, which was the creation of a dynamic young curate named Edward Thomas O'Dwyer, destined to be the future controversial but highly influential bishop, who would continue to hold Finlay's ability in high esteem. Another pamphlet was published in London, in 1879. *Freedom of education under the French Republic: the principles of liberty, equality, and fraternity applied to the school*, dealt with Jules Ferry's proposed legislation to deny to the Jesuits, the Marists, and other 'unauthorised' religious groups the freedom to teach.[14]

The following year, 1880, Thomas A. Finlay was ordained priest, and, after a further year of theology, he returned to Ireland. He was immediately appointed to a teaching post. His life was to be devoted to teaching.

2

University professor and rector of Belvedere College

When Finlay emerged from his theological studies in 1881, the Irish Jesuit province was facing a new challenge. It arose from the history of the struggle for university education for Catholics. The Queen's University Colleges, founded by the government more than thirty years previously, had been opposed by the Irish Catholic bishops as not suitable for Catholics because they were non-denominational in character. They sought to meet the requirements of their people by establishing in 1851 a Catholic University, with John Henry Newman as rector. Its degrees, however, were not recognised by the government, and the venture failed so far as practical results were concerned. But the long struggle by the majority population for equality of rights in university education met, in 1879, with a partial response from the government. The Royal University of Ireland was founded as an examining body, governed by a senate containing representatives from the main religious denominations. This institution, which became active in 1881, offered fresh opportunities to Catholics. The Jesuit general, Fr Pieter Beckx, eager that the order should play a leading role in forming the new generation of graduates, instructed the provincial, James Tuite, to embark on a university college in Dublin, and he recommended that it be placed under the guidance of Fr William Delany. The latter had been highly successful as headmaster/rector of St Stanislaus College at Tullabeg in the Irish midlands, where he had been effective in preparing students for the examinations of London University. In 1880–1 he had had a break-down in health, and his place at Tullabeg was entrusted to Finlay. Then, faced with the prospect of developing a college in Dublin that would enter its students for the examinations of the new Royal University, Delany found a new lease of life. The provincial had acquired a premises at Temple Street, which he envisaged as a college and, also, as a hostel catering for students, drawn mainly from country areas, whose social and moral well-being was thought to be at risk in the big city. In December 1881 Delany was appointed to Temple Street.[1]

Before long, Finlay was called to Dublin to meet a vacancy at University College Dublin, then being run by Monsignor Henry Neville on behalf of the bishops. To fill the college's need, he was offered a fellowship of the Royal University in classics. Although he was living in the Temple Street community, the fellowship precluded him from teaching there. His services were reserved for University College. In 1883 his teaching role was changed from classics to philosophy. He, and his brother, Peter, were appointed joint professors of mental and moral science. At the same time, he was made rector of Belvedere College, a well-established Jesuit secondary school in the north of the city. From 1883-8 he carried the dual responsibility of rector at Belvedere and professor at University College. His success in both roles became legendary.

RECTOR OF BELVEDERE

Although scarcely any of his letters are extant, a few, from his Belvedere years, written in lapidary Latin, have survived.[2] They provide an account of the college and were addressed to the Jesuit superior general, Pieter Beckx.

In his annual report to the general, on 8 January 1884, the youthful rector indicated what was needed for the Jesuit community and the pupils, what was required in the way of school structures and for the improvement of school studies. He then explained what he had done to achieve these objectives. For the Jesuit community he had established a special refectory, reintroduced the order's custom of having a book read during meals, provided a place for recreation after dinner, arranged for spiritual talks at regular intervals, and arranged fixed times for prayer together. For the pupils he had instituted a sodality of the Blessed Virgin and provided a Mass for them each day. With the pupils in mind he had also introduced certain structural and material improvements. He obtained a loan of £800 from Fr William Ronan, rector of Mungret College, Limerick, with which he improved the condition of the school toilets, built dividing walls, and provided some new school furniture. He had embarked on further expenditure to meet the problem posed by pupils who came to the city by train and then had a long walk from the station to the school. A number of parents were concerned for the health and safety of their children, and others hesitated to send their children to Belvedere because of the situation. He solved the problem by investing in a horse-drawn bus, driven by one of the college staff, which met the pupils at the station in the morning and returned them in the afternoon. The outlay was £150, which, however, was more than recovered by charging each benefiting pupil £6 per annum. The initiative, moreover, had increased the number of pupils coming from a distance. As a result, overcrowding had now become a problem, especially in the school chapel.

Expanding on the space problem, he reported that the greater part of the pupils now had their classes in a neighbouring building that was rented at £100 a year and was in poor condition. The owner refused to make repairs. Consequently, he had decided to construct a building that would contain a chapel, a large hall, and classrooms. The cost would be £3000, but it would be met by raising the emolument. The presence of these facilities, he believed, would attract additional numbers to the school.

Apart from the information on developments in this letter to the general, Finlay also appears to have acquired a playing field for the pupils: a suitable piece of ground between the Jesuit property at Miltown Park and a line of railway running parallel to the Palmerston Road. He persuaded the Irish Jesuit province to purchase the land, which was then rented to him for the use of Belvedere. With the confident vision that became associated with him, he had a bicycle track laid round the spacious field and made provision for tennis courts and a pavilion. Besides, a bridge giving access to Palmerston Road was thrown over the Wicklow and Wexford railway that skirted the property.[3]

In relation to school studies, Finlay explained to the general that the introduction by the State of a system of payment based on results in the Intermediate (secondary school) examinations had led to intense competition between schools. To improve the standard of work at Belvedere, and to prepare the pupils more effectively for the public examinations, he had inaugurated a weekly test for all classes, a practice in vogue in the Jesuit colleges in Paris. It had proved a great success. 'There was ardour among teachers and boys', he emphasised, and 'maximum industry'. Most of the pupils, however, were young and in the lower school. Once boys reached the ages of fourteen or fifteen they tended to leave for boarding school or for work in business. 'We will never achieve a reputation', he declared, 'unless we can keep them (on) for three or four years.' The way forward was 'to convince the parents that we teach better than the boarding schools'.

He concluded on a more personal note. Although all were working well in the college, he scarcely had strength for all his duties. He was carrying out the requirements of rector at Belvedere and of a professor at University College where he was also in charge of a body of young people known as the Lyceum Club. He feared that with so many things to do he would be deficient in carrying out his responsibilities as rector and professor.[4] He might have added, for the general's understanding, that the rector of Belvedere in that era had a conspicuous social standing, which involved attendance at a variety of functions. That status was reflected in the young rector's practice of riding a fine black horse through the streets of Dublin *en route* to exercise in the Phoenix Park.[5]

Five months later, on 12 June 1884, he provided further information about the school. It was continuing to do well. Numbers were up, teachers and boys were working hard, and there were good prospects of success in the public examinations next year. This year the pupils were too young. 'In the first (examination) class', he explained, 'we have only one pupil, in the second four, all the other pupils, some 230, were in the lower classes and would not be properly prepared for the public examinations for another two years.' The new building, he added, was almost ready. The pressure for classroom space, however, had excluded the *aula maxima*, or great hall from their plans. Such a hall, nevertheless, was necessary for public presentations and to hold the public examinations. The provincial had encouraged him to buy a neighbouring house and to construct a hall in its place. He would follow this advice if there was a chance of doing so. He would forward as soon as possible all the information relating to this possible development. Finlay, plainly, was not afraid of venturous decisions, or of spending money, but he did so shrewdly.

His initiatives, however, did not go without criticism nearer home. As he had warned the general in his previous letter, his wholehearted commitment to the role of rector and, a couple of miles away, to the demands of professor of philosophy and to involvement in student activities, was sure to lead to neglect in some areas. Members of the Belvedere community complained to the provincial, Fr Thomas Browne, who passed on the complaints to the rector. He had been remiss, it was said, in not having regular meetings with his consultors, in not ensuring that the spiritual talks to the community took place, and in not communicating to the bursar the origin of the money for the new building. In his letter to the general, on 12 June 1884, Finlay acknowledged the truth of the complaints. In future he would hold regular meetings with his consultors. The money for the new building had come from a friend. The spiritual talks to the community depended on the spiritual father of the community, who had not been well. He added, humanly, that there had not been any spiritual exhortations for ten years prior to his arrival!

The remaining extant letters from Finlay's time at Belvedere date from 1888, his final year as rector. On 10 June 1888 he was pleased to inform the general that his community were well and were men of zeal. The pupils were working earnestly and he hoped for many honours in the public examinations. Their spiritual development was also being cultivated. Fr James Cullen (founder of the Pioneer Total Abstinence Association) was their spiritual director, and he fostered piety in young people. Many boys made their first communion on the feast of the Sacred Heart, and their parents attended. He went on to refer to a recent letter of his asking to be relieved of his position as rector.

The large number of schools entered for the Intermediate examinations had given rise to a demand for common textbooks in a range of subjects. He, on top of his other responsibilities, had endeavoured to meet this need. 'I asked to be allowed free of rectorship', he reminded the general, 'so that I could write and edit books. In the past year I edited five books for the lower schools, of which 9000 copies were sold. I have nine in hand, and I have also put together headline copies to teach handwriting, which the schools founded by the government (the National Schools) will use. All these should bring in a good income.' He had also produced, he added, two periodicals, the *Lyceum* and *The Messenger of the Sacred Heart*, which, he hoped, would, in time, gain a wide readership.[6] 'If your Paternity wished to promote these new ventures', Finlay went on, 'the best way was to set up a small school of writers whose function would be to produce books for use in schools and to promote the periodicals already founded. Before long, the books would be in use in all the schools of the kingdom, and the periodicals would be read by Catholics everywhere. If these proposals meet with your Paternity's approval', he concluded, 'I and Fr Cullen, who have already commenced the task, will gladly move it forward.'[7]

A reply was sent from Rome on 12 July. On 15 July Finlay reported its arrival. The general's letter is not extant, but Finlay's reply indicates that his request received a favourable response. He was happy to accept the requirements stipulated by Fr Beckx with regard to the editing of books. He would request, however, that a suitable bursar be appointed to take care of the business, which was likely to generate a good deal of money. It was important for the good of the province to have such a person.[8]

The development of a school of writers at Belvedere did not take place. Finlay's request that he be removed from rector was granted, but he was also moved from Belvedere. He was appointed to the Jesuit residence attached to University College, St Stephen's Green. Thereafter, his main focus was on his students at the college. He continued, nevertheless, to find time to produce books for primary education. 'Father Finlay wants to bring out a series of 4 copybooks for [National] schools as a supplement to the present series', Hugh MacNeill informed his brother John (Eoin) on 7 November 1895. 'They are all to be in Irish characters, suitably graduated from letters up to sentences ... He has been in communication with teachers on the subject and wants to get them produced at once as he anticipates little difficulty about their adoption by the Board [of Education]. He would like you to write the headlines, and he will at once have them engraved ...' Two days later Finlay sent four copybooks to John MacNeill. On 22 November, he forwarded two letters about copybooks that he had received from Dr Douglas Hyde, and a year later, 12 November 1895, thanked MacNeill 'for the Irish headlines' and suggested that they 'issue a small Irish primer in connection with the copybooks which would help the pupil to understand something of what he was copying and lead him on to a wider study of the language.'[9] Finlay frequently availed of Messrs Fallon, Dublin, as publisher. It is not clear that he employed them for the copybooks. It is evident, however, that Messrs Browne and Nolan, Dublin, published such material. In the MacNeill papers, in which the Finlay letters are found, there are two typed letters from Browne and Nolan's, one to Dr O'Hickey, of Maynooth, and one to John MacNeill, referring to Gaelic publications. The Hickey letter, dated 28 December 1899, mentions, 'We have within the past year brought out a series of writing copybooks which have met with great success amongst the National Schools.'[10]

Finlay, incidentally, as a colleague in University College and particularly as editor of the *Lyceum* and of its successor, the *New Ireland Review*, kept in touch with MacNeill, who reviewed books for him, and provided articles on a range of Gaelic topics, including aspects of early Irish literature, the Fenian cycle, and 'Phases of Irish history'.[11] On 13 April 1916, with never a hint of politics or projected conflict, he thanked MacNeill for taking so much trouble in answering his question on 'the destruction of Tara' and the 'legend of the cursing of Tara'.[12]

Meantime, Finlay's dual role between Belvedere and St Stephen's Green, from 1883 to 1888, had allowed him little time for writing. He managed two articles in 1883 – 'Liberty of thought' in the *Irish Ecclesiastical Record*, of March 1883, and 'The sin of unbelief' in the *Irish Monthly* in June. The *Sources for the*

History of Irish Civilization contain no further record of his writings until 1890. In fact, in 1886 his growing interest in political economy resulted in the publication of a pamphlet on a pressing and emotive problem, *Rent and the Payment of Rent*, which was printed by Gills of Dublin. He examined David Ricardo's theory of rent and applied it to the Irish scene. In a tightly argued presentation, he pointed to the fact that the Land Court had been hampered in applying a 'fair rent' policy across the board by the harsh fact that the small tenant was often unable to pay any rent, his holding was so small 'that its entire produce' was 'necessary to maintain the cultivator'. The law did not recognise this, and the landlord was entitled to evict the tenant from land and home. There was, however, a resource left to the legislator to avoid the extreme evils surrounding such evictions, namely, to exclude the tenant's homestead from the contract. Such a homestead law was in operation in North America; and even under Turkish rule in Bosnia, where landlords had 'practised indescribable cruelties' on Christian peasant farmers, 'a creditor cannot seize his debtor's home, nor even take from him the land indispensable to his subsistence'. We might not 'have much to learn from the Turk in the matter of humanity or of natural justice', Finlay commented, 'but comparing the law of eviction as it prevails at Sarajewo with the law of eviction as it obtains at Gweedore, ... there is at least one leaf in the Mussulman statute-book we might with profit add to our own' (p. 19). Finally, with characteristic independence, he raised the thorny issue of the 'nationalisation of land'. Having discussed the benefits and problems associated with nationalisation, and surveyed developments in some other countries, he observed that under nationalisation a wide variety of landlords would be replaced by one landlord, the State, which, for its own financial survival, would require some payment from tenant proprietors. But the problem of being unable to pay would still remain for the small tenant. Hence, the State would either get rid of such, or else, endeavour to favour all classes of cultivators by 'a scheme which made the large occupiers tenants of the State and made the small occupiers, in fact, if not in name, peasant proprietors' (p. 23).

3

At University College, St Stephen's Green

In October 1883, William Delany, on behalf of the Society of Jesus, signed an agreement with the episcopal trustees of the Catholic University whereby he took over the running of University College, Dublin with a view to making it a thriving educational institution. He aimed to combine a wide education in the tradition of Newman with success in the Royal University examinations so that an irrefutable argument might be presented in support of a fully constituted university acceptable to Catholics.

Within a short while, Delany's college surpassed in examination results the three well-subsidised Queen's Colleges combined – Cork, Galway, and Belfast – and, in the end, such success, and Delany's ability and skill, were to play a large part in the settlement of the University Question. A key figure in the life, work, and success of the college was Tom Finlay. Once he became resident at Stephen's Green, his infectious energy, ability, and enthusiasm found extra-curricular expression in a religious sodality, a Shakespearean reading society, a dramatic society, and a vigorous debating society. Prior to that, however, while rector of Belvedere as well as professor and organiser of studies at University College, the very spread of his engagements contributed to an error that threatened the future of the college.

PROBLEMS IN PHILOSOPHY

The bishops at their meeting in Clonliffe College, on 1 October 1884, complained that the questions set in the metaphysics examinations of the Royal University practically necessitated 'the reading of anti-Catholic works, most dangerous to the Catholic faith'. The questions, which had been set by Finlay and Professor Park of Queen's College, Belfast, were designed to cater for all candidates, those who studied under professors acquainted only with modern systems of philosophy and modern terminologies, and those who attended Catholic institutions and studied both scholastic philosophy and modern systems. Finlay acknowledged they had made 'a deplorable blunder'. They did not allow for the fact that in the Catholic seminaries scarcely anything was done on the modern systems; and that, besides, there were as yet no textbooks in English dealing with the modern philosophies from the Catholic point of view, and none on scholastic theology. Finlay, presumably, provided his own text notes, and translations from the German, for his students. In the circumstances, the general body of Catholic students were placed at a disadvantage, and it was feared that were the form of examination to continue the bishops might withdraw their students from the Royal University courses. Conscious of this, the senate of the university appointed a sub-committee on 24 October to devise a programme that would give equal advantage to all the candidates. Dr Woodlock of Ardagh was the bishops' representative.[1] Meanwhile, the issue became public when the fairness of the papers was impugned by Dr Thomas McGrath of Clonliffe, and later by Drs William Walsh and Walter McDonald of Maynooth in the *Irish Ecclesiastical Record*. There were attacks also in the *Tablet*, which, as Delany explained to Lord Emly, chairman of the senate of the university, were likely to have been 'inspired by Maynooth' as Dr Walsh was known to be hostile and was prepared to appeal to Rome 'to assail us on our programme'.[2]

Early in the new year, largely through the efforts of Finlay, a satisfactory and effective compromise was worked out. Some changes were made in the courses, and a choice of alternative questions was offered. These proposals, drawn up by the sub-committee, were approved by the senate on 6 February 1885.[3] Emly had favoured challenging the bishops on the matter, but Delany had impressed on him the need to satisfy them 'temporarily'. He used the word 'temporarily' because he hoped that within a few years there would be suitable handbooks available, and that by then the Royal University, 'now on its trial and suspected', would have grown and established itself, and Catholics would have won such a position at University College that it would be plain that the system involved no unfairness and no religious danger. Meantime, it was his 'primary object' to make University College 'deserve the confidence of the Catholic ecclesiastical authorities' and he was prepared to subordinate his own views to those of the bishops. For the rest, in accordance with the lines laid down by the pope, he was committed to making the college's philosophical teaching 'distinctly and thoroughly scholastic and thomistic', whilst yet doing his best to make his young students 'able to defend their faith against the errors of the day'.[4]

That same year, Delany and Finlay experienced further evidence of vigilant hostility towards themselves and the College on St Stephen's Green. In August 1885, when the Education Endowments Bill was being prepared, Lord Justice Fitzgibbon proposed that Fr Thomas A. Finlay SJ, be appointed assistant commissioner of education. Rumours in certain Catholic quarters in Dublin suggested that this was due to Delany's influence, but the latter was at pains to make it clear that the opposite was the case. He was determined not to give any grounds for criticism to those bishops who were critical of University College under his leadership, and especially to Dr William Walsh, now archbishop of Dublin, who was poised to find fault with the Royal University and was not well-disposed towards the college. The rumours, however, did not develop beyond Dublin gossip, and they dissolved when Dr Gerald Molloy, a close friend of the archbishop, rather than Fr Finlay, was appointed assistant commissioner.[5]

HIS STANDING AMONG COLLEAGUES AND STUDENTS

In this difficult year, Finlay, as has been seen, was prefect of studies in University College, as well as being professor there and rector of Belvedere. Prefect of studies was a sensitive position, as he was dealing with a varied staff, whose overall commitment was essential to the success of the undertaking. Delany had inherited a group of nine fellows from the Catholic University, many of whom were no longer competent as teachers. They did include, nevertheless, men of eminence like Dr Casey, the mathematician, and Thomas Arnold, who professed English and was a younger brother of the poet, Mathew Arnold. Among the Jesuit staff, too, at the time, was an unusual range of ability. Père Mallac, who lectured in philosophy, had practised at the French bar, and had been at one time a confirmed free-thinker. Fr Kieffer, from the German Jesuit province, was a specialist in electrical science.[6] Fr Martial L. Klein, from the English Jesuit province, taught science, and was an eloquent writer and preacher; unfortunately, he had delusions of grandeur (claiming, *inter alia*, that he was a grandson of Napoleon's Marshal Klein), which occasioned embarrassment and led to his recall by the English provincial.[7] Also from the English province were Joseph Darlington and Gerard Manley Hopkins. The former became a legend for his capacity to relate to students and his encouragement of them; open to every new idea, he was, as assistant to Delany, both a considerable support and an occasional trial. The brilliant but eccentric Hopkins had some unhappy years in Dublin; his darkest poetry was written there; as a teacher he did not endear himself to a prefect of studies; he could not keep discipline, a circumstance assisted by his insisting not to teach anything that would be asked in examinations![8] The Irish Jesuit lecturers included Denis Murphy, the author of a number of historical works, including a pioneering book on the Irish martyrs; Edmund Hogan, highly regarded for his research and teaching on the Irish language and Irish history; and John J. O'Carroll, who claimed competence in eighteen European languages.[9]

Delany maintained, as C.P. Curran recalled in *Under the Receding Wave*, that the philosophy faculty should be the heart of any university. This made Finlay a fulcrum point. He translated Stöckle's *History of Philosophy* from the German for the benefit of his students, and worked to bring the subject alive. Through his efforts, and those of his assistant lecturer and later successor, William Magennis, and Professor Park of Queen's College, Belfast, the standard of philosophy in the university was raised, and at Stephen's Green classes in the subject attracted 'a large portion of the best brains in the college'. 'None of us escaped its tincture,' Curran added. The Aristotelian and Thomist undercurrent ran through the institution, and influenced those like James Joyce and Curran who did not follow any course in philosophy.[10] The Aquinas Society, founded by one of Finlay's brightest students, W.P. Coyne, provided a forum for additional discussion.

Finlay's standing among fellow philosophers was underlined when, years after he had ceased to teach the subject, he was called to give evidence before the privy council following the establishment in 1908 of the National University of Ireland

and of Queen's University, Belfast. The commissioners of the new Belfast university decided to fund a chair of Scholastic Philosophy, to be held probably by a Catholic clergyman, and to have, as a result, a dual course such as had existed in the Royal University. The proposal was strongly opposed by the Presbyterians, who determined to appeal to the privy council to have the proposal quashed. Finlay, 'who was practically the founder of the dual system in Ireland', was called by the defence. He maintained against the counsel for the petitioners that in his experience as professor of Mental Philosophy at University College, Dublin, where he had students of every religion, there had been no difficulty on the score of religious belief. There was no necessity, while teaching philosophy, to maintain any religious doctrine. In upholding this position, Finlay had to undergo a severe and complicated cross-examination of several hours; but his answers were sufficiently clear and to the point, and his assertion of Catholic freedom in the purely intellectual sphere so assured, that the judges by an unanimous verdict dismissed the appeal. The chair of Scholastic Philosophy was established and met with success. Finlay's performance was considered of sufficient importance to the cause of Catholic higher education that his evidence was reprinted in pamphlet form and widely circulated by the Catholic Truth Society.[11]

His influence from the start, however, among staff members and students at University College, spread far beyond philosophy. Various colleagues, and past students of the college on Stephen's Green, testified to his remarkable influence from approximately 1884 to 1909. 'As the years went by,' Professor Aubrey Gwynn was to write after his death, 'his position in University College was hardly less important than that of the president himself, and his influence on the abler type of student was immensely stimulating. In the end Fr Finlay became almost a legend.'[12] William Dawson, a prominent student in the early years, recalled vividly:

> The influences strongest upon us in those young days were Father Delany, Father Tom Finlay and Professor Magennis. And the greatest of these was Finlay. We strove to talk like him; perhaps, even to think like him.[13]

Finlay spoke in a clipped, clear manner. C.P. Curran remembered him as 'a formidable logician gifted with style ... In logic, political economy and political science, he was more than competent, and what he had to say he said with authority, precision and a mordant wit. Walter Bagehot, his fellow economist, once divided men into molars and incisors. Father Tom was one of the incisors. His was the way of short definition and analysis. Popular slogans and the easy phrases of the platform shrivelled under his cool humorous dissection, curled up and died ... At first contact [Curran went on] he shocked my credulous youth, and he was a pain to platform politicians. But he was far from being the negative, corrosive-academic type. Whenever possible he directed the activities of his students into writing and into public affairs. One way of judging him is through the careers of his pupils; another is by reference to the monthlies which he founded and edited: the *Lyceum* and the *New Ireland Review*, predecessors of *Studies*.'[14]

Something similar was recalled by a later student, Finlay's successor in Political Economy. George O'Brien, unlike other students, had a boyhood memory of Finlay. While at Belvedere, he attended a retreat given by Finlay at Gardiner Street church and was impressed by 'his cold handling of spiritual questions'. He had no premonition that the preacher was to become one day, his 'kindest friend'. As a university student, he recalled going to his professor about his thesis. By then, Finlay was combining ceaseless work for the co-operative movement with his lectures and supervision as professor. 'He was a very busy man, with endless interests outside the college', O'Brien commented, but 'he did not discourage me, and I call to mind his example when I am tempted to discourage young graduates who seek my advice in similar circumstances.' He was not encouraging, his manner, rather, was 'distantly civil'. Later, when he saw the amount of work O'Brien had done for his MA thesis, he became positively helpful, urging him 'to publish his thesis and to present for the degree of DLitt'.[15]

Returning for a moment to Finlay as preacher and 'handler of spiritual questions', he was clearly much in demand as a preacher for major clerical and social occasions. He adapted his style to the occasion, but his characteristically reasoned approach did not meet with the unanimous approval of churchmen. Patrick Foley, bishop of Kildare and Leighlin, in the course of inviting Fr William Delany to Carlow, in November 1897, to meet Dr William Barry, the Burke Centenary lecturer, observed: 'Dr Barry, like your own Fr T. Finlay, sadly lacks dramatic power. I fear the people wont hear a word from him on Sunday.'[16]

At college, nevertheless, Finlay's rational handling of spiritual questions found favour with most students, who were conscious that they were not equipped to defend their Catholic beliefs philosophically or theologically and welcomed responses to their queries.[17] The Finlay brothers gave lectures on religious doctrine in the college over a number of years. All Catholic students were expected to attend. As the lectures were in the great hall, or *aula maxima*, women students were able to be present. The position of women in higher education was a pressing issue in the later years of the nineteenth century and the commencement of the twentieth century.

WOMEN STUDENTS

The act establishing the Royal University of Ireland in 1879 went beyond London University, let alone Oxford, Cambridge, and Dublin University, in expressly stating 'that all exhibitions, scholarships, fellowships, and other emolument are to be open to women equally with men'. This, in addition to university membership, degrees and honours. As they were competing with men, the women naturally sought the same quality of teaching as the men, and especially the opportunity to follow the lectures of the men's professors who had the setting of the examinations. The authorities at University College pointed out that they did not have suitable accommodation for women students or women lecturers. Certainly the place was over-crowded and poorly equipped, and money was not available for an overhaul of the building. In 1888, however, the standing committee of the senate of the university responded to a complaint from women graduates and undergraduates in Dublin that they were not allowed to attend the lectures of the university fellows and wished the senate 'to take some steps to remedy this hardship'. The senate announced that it had no right or power to interfere in any college in which the fellows taught, but if any of the women concerned, or other female students, 'could arrange with any of the fellows to deliver courses of lectures especially for female students, a room for the delivery should be provided in these buildings'.[18]

No more than two or three of the fellows in University College availed themselves of the senate's suggestion. 'Among them were the Abbé Polin, who lectured in French, and Fr Finlay in philosophy.' The author of the relevant section in the published memoir of the college, *A Page of Irish History*, observed that Finlay 'had always shown himself most sympathetic and helpful in regard to the claims of women to higher education, and took this opportunity of proving his devotion to their cause. There was no remuneration for this service.'[19]

He worked closely with women on a number of committees, and on a variety of occasions, especially in the co-operative movement, as will appear later. In University College he unwittingly helped to overcome the lack of space for women. In 1907 there was constructed at the rear of 86 St Stephen's Green what was termed alternatively the 'garden classrooms', or 'Fr Finlay's tin university' – in reference to an article of his in the *New Ireland Review*, in May 1905, which had urged that instead of waiting for ever for the government to move they should start constructing their own temporary university buildings. Shortly after the article appeared, Padraic Pearse spoke in it favour, and T.M. Kettle in the *Nationist* pressed the merits of the scheme. In 1906 Fr Delany obtained approval from the bishops to build temporary dwellings. The new buildings catered for the increased student population arising from scholarships established by the county councils and also provided additional room for women students.[20] Moreover, 'an adjoining house was brought into the scheme, in which apartments were provided for the women, with cloakrooms and a comfortable waiting-room; and a woman was appointed to take charge of the area'.[21]

In a more direct manner, Finlay and Delany assisted also in the development of the women's university colleges. The *Lantern*, the year book of the Dominican College at Eccles Street, Dublin, noted, in its 1916 issue, both men's work for university education in Ireland, adding: 'It is as dear and valued friends of the early founders of Eccles Street College that we wish to recall them'. In the early years of Eccles Street, 'as the pioneer in the higher education of Catholic women, the first teachers and students had the inestimable benefit of the guidance and help of both Dr Delany and Father Finlay. Their counsel and guidance was always generously given, and to it much of the success which attended the early efforts of the university students may be attributed.' Both men were also members of the college council of the other Dominican institution, St Mary's

University College, and High School, 28 Merrion Square North, founded in 1893 for the higher education of ladies. The president of the college council was Archbishop Walsh, who nominated Delany and Finlay to the council.[22] At that stage, Delany was no longer president of University College.

Finlay's involvement in many strands of education and his rectorship of Belvedere gave him a reputation as an educationalist quite early on. His influence at University College, however, depended largely on his ability as a lecturer.

THE PROFESSOR

If his lectures had not been stimulating, his standing in other areas of college life would have been much less. 'My predecessor, Father Finlay, was a man of good general education', George O'Brien observed, 'a friend of many people drawn from all ranks and classes, and a man of the world rather than a dry-as-dust pedant. Nobody meeting him would have taken him for a professor. I hope that nobody would have taken me for one!' But he transmitted much that was special. Seeking to convey his ideal professor, and evidently reflecting Finlay, O'Brien was of the opinion that a professor should be an interesting teacher rather than a research-worker or a deep original scholar. In his view:

> A professor transmits to his students far more than the information conveyed in his lectures, much of which can be derived from text books. He conveys his outlook and valuations on all sorts of subjects. His lectures are coloured by his own personality, which is the result of millions of influences derived from his background, his contacts, his reading and his reflections. Every activity that improves a professor in any respect will improve his competence in his vocation.

Such activities, especially for a professor of political economy were particularly those of a complementary nature, including 'work in commissions and in the senate, writing and journalism connected even remotely with his subject, and business and social contracts'.[23] Finlay's interest in social justice, his involvement in the practical details of the agricultural co-operative movement, his openness to new ideas, and his width of learning, enriched his classes and, in turn, made him acceptable in most student gatherings, even in the Literary and Historical Society, which, in the eyes of a considerable number of students, was the centre of the college's activities and a forum for free and critical expression.

THE L AND H

The Literary and Historical, which had been allowed to lapse, was revived in the first session of the Jesuit regime, 1883–4. Tom Finlay was elected auditor, with an expression of hope that the post would be filled by a student in the future. Finlay, as one student recalled, 'saw to it, characteristically, that rules were adopted', and later he 'read an inaugural on "The relation of the proposed work of the society to the university"'. Having completed the re-organisation and ended his term of office, he stepped down. Thereafter, there were lay auditors, though members of the Jesuit community held office on the committee for the twenty-five years of the Jesuit university college. For fifty years Finlay maintained his interest in the History and Literary Society; and as late as 1929 suggested a subject for an international inter-university debate, namely, 'That the recrudescence of autocracy in Europe is due to abuses of democracy'. 'He was', William Dawson averred, 'one of the formative influences on generations in the society.'[24]

The onset of lay auditors led to some squalls with college authorities. Differences of opinion became marked in 1886. The president, Dr Delany, intervened to replace a motion calling for 'Separation from England' with the interesting but anodyne proposal 'That the federation of the colonies would tend to strengthen the British Empire'. At its next meeting the committee of the society adopted the resolution – 'That subjects appointed for debate be submitted for the approval or disapproval of the president of the society [Delany] before a date be fixed for their discussion'.[25] The problem would arise again. Students naturally wished to discuss the pressing events of the day and, as Dawson acknowledged, they 'liked scenes'. By and large, the student body, at the turn of the century, was strongly nationalist. 'Here', Tom Kettle proclaimed, 'I have a home for my disaffection.'[26] William Delany and the College, however, could not afford 'scenes', especially on nationalist issues. Delany had not been appointed president of the college to promote the cause of Home Rule, still less of separation. His was to do his utmost to bring to a successful conclusion the long struggle for a university settlement, and to that end he was determined that the goal would not be prejudiced by discordant activities on the part of the students.[27] Finlay, always loyal to Delany, directed his wit and cool reasoning to the problem.

In 1903–4 the 'scenes' attracted public notice. It was a restless time. Among those who came to college in that year were Patrick Little, Francis Cruise O'Brien, and Timothy Mangan, a trio with a talent for disruptive activity. They were part of a group that stopped the playing of 'God Save the King' at a conferring attended by numerous distinguished guests.[28] Delany was angry and upset. Subsequently, there was a split in the L and H. The main body worked with the authorities, partly, it seems, through Finlay's influence. The alternate group, led by Cruise O'Brien, held their inaugural outside the college, in the Antient Concert Rooms; and in December 1906 they disrupted a paper read by Maurice Healy at the traditional inaugural in the Aula Maxima. A number of non-conformists came to the meeting, Michael McGilligan recalled, 'and we made ourselves heard almost as often as Maurice with interruptions, which we thought witty but of which Father Tom Finlay, the formidable chairman, took a much poorer view'.[29]

The model for the debates was the House of Commons. George O'Brien recalled that though in his day, 1911–12, the L and H was not what it had been at the turn of the century, when Joyce, Kettle, Clery, Curran and Hugh Kennedy were among its members, it still encouraged its members to think on ambitious political lines. 'There are only three positions for which we are being fitted in our education', Arthur Cox remarked to O'Brien, 'prime minister, leader of the opposition, and speaker of the House of Commons'.[30] There was an inducement to preening oratory, moreover, on occasions when ambition was stirred by John Dillon, or some other future prime minister taking the chair. Distinguished guests were not unusual at the L and H debates. Already in 1888–9, a notable gathering attended to hear William Magennis read what was judged 'a brilliant paper' on democracy. The platform and audience matched the address: 'Father Finlay in the chair; the speakers, John Pentland Mahaffy, John Dillon, Charles Dawson; in the audience, John Redmond and Father Gerald Manley Hopkins.'[31] Finlay, Delany, and Professor Magennis presided over many of the society's debates, but outsiders presided from time to time. Among these were Padraic Pearse, George W. Russell (Æ), John O'Leary, Monsignor Molloy, and Stephen Gwynn. John O'Leary, the highly literate old Fenian, was in the chair on 23 January 1904 when the motion before the house read: 'That parliamentary agitation, as a means of redress for Irish grievances, is a failure'. Summing up, he was of the view that nothing could be got from England except by force, adding 'the Fenians would only declare war on England when the country was engaged in a life or death struggle with Russia, France, or the United States'. Ironically, Germany was not envisaged as a possibility.[32]

All the atmosphere of 'bright intellectual life', noted by William Dawson and others, was to be found in a college that totalled no more than 500 students, who spilled over in late night conversation into a city that had its boundaries between the Royal and Grand Canals. 'The vast majority of the students lived inside those boundaries', the former student, Felix Hackett, recalled, 'within easy walking distance of the college. Only two tram-lines were electrified. The motoring age had not arrived. The streets sank to silence much earlier than today. Talk, merging into discussions of the problems of the day, or of the theatre, or of the more abstract topics of the lecture-room, went on easily, walking across St Stephen's Green, or homeward from L and H debates, or from the closing of the National Library.'[33] Despite this afterglow of brilliance and sparkle ascribed to the years in Stephen's Green, it is likely that only a minority of the student body participated in the excitement of this 'bright intellectual life'. The excitement of the L and H and its association with colourful and talented public speakers, is also overdrawn. The standard of speaking in debates at the turn of the century was not 'really good' in William Dawson's judgment.[34] The best were Kettle, Clery and Skeffington. The latter was unusual but impressive. A senior student, bearded and wearing knickerbockers, quick-firing in speech, and conscious of every social problem, his opinions were more formed than those of most students. His impressive inaugural address, 'Realism in fiction', was given in the college's physic's theatre, with Fr Finlay in the chair.[35] Of other prominent members of the L and H, Dawson was perfunctory. Hugh Kennedy, future attorney general in the new Irish state, was solemn and didactic, Felix Hackett, later dean of the Royal College of Science, and James Murnaghan, a future judge, 'had that curious northern hesitancy of speech', and John M. Sullivan, later professor of History and minister for Education, 'was jerky, scrappy and Socratic'.[36] Whatever the standard of the speakers, and the relatively small number participating, most of those who did participate were part of the particularly brilliant student body who attended at University College from the late 1880s to the start of the First World War, and among them Tom Finlay was a highly regarded and formative figure.

4

Finlay and literature; George Moore and D.P. Moran

Among the factors that earned Finlay respect was the width of his interests. Philosophy, science, social and political reform, economics, drama, literature, and journalism: the range made him a man for most occasions. On the literary and journalistic side he had numerous friends. The fact that he had been co-editor of the *Irish Monthly*, and was editor, in turn, of the *Lyceum* and the *New Ireland Review* gave him a standing which his intelligence, imagination and wit enhanced. The *Lyceum*, though conservative in approach, published articles on Russian and Scandinavian writers, on European literary figures from Jacapone da Todi to Zola, and on English and American writing – Tennyson, Arnold, Meredith, Pater, and Whitman.[1] The *New Ireland Review* serialised Douglas Hyde's celebrated *Love Songs of Connacht*, and carried studies by Professor Darlington on *Hamlet*, a series by William Sutton advocating the Baconian theory of Shakespeare, and eclectic contributions by Professor George O'Neill on French authors from Pascal to the younger Dumas and his contemporaries, and on such Irish poets as Goldsmith and Aubrey de Vere, about whom he was enthusiastic. Other contributions of note – apart from those of regular student and staff writers such as William Magennis, W. P. Coyne, and, to a lesser degree, Tom Kettle – included essays from Thomas Arnold and Dr William Barry, short stories from novelist, George Moore, and an article from John Millington Synge.[2]

It is not surprising, therefore, that at the foundation meeting of the National Literary Society in 1892 one of the speakers was Tom Finlay, along with W.B. Yeats, Maud Gonne and John O'Leary. The last-mentioned, who had an abiding interest in literature, was president of the new society and a key personage in the emerging literary revival.[3] He and Finlay became good friends, and, through Finlay, he eventually, after many years of estrangement, became reconciled to the Catholic Church.[4]

There are many examples of the regard with which Finlay was held in literary circles. When Yeats' *Countess Kathleen* was being roundly criticised by Gaelic enthusiasts and many clergy, Finlay and Fr William Barry were appealed to and gave their verdict in favour of the play being performed. Finlay's wit and humour was much appreciated by literary friends. A public lecture in

Dublin by George Bernard Shaw provided an occasion for his puckish sense of fun. Shaw lectured on 'Equality' and answered questions in brilliant style. The following day, at lunch in Horace Plunkett's house, Kilteragh, a lady in the party ventured to doubt his sincerity in advocating socialism. Shaw replied, protesting his belief in what he had said the previous evening. Then, Finlay 'surprised the table by saying that he agreed with Shaw about the virtues of communism, adding that the only difference between them was that Shaw talked about it while he himself practised it'! He went on to explain the difference between the socialist support for universal compulsory communism and the Catholic position that communism, like celibacy, could only be practised by a few.[5]

When there was a principle at stake, or something that seemed subversive of religious belief, he could be adamant in the face of protests, and arguments and persuasion from colleagues or respected literary figures. A case in point was Lennox Robinson in 1924. He had been encouraged by Yeats to present an article to the short-lived periodical *To-morrow*. The article was entitled 'The Madonna of Slieve Dun', on the theme of an Irish farm-girl, named Mary, who, having been raped, imagined herself to be the Virgin Mary. The young man who wanted to marry her was named Joseph. The printer refused to print the story, seeing it as a blasphemous parody of the Gospel. There was a public outcry. Pressure was brought on the government to institute a prosecution. The relevant minister, Kevin O'Higgins, refused to take any action. Instead, Robinson's dismissal was secured from the position of secretary to the Carnegie Library Trust. Robinson denied any intention of presenting a parody of scripture. Thomas McGreevy, in the course of a long and eloquent letter to Finlay to secure his intercession for Robinson, observed, 'There is more Christian charity in one day of Lennox Robinson's life than there is in the whole lives of *some* of those who would urge on the fight against him in the name of Christianity.'[6] George O'Brien also sought Finlay's support for Robinson.[7] Both were unsuccessful.

The most striking indication, however, of how Finlay was viewed in literary circles is, perhaps, George Moore's *Hail and Farewell. Ave, Salve, Vale*. Moore – an Irish landowner in the west of Ireland, who had lived overseas, a *poseur*, a brilliant conversationalist, and, perhaps, the outstanding novelist of his generation – prided himself in saying exactly what he thought. He indulged himself in *Hail and Farewell*, presenting a number of his friends and contemporaries in an unfavourable light. Finlay appeared at some length, but, though some of the observations about his appearance were less than complimentary, he emerged with, if anything, an enhanced reputation. One gets the impression that he bore Moore's peacock vanity and switchback moods with patience and, possibly, with humour.

'HAIL AND FAREWELL'

In the course of this three volume work, published 1911–13, Moore noted how Yeats' play *The Countess Cathleen*, which had been publicly criticised by members of the Gaelic League and of the clergy, had 'found a backing in Father [William] Barry and Father Tom Finlay'.[8] He had 'long desired to make Father Tom's acquaintance,' he declared, for all that he had heard about him had excited his curiosity. 'My friends were his friends, and they spoke of him as a cryptogram which nobody could decipher.'

Then one day in Merrion Street, when he was with Æ, the latter stopped to speak to someone, and 'turning suddenly, he said: "Let me introduce you to Father Tom Finlay".'

Moore, at this point in the narrative, provides an unreserved depiction of Finlay, then about sixty three years of age, which, though helpful to the biographer, must, like many of Moore's accounts, be taken with reserve:

> I felt a look of pleasure come into my face, and I knew myself at once to be in sympathy with this long-bodied man, fleshy everywhere – hands, paunch, calves, thighs, forearm, and neck. I liked the russet-coloured face, withered like an apple, the small, bright, affectionate eyes, the insignificant nose, the short grey hair. I liked his speech – simple, direct, and intimate, and his rough clothes. I was whirled away into admiration of Father Tom, and for the next few days thought of nothing but when I should see him again. A few days after, seeing him coming towards me, hurrying along on his short legs (one cannot imagine Father Tom strolling), I tried to summon courage to speak to him. He passed, saluting me, lifting his hat with a little smile in his eyes – a smile which passed rapidly. One sees that his salute and his smile are a mere formality. So I nearly let him pass me, but summoning all my courage at the last moment I called to him, and he stopped at once, like one ready to render a service to whoever required one.

The passage in *Hail and Farewell* continues:

> 'I thought of writing to you, Father Tom, about a matter which has been troubling me; but refrained. On consideration it seemed too absurd.'
> Father Tom waited for me to continue, but my courage forsook me suddenly, and I began to speak about other things. Father Tom listened to Gaelic League propaganda with kindness and deference; and it was not till I was about to bid him goodbye that he said:
> 'But what was the matter to which you alluded in the beginning of our conversation? You said you wished to consult me upon something.'
> 'Well, it is so stupid that I am afraid to tell you.'

'I shall be glad if you will tell me,' he answered, taking me into his confidence; and I told him that I had been down at the *Freeman* office to ask the editor to publish a letter from me.

'But, Father Tom, what I'm going to say is absurd.'

Father Tom smiled encouragingly; his smile seemed to say, 'Nothing you can say is absurd.'

'Well, it doesn't seem to me that people are dancing enough in Ireland.'

'You mean there isn't enough amusement in Ireland? I quite agree with you.'

'It's a relief to find oneself in agreement with somebody, especially with you, Father Tom.' Father Tom smiled amiably, and then, becoming suddenly serious, I said, 'Ever since I've been here I find myself up against somebody or something. [...] What is one to do?'

'One mustn't pay any attention to criticism. The best way is to go on doing what one has to do.' In these words Father Tom seemed to reveal himself a little, and we talked about the cross-road dances [it was the era of episcopal letters on the danger of such meetings for young people]. He said he would speak on the subject; and he did, astonishing the editor of the *Freeman*, and, when I next ran across Father Tom, he told me he had just come back from his holidays in Donegal, where he had attended a gathering of young people – the young girls came with their mothers and went home with them after the dance. These words were spoken with a certain fat unction, a certain gross moral satisfaction which did not seem like Father Tom, and I was much inclined to tell him that to dance under the eye of a priest and be taken home by one's mother must seem a somewhat trite amusement to a healthy country girl, unless, indeed, the Irish people experience little passion in their courtships or their marriages. These opinions were, however, not vented, and we walked on side by side till the silence became painful, and, to interrupt it, Father Tom asked if I had seen Peter lately.

'Peter?' I answered. 'What Peter?' For I had completely forgotten him. Father Tom answered, 'My brother,' and I said, 'No, I haven't seen him this long while,' and we walked on, I listening to Tom with half my mind, the other half meditating on the difference between the two brothers. Whereas Peter seemed to me to be sunk in the Order, Father Tom seemed to have struck out and saved himself. It was possible to imagine Peter reading the *Exercises of St Ignatius*, and by their help quelling all original speculation regarding the value of life and death; for he that reads often of the beatific faces in Heaven, and the flames that lick up the entrails of the damned without ever consuming them, is not troubled with doubt that perhaps, after all, the flower in the grass, the cloud in the sky, and his own beating heart may be parcel of Divinity. Tom must have studied these *Exercises* too, but it would seem that they had influenced Peter more deeply, and, thinking of Peter again, it seemed to me that to them might be fairly attributed the dryness and the angularity of mind that I observed in him. But how was it that these *Exercises* passed so lightly over Tom's mind? For it was difficult to think he had ever been tempted by pantheism. He has had his temptations, like all of us, but pantheism was not one of them, and, on thinking the matter out, the conclusion was forced upon me that he had escaped from the influences of the *Exercises* by throwing himself into all manners and kinds of work. He is the busiest man in Ireland – on every Board, pushing the wheel of education and industry, the editor of a review, the author of innumerable text-books, a friend to those who need a friend, finding time somehow for everybody and everything, and himself full of good humour and kindness, outspoken and impetuous, a keen intellect, a ready and incisive speaker, a politician at heart, who, if he had been one actually, would have led his own party and not been led by it.

The *Spiritual Exercises,* it should be said, which, perhaps, Moore had read or read about, but had never experienced, were very different from the picture he presented. They were scripture-based and sought to lead people, by means of intense reflection and prayer over some thirty days, to a deeper personal knowledge of Jesus Christ, a more faithful following of his teaching, and to the capacity to find God in all people and things. In the light of that aim, Tom Finlay, as presented by Moore, was a more obvious product of the *Spiritual Exercises* than his brother, Peter, as he was depicted.

Moore then went on to weigh Tom Finlay in the context of the Jesuit order. Once again, he did not burden himself with a prior inquiry into the nature of the subject, though he probably adds to the reader's knowledge of Finlay's mannerisms and even, perhaps, of his character. Moore mused:

> One has to think for a while to discover some trace of the discipline of the Order in him. If he were a secular priest he would not bow so elaborately perhaps, nor wear so enigmatic a smile in his eyes. Father Tom is a little conscious of his intellectual superiority, I think. He is looked upon as a mystery by many people, and perhaps is a little eccentric. Intelligence and moral courage are eccentricities in the Irish character, and one would not look for them in a Jesuit priest. It seems to me that I understand him, but one may understand without being able to interpret, and to write Father Tom's *Apology* would require the genius of Robert Browning. He could write his own *Apology*, and if he set himself to the task he would produce a book much more interesting than Newman's. But Father Tom would not care to write about himself unless he wrote quite sincerely, and it would be necessary to tell the waverings that preceded his decision to become a Jesuit. He must have known that by joining the Order he risked losing his personality, the chief business of the Order being to blot out personality.[!]

Now, how was this problem solved by Father Tom? Did the Order present such an irresistible attraction to his imagination that he resolved to risk himself in the Order? Or did he know himself to be so strong that he would be able to survive the discipline to which he would have to submit? If he wrote his *Apology* he would have to tell us whether he does things because he likes to do so efficiently, or because he thinks it right they should be done ... But oneself is a dangerous subject for a priest to write about, and perhaps Father Tom avoids the subject, foreseeing the several difficulties that would confront him before he had gone very far ... Any misunderstanding which might arise out of the *Apology* would revert to the co-operative movement of which he is so able an advocate. All the same, I reflected, it's a pity that so delightful an intelligence should be wasted on agriculture, and I thought how I might ensnare Father Tom's literary instincts.

'I've been thinking, Father Tom,' I said, in our next walk, 'about the book you told me you once wished to write – *The Psychology of Religion*. A more interesting subject I cannot imagine, or one more suited to your genius, and I am full hope that you will write that book.'

Father Tom muttered a little to himself, and I think I heard him say that there was more important work to be done in Ireland.

'What work?'

Father Tom did not seem to like being questioned, and when I pressed him for an answer, he spoke of the regeneration of the countryside.

'Mere agriculture, that anybody can do; but this book would be yourself, and Ireland is without ideas and literary ideals. We would prefer your book to agriculture, and you must write it. And ... I wonder how it is that you have never written a book; you are full of literary interests.'

Then, very coquettishly, Father Tom admitted that he had once written a novel.

'A novel! You must let me see it!' And I stared at him nervously, frightened lest he might refuse.

'I don't think it would interest you.'

'Oh, but it would.' I was afraid to say how much it would interest me – more it seemed to me than any novel by Balzac or Turgenev, for it would reveal Father Tom to me. However inadequate the words might be, I should be able to see the man behind them; and I pleaded for the book all the way to the College in Stephen's Green.

'I shall have to go upstairs to my bedroom to fetch it.'

'I'll wait.' And I waited in the hall [...] [H]e appeared on the staircase with the book in his hand – a repellent-looking book, bound in red boards, which I grasped eagerly, and stopped under a lamp to examine. The print seemed as uninviting as tin-tacks, but a book cannot be read under a street lamp and in the rain, so I slipped the volume into my overcoat and hurried home.

'Æ, I've discovered a novel by a well-known Irishman – a friend of yours.'

'Have I read it?'

'I don't think so; you'd have spoken about it to me if you had. You'll never guess – the most unlikely man in Ireland.'

'The most unlikely man in Ireland to have written a novel?' Æ answered. 'Then it must be Plunkett.'

'You're near it.'

'Anderson?'

'No.'

'Father Tom?'

I nodded, very proud of myself at having found out something about Father Tom that Æ did not know.

'If Father Tom has written a novel I think I shall be able to read the man behind the words.'

Just what I said to myself as I came along the Green, and I watched Æ reading.

'With a cast-iron style like that, a man has nothing to fear from the prying eyes,'' and he handed the book back to me.

'But let us,' I replied, 'discover the story that he has to tell.'

Æ looked through some pages and said, 'There seems to be an insurrection going on somewhere; the soldiers have arrived, and are surrounding a castle in the moonlight.' Æ always finds something to say about a book, even if it be in cast-iron, and I loved him better than before, when he said, 'Father Tom loves Ireland.' That Father Tom's love of Ireland should have penetrated his cast-iron style mitigated my disappointment.

'I wonder why he lent me the book?'

'Possibly to prevent you worrying him any more to write *The Psychology of Religion.*'

'Every time I go for a bicycle ride with him, or a walk, I am at him about that book – but it's no use.'

A cloud appeared in Æ's face. He suspects Father Tom, I said to myself, of angling for my soul; and, to tease Æ, I told him that I often spent my evenings talking to Father Tom, in his bedroom, on literary subjects, and that I had arranged with him for the publication of several short stories in the *New Ireland Review.*

'These stories are to be translated into Irish by Taidgh O'Donoghue, and Father Tom will probably get the book accepted as a text-book by the Intermediate Board of Education.'

'But do you think that it was to write these stories that you came from England?'

'Well, for what other purpose do you think I came? And to what better purpose can a man's energy be devoted, and his talents, than the resuscitation of his country's language? What do you think I came for?'

'I hoped that you would do in Ireland what Voltaire did in France, that, whenever Walsh or Logue said something stupid in the papers, you would just reply to them in some sharp cutting letter, showing them up in the most ridiculous light, terrifying them in to silence.'

'I'm afraid you were mistaken if you thought that I came to Ireland on any enterprise so trivial. I came to give back to Ireland her language.'

The conversation went on between them without further reference to Fr Finlay.

Later in the work, Moore referred to an occasion when he was walking round St Stephen's Green with Finlay, and he said: 'It is strange that Catholics have written so little in Ireland.' 'It is, indeed,' he answered, 'and Maynooth is a case in point; after a hundred years of education it has not succeeded in producing a book of any value, not even a theological work.' Moore commented: 'I don't know that Father Tom has produced anything very wonderful himself. Very likely he hasn't. Father Tom's lack of original literary inspiration is a matter of no importance to anyone except to Father Tom. The question before us is, Which is at fault – race or Catholicism?'[10] Subsequently, Moore quoted Finlay's alleged comment about the absence of a book of value from Maynooth as a spear with which to jab T.P. Gill into thinking, with his 'somewhat meagre mind', that he had an obligation to write a defence of Catholicism.[11]

Moore's final reference to his friend Father Tom was in relation to Douglas Hyde, the founder of the Gaelic League, concerning whom Moore was slighting and defamatory. He was 'soft and peaty ... the softest of all our natural products, a Protestant that Protestantism had not been able to harden!' He sought out the company of priests, and 'melts like peat into a fine ash before his Grace's ring'. Moore admitted, however, that Hyde's 'prose translations of the *Love Songs of Connacht*' were 'as beautiful as Synge's'; and then, with scant regard for historical accuracy, observed, 'It is a pity he was stopped by Father Tom Finlay, who said: "Write in Irish or in English, but our review does not like mixed languages." And these words, and his election to the presidency of the Gaelic League, made an end to Hyde as a man of letters.'[12]

D.P. MORAN

Another unusual, larger than life literary figure, who was friendly with Finlay, was D.P. Moran. The latter produced a new weekly review, the *Leader*, in 1900, the year, also, in which the split in the Irish Parliamentary Party was healed. His frank, critical comment won a wide following, and his *Leader* became associated with the new national revival. He had no time for patriotic rhetoric or what he termed the national 'sunburstry' in 'platform oratory, newspapers or elsewhere'.[13]

Some years previously, on his return to Ireland from England, he wrote in the *New Ireland Review*, and when he came to establish his weekly, he approached Finlay in search of fresh minds. Finlay directed him to the members of the L and H, and among his earliest contributors were William Dawson ('Avis') and Arthur Clery ('Chanel'). Later contributors included Francis Cruise O'Brien.[14]

Moran first caught the public interest in Finlay's review. In December 1898 he raised the question 'Is the Irish nation dying?' and left few of his readers unchallenged. 'It is scarcely necessary to point out,' he declared, 'that of the things which go to the making of a nation, some, such as arts, practically do not exist in Ireland, others, such as the language we speak and the literature we read, are borrowed from another country.' There was a constant tendency, he added, 'to explain away our shortcomings' by blaming past history, and those who did not see eye to eye with the 'national' politicians were 'held up as enemies of their race'. With reference to the Irish party's policy of putting off reform until Home Rule was granted, he questioned acidly whether 'all the national life is to be left to bleed out of us, until we come by our right to make laws for the corpse'.

Not surprisingly, such independent, trenchant comment was popular with the students at University College, but it was not calculated to make friends for Moran, or for the editor who published such criticism, among the supporters of the Irish party. The following year, in February 1889, Moran returned to the charge in 'The future of the Irish nation'. 'We must be original Irish', he proclaimed, 'and not imitation English ... The time has come when people and politicians are made to recognise that there are two other Irish movements ... (with) an equal right to as much public attention as Home Rule ... One is the movement which aims at making the best of Ireland's economic opportunities, and the other, that for reviving a universal interest in all that appertains to the Gael and his language.'

The sentiments were close to Finlay's own. To him the economic, social and moral development of the people and the country were the primary aims, and Home Rule was desirable mainly as a means towards them and towards building national self-confidence.

Finlay's journals, the *Lyceum* and the *New Ireland Review*, as has been indicated, added to both his influence and his problems. They loomed large during his most vigorous years and merit particular attention.

5

The editor of journals

The editorial in the first issue of the *Irish Homestead*, the periodical Finlay founded to serve the Irish Agricultural Co-operative Movement, conveyed his views on the importance of publications: 'There is hardly any interest now days worth representing before the public which has not its organ in the press. Not to have a publication is to be in danger of being thought insignificant.' He planned to achieve for the Irish Agricultural Co-operative Society by means of the *Irish Homestead* what he had already endeavoured to encompass for University College, its reputation, its interests and its students, by means of the *Lyceum*, from September 1887 to February 1894, and the *New Ireland Review*, from March 1894 to February 1911.

THE 'LYCEUM'

The *Lyceum* was a monthly educational and literary magazine and review, which was started by four people: the Finlay brothers, Fr John Carroll, and a Jesuit scholastic, Robert Curtis. Between them they wrote practically the whole of the first number, Tom Finlay contributing almost 50 per cent. The subsequent issues, carried articles, all unsigned, by a Mrs O'Gorman, and by W.P. Coyne, Thomas Arnold, William Magennis, Robert Donovan, and the Jesuits, Robert Curtis and Denis Murphy. These eleven were the team, captained by Tom Finlay, which ran the periodical from September 1887 to October 1891, when William Magennis took over as editor.

The first number of the *Lyceum* set out the programme to be followed: 'To promote a higher Catholic literature, to discuss questions of scientific and literary interest from the Catholic point of view, and under guidance of Catholic teaching to contribute something … to the solution … of the great problems …' He added, 'We shall examine principles, not champion men; we shall seek the solution of problems, practical or otherwise, not advocate party interests or strive for mere party ends.'[1] The programme was pursued to the point of omitting any *direct* treatment of the land agitation, the Home Rule movement, or the Parnell split, burning issues during the magazine's existence. To C.P. Curran, looking back after many years, the *Lyceum* was 'peculiarly sensitive to the atmosphere in which it was born', and was 'conservative without being reactionary'. Given its aim, 'to promote a Catholic solution of the educational and social problems which were pressing themselves, at home and abroad, on public attention, ... it gallantly discharged this task.'[2] In addition to its emphasis on educational and social matters, however, it carried regular reviews of new publications, and literary articles, notably on Russian literature, concerning writers such as Gogol, Dostoievsky, and Turgenev, and from July 1890 a sonnet was published in each issue.[3]

OCCASIONS OF EMBARRASSMENT

Tom Finlay's strong demand for high moral standards in public life led him to criticise Parnell and to argue against his continuance as leader of the Irish party,[4] but none of this was given expression in the *Lyceum*. His brother, Peter, however, was not as 'peculiarly sensitive to the atmosphere' of the time, and in his use of the periodical was more involved in live issues than Curran indicated, and was more inflexible than Tom. In 'The bishops and political morality', in November 1892, Peter asserted, and could not conceive how any Catholic could question his assertion, that the Parnell situation necessitated episcopal intervention. 'And', he added, in sweeping rigorist vein, 'since Catholics believe that sin brings down upon the sinner God's anger here and punishment hereafter, might not the Bishops go on to warn their people of the spiritual penalties they are certain to undergo, should they aid, even by their votes, the Church's enemies.'[5] It was the kind of statement that strained his brother's patience, and not for the first time. Earlier, in the second issue of the *Lyceum*, Peter produced the first of two articles on 'The theology of land nationalisation', which caused a ripple of excitement even on the Tiber. Henry George, in his own journal, expressed his pleasure that the *Lyceum* had accepted his 'new theory' – that there should be no private ownership in land.[6] Tom came to his brother's rescue in 'Mr Henry George and the *Lyceum*', December 1887. At the close of a strong article, he declared:

> We have not, then, accepted any 'new theory' from Mr George. What is new in his theory – the doctrine of the immorality of private ownership in land – we reject as repugnant alike to social philosophy and traditional theology. What remains when this doctrine has been rejected – his scheme of taxation – is not new in theory, and not new in practice. And further, whether it be new or old, we have expressed no opinion on its merits.

On another occasion, however, on an issue remote from Irish politics, he was unable to save the magazine and himself from Peter's sharp pen. The occasion was a review of *Our Christian Heritage* by James Cardinal Gibbons.[7] In the February issue, 1890, Peter Finlay commented:

> The object of the work is to bring home the claims of Theism and Christianity to minds estranged by training, association, and other more or less excusing causes 'from the specific teachings of the Gospel', and from the truths even of 'natural religion'. How far does it succeed? If the

reader had the wish to believe, *Our Christian Heritage* may aid him to realise his wish; but if he should be unwilling to believe, or even coldly critical, the work, we are afraid, will have little weight with him. Worse even: it may prove injurious. For, next to convincing proofs that he is right, nothing is more calculated to strengthen a man's faith in the soundness of his position than a weak argument that he is wrong. We would not be understood to mean that the Cardinal's arguments are generally inconclusive – though we should be sorry to have to maintain them all against a clear-sighted opponent.

He went on to demonstrate how this was so![8]

The review was noticed and given publicity by a Chicago newspaper, and some American Jesuits complained of it to the Jesuit general, Anton Anderledy. The latter felt it necessary to send a personal apology to the cardinal. In addition, he wrote strongly to the Irish provincial, Timothy Kenny. His letter was read to the consultors of the province on 20 February 1890.[9] The minutes of the meeting noted: 'There followed a series of consultations about the *Lyceum*, especially a review of Cardinal Gibbon's *Christian Heritage*. The end was a suspension from writing of Frs Thomas and Peter Finlay. A letter of apology was written to Cardinal Gibbons by order of Father General.'[10] Gibbons replied to the vice-provincial, Alfred Murphy, who had sent the letter, on 7 May 1890:

> The work *Our Christian Heritage* received undue praise. I have no unkind feeling for the article in the *Lyceum* … Surprised that your General should have taken the trouble to apologise.[11]

After an interval to arrange matters, the financial and editorial responsibility for the *Lyceum* passed from the Finlays to William Magennis. It had been Tom Finlay's policy from the start to invite contributions from more gifted students with a view to encouraging and schooling them as writers. The most prominent of these were Robert Donovan, a future professor of English, W.P. Coyne, later a lecturer in Economics and the first director of statistics in the Department of Agriculture, and William Magennis, destined to become professor of Philosophy at University College. Magennis graduated in 1888. The *Lyceum* remained in his charge from October 1891 until it was discontinued in favour of the *New Ireland Review* in February 1894.

The ban on the Finlays seems to have lasted only for a short time. Indeed, it did not prevent Tom Finlay writing a number of articles for the *Lyceum* following the suspension. It is possible that he had been privately excused by the provincial, as a result of the cardinal's letter, or he had excused himself on the grounds that he was writing anonymously. Doubtless, had George Moore known of the matter, it would have been construed as a template of Finlay's alleged advice to him – 'One must pay no attention to criticism, but go on doing what one has to do.'[12]

Peter Finlay was not the only lightning conductor. The *Lyceum*, for a supposedly conservative monthly, generated its share of criticism and opposition. In the very first issue, Fr John O'Carroll, a noted linguist and a member of the University College teaching staff, commenced a projected series of articles on the history of the Royal University. He had no premonition of trouble. 'The Education Question', he opined, 'has no hold on human passions ... The long steady injury of a bad educational system is temperately condemned and quietly endured.' And 'if by speaking on the subject we cannot hope to do much good, we are at any rate sure not to do any harm.'[13] The series was discontinued after the second article! O'Carroll had made the mistake of praising the fairness of the senate of the university. Even though weighted numerically against Catholics, the senators had been 'astonishingly and nobly just to Catholics', especially in the allocation of fellows of the university. Archbishop Walsh perceived in this presentation an attack on himself. As president of Maynooth he had been on the senate of the university and had resigned because of its policy of distributing virtually all the Catholic fellows to the bishops' college, University College, St Stephen's Green. He wanted some fellows to go to Blackrock College. Subsequently, decrying the monopolistic policy of the senate, he brought his grievance into the public press to the embarrassment of the bishops and eventually to his own humiliation.[14] He became, as a result, a persistent critic of the Royal University and its senate, and less than friendly towards University College. He was incensed, moreover, by the promise in the second article that in the next issue there would be proposals relating to a system of endowments for Catholic education in connection with the Royal University. The question of endowments, the archbishop declared, pertained strictly to the hierarchy. Angry at the articles, he blamed Tom Finlay, as editor, for their publication, and conveyed his displeasure to the Jesuit provincial, Thomas Browne, who, in turn, conveyed to Finlay his Grace's opposition. The proofs of the next article, which avoided the subject of endowments, were forwarded to Dr Walsh who returned them unread. The article was not published, and the series ceased.[15] Archbishop Walsh, nevertheless, remained suspicious of the editor of the *Lyceum*, and subsequently transferred his suspicions to the *New Ireland Review*.

FINLAY'S OWN CONTRIBUTIONS

So far, the contributions of others than Tom Finlay have been mentioned. His own articles covered a wide field. An adequate description would require a separate volume. The following titles from just eight months of one year suggest the range: 'Unearned increment as a basis for taxation' (January 1888); 'The successful preacher' (February 1888); 'The school examiner' (March 1888); 'Social science in the slums' (April 1888); 'The growth of an empire (Russia)' (April 1888); 'The burden of pauperism' (May 1888); 'A scheme of denominational school endowment' (June 1888); 'The law of demand and supply in danger' (in collaboration with William Magennis), and the start of a series on 'The witch before the law' (July 1888); and, in August, 'The depopulation of Ireland'. The foregoing point to the variety of his interests and to his leaning towards social economics. An alternative to capitalism was one of his abiding concerns. He wrote a number of articles on socialism. The extreme form, which sought the abolishment of social and economic institutions, by violence if necessary, he viewed as chimerical, but he looked with sympathy on a form of socialism which accepted the existing framework of industrial society and sought, 'by gradual and peaceful change', to 'bring labour and capital into the hands of the actual workers, and thus abolish capitalist employers as a distinct class of society'. He linked this form of socialism to co-operation: the latter seeking 'by gradual and voluntary change' what socialism would effect by actual state legislation.[16] His commitment was to co-operation as a remedy for social ills and, as will later appear, he wrote a long and vigorous article on it in the *Lyceum*. Apart from such social issues, education, as might be expected, occupied a large part of his contributions. His articles in this area had frequently a searching quality which give them a relevance more than a century later. Among them were: 'Recent developments in the art of teaching' (June 1888); and 'Education and examination' (in volume 2, pp 77ff); also in that volume, a powerful plea in support of primary teachers; 'University extension' and 'Some educational reform' (August 1891); 'Women's higher education in Ireland' (April 1893); and 'Anomalies in our Intermediate system' (October 1893).

On certain issues, notably those of a social and religious nature, his independent thinking and expression were likely to upset influential sections of society.

SEMINARIES. THE MASONS

In some articles concerning Cardinal Manning he pointed out that ecclesiastical training tended to dwell in the past, and that the clergy 'ran the risk of growing up more intimately conversant with ways of thought and conditions of existence' which had passed away than 'with the realities around them'. This was particularly so regarding the social order, where there was a process of ceaseless change, and 'the most commonly accepted social truths today were innovations yesterday' and objects of suspicion to good men. He concluded:

> Rapidity of communication, the diffusion of books, the daily press, above all the spread of education and combination for common ends, have lifted the masses from the position of hopeless inferiority in which they lay. They are the true masters of the modern world, though they scarcely realise their power, and have not yet learned to use it. And religion, if it is to carry on its mission must join forces with them.[17]

In this analysis and conclusion he could appeal to Pope Leo XIII's social encyclical, *Rerum novarum*, which had been influenced by Manning's example and teaching. Writing of the encyclical in July 1891, he succinctly observed:

Statesmen and labourers may alike study it with advantage. The one will find in it an accurate definition of the range of his powers and the measure of his responsibilities; the other a lucid statement of the claims he is justified in making upon the owners of capital, and the limit to which he may go in enforcing his demands.[18]

Certain delicate areas likely to generate strong public feeling were tackled directly but sensitively. One of these was the Masons. A meeting of the Freemason Brotherhood in Dublin had given rise to public comment. On 15 June 1892, Finlay wrote on 'Our brothers the Masons'. He felt it necessary to explain why the Catholic Church opposed Freemasonry. The subject extended over three articles. At the close of the first he observed:

It will be noted, then, that Freemasonry is disposed to make use of the public positions attained by its members to further secret ends; that it obliges them to use the trust conferred on them by the people for the service of the people as an opportunity to do the business of the lodges, and to carry out their decrees.

Accordingly, the Church was doing a service to society in pointing out the failings of the Masonic organisation. The second article appeared in July and dealt in some detail with Freemasonry's history of hostility to Catholicism, and with the Church's critical response. The final article appeared in the August/September issue, 1892.

Another area of public sensitivity was the activity of Jews in society. Finlay wrote three articles entitled 'The Jew in Ireland', which caused something of a stir and brought him into conflict with Michael Davitt.

THE JEWS AND IRELAND

The first article appeared in July 1893 in connection with a difference between a local politician in Bandon, County Cork, and Michael Davitt. The local politician, in the context of a fresh influx of Jewish immigrants, had made a speech advising his audience to 'keep the Jews out of Ireland'. Davitt took the orator to task in the *Freeman's Journal*, 13 July 1893, for this display of intolerance. The orator, in reply, explained away his words, disclaiming any intention of hindering the influx of Jews into Ireland. Finlay regretted that 'the Bandon orator gave up his case so readily', because the matter deserved to be 'raised and discussed'.

He agreed with Davitt that Irish people did not have a record of intolerance towards the Jews, had no conceivable motive for racial hatred against the Jews, and should spurn the myths emanating from Eastern Europe which accused the Jews of sacrificing Christian children in their liturgies. Nevertheless, the prospect of an increased number of Jews coming into Ireland was one that needed to be discussed, and it was better to discuss it calmly now 'when passion has not been wildly excited' and when people can reason without the bias that comes from a sense of serious grievances – even a mistaken sense. The issue, he insisted, was not simply one of racial or religious intolerance. It might well be one of self-defence. In public as in private relations, 'charity began at home', and it might be necessary in self-defence to take measures against immigrants whose settlement in the country would constitute an economic danger.

The danger was not that mentioned by Mr Davitt, namely, 'the competition of the Jewish labourer with the native wage-earner, and the consequent reduction in the standard of wages and standard of comfort for the latter'. Although the Irish Jews were not a danger in that sense, the point needed to be made that 'competition with labour which will submit to any conditions of hardship, and accept any scale of remuneration, must force the well-to-do labourer down to the level of the most indigent, and when the labourer is well-to-do he can rightly protest against being thus degraded, and appeal to the public authority to save him from the competition which leads to his degradation'. 'State interference in such a case', Finlay emphasised, was 'distinctly justifiable, and the more democratic the state, the more sensitive the government to popular influences, the more readily' would 'such interference be accorded.' No one complained when the American government took effectual measures to check the influx of Chinese workmen into the United States. But, he reiterated, the penniless Jewish workman was not the problem in Ireland. The Jews in Ireland, and the recent influx of such, were reasonably well off. They were the type of Jew that had given rise to an anti-Semitic party in Germany and had led the German Catholic party to criticise them as not contributing to the productive industries of the country but having 'by tricks of trade and the devices of the money-lender' continued 'to get possession of the wealth which the toiling Christian creates'. The evidence in support of this contention was, in Finlay's own recollection, 'abundant'.

'If we are ever to have an anti-Semitic party in Ireland', he declared, 'it will, most probably, owe its origins to causes like those which have been at work in Germany.' Already, the Jew had begun in Ireland as a petty trader, using the methods that brought unpopularity in Germany. Already, he was traversing the lanes of Irish cities, or visiting country farmhouses, when the farmer was out and only the women of the house were to be dealt with, carrying bundles of cheap wares at prices which appeared very low to the purchaser because the payment was spread over a considerable time. He was prepared to call weekly for his payment, and thereby obtain knowledge of various households and opportunities for money lending. Once he had lent money, he could, by pressing for repayment at inconvenient times, almost oblige the borrower to let the debt grow until ultimately the borrower was 'burdened to the point at which his interest in his farm passes to his creditor.' This was the process followed among peasant proprietors in Germany, Finlay explained, and it was successful to the extent of creating an anti-Semitic party in the Reichstag.

It was significant, he thought, 'that the appearance of the Jew in Ireland as a trader and money-lender on a large scale' coincided 'with the change in law which gave the Irish tenant a saleable interest in his farm'. He had noticed, moreover, 'that certain well-known figures of the Jewish quarter in Dublin' were to be 'encountered frequently in certain southern counties, driving in smart vehicles, making calls at the houses of some of the farmers as they went. They were not encumbered by the familiar pack and its contents, and their visits were not out of friendship or philanthropy'. Hence, in answer to the question with which he had begun – 'Should the Jew be made welcome in Ireland?' – his reply was:

> If he will come to take a share in our industries, to be an honest producer amongst us, to contribute by his labour to the general sum of our wealth, let him be welcome even though the field of labour amongst us is pretty well crowded already. But if he comes merely as a parasite, not to produce by labour in the field or workshop, but to live upon the fruits of labour of others, which he secures by the arts of doubtful traffic and dangerous money-lending, then let him not be more welcome here than he is among the peasants of Germany or among the labourers of France.[19]

Finally, in the September issue, he emphasised that 'reasons of expediency alone, and the natural desire to see our people exempt from the consequences which have usually followed the advent of the Jew among poor populations, influence us in our suspicion of the benefits to be derived from the widespread establishment of the Jew in our midst, and render us slow to make him welcome.'[20]

The *Lyceum* endeavoured to lift Irish Catholics out of a blinkered political groove, and to develop a Catholic consciousness and a critical sense which would enrich life and extend horizons. It encountered opposition, as has been seen. Although to some it seemed conservative, to others it appeared too progressive, 'too full of ideas'.[21] W.H. Stead, perhaps, viewed the *Lyceum* in a clearer light than its Irish readers. Again and again he referred to it in his *Review of Reviews* and, thereby, added to its stature. He was attracted by its touch of novelty and venturesomeness, the quality which disturbed the conventionalists and heresy-hunters. The anonymity of the articles gave the contributors greater freedom, but it had the drawback of throwing the main responsibility for the contributors' views on the organ and those credited with its control. It gradually came to be appreciated that it was desirable to have the articles signed, and also to change the format from the old quarto double column, which was thought more suitable for a weekly paper than for a magazine. It was also felt, however, that Ireland had changed much in recent years and had grown in the number of educated readers and that there was scope for a review that appealed to all class of readers.

Announcing the closure of the *Lyceum*, in the editorial in February 1894, Finlay noted that their list of contributors would enable them provide in the new *Review* 'a treatment of all current questions of interest, theological, historical, scientific, economic, and educational, as well as the lighter and more popular social and literary topics'. The *New Ireland Review*, he declared, would appear the following month, March 1894. The principal articles would 'be signed with the names of the writers, who' would 'be individually responsible for the views which they express'. 'Beyond this requirement', Finlay promised, 'only one restriction will be placed on liberty of discussion: there shall not appear in our pages any attack upon the religious convictions or the national character of our people.'

THE 'NEW IRELAND REVIEW'

The *Freeman's Journal*, of 1 March 1894, welcomed the *New Ireland Review*, observing that the title acknowledged the 'political and social changes, educational developments, the stirring of new ideas, and the growth of new wants' that made Ireland a very different place from twenty years ago. The paper concluded that the first issue lived up to the editor's promise, and that there was matter in it 'of a worth beyond that of fugitive topics however important'.[23]

In the *Review*, as in the *Lyceum*, a number of the contributors and joint-editors had been students taught by Finlay, or brought into connection with him. Among them, besides W.P. Coyne and William Magennis, Arthur Clery and Tom Kettle, were P.T Hogan, James Meredith, Vasey Hague, and the poet Frank Little whom Finlay greatly encouraged. But the *Review* was not confined to friends of the editor. It claimed that its pages were open to all who had something to say and knew how to say it. The magazine, in fact, came to exercise a strong influence upon many reflective men and women. In addition, it produced two series of articles which, published later in book form, were recognised as contributions of significance to Irish history and letters. The first of these was Douglas Hyde's *Religious Songs of Connacht*, which appeared almost uninterruptedly from June 1895 to June 1905. The second publication was the series of lectures on early Irish history, by Eoin MacNeill, delivered in University College in 1904 and published in the *New Ireland Review* the same year. The epoch-making series appeared in two books: *Phases of Irish History* and *Celtic Ireland*. MacNeill, it has been said, 'cleared away the debris of barren legend and showed what the history of pagan Ireland certainly was not', and then 'applied himself to the task of reconstruction'.[24]

To describe Finlay's own articles in the *Review* would, as in the *Lyceum*, require a separate publication. He wrote much on the industries of the country, especially those connected with agriculture and co-operation, and also with more general questions of political economy but always with reference to their practical application in Ireland. Finlay, according to his friend and successor, George O'Brien, 'was impatient of discussion that did not lead to practical results'.[25] Among his many articles on economic matters was a series of five on the 'Art of rent fixing' (March–November 1901), then a thorny question as it dealt with a question of fair rents as fixed compulsorily by the Land Commission then sitting, and with cases where its judgments were revised by the Court of Appeal. A later series, from February to April 1904, dealt with 'Ireland and free trade', a subject being debated actively in Britain and Ireland. His articles were mainly historical, but from current historical knowledge of the period he drew conclusions relating to modern economics and free trade. Reflecting on the prosperity achieved under the Irish parliament at the end of the eighteenth century, he concluded that the Irish statesmen of the period, nine years after the publication of Adam Smith's *Wealth of Nations*, 'believed that their duty was, not to work out or apply brilliant scientific theories, but to study carefully the particular conditions of their own country, and to devise by the light of practical common sense what policy would, in these conditions, best promote its interests'. Their approach, Finlay observed pointedly, was at variance with economic theories 'which have since become fashionable, and which were framed as an economic gospel for an England that held the supremacy in the world of industry and commerce'.[26] Free trade in the past, he insisted, had been ruinous of Irish industry. He saw no reason to believe that the proposed modifications now being put forward by British conservatives would be of benefit to Ireland. 'They would secure our markets for British manufacturers; they would not help us to create manufactures of our own.'[27]

Economic and social issues received wide coverage in the *Review*. Horace Plunkett, in August 1896, wrote about 'The Report of the Recess Committee', of which he was the chairman and inspiration; W.P. Coyne, now lecturing in economics in University College, contributed articles, *inter alia*, on 'The future of industry' (1899); Marian Mulhall wrote on 'Workhouse reform', and Charles Stannwell on 'The railway system'. There were articles on philosophy from W.P. Coyne and William Magennis, and from Vesey Hague who, in 'Wanted: a philosophy of duty', 1902–3, defended Aristotle against modern Idealism, and James Merideth who, from July 1904 to February 1906, examined Haeckel's presentation of Materialism in a series of eleven articles with different titles. Tom Finlay dealt benignly with Arthur Balfour's *Philosophic Doubt* in contributions entitled 'Mr Balfour and his critics', July and August 1895. There were also, apart from Hyde's 'Religious songs of Connacht', a variety of articles on literary and cultural topics. These included Æ on the 'Cuchulann saga', Charles Gavan Duffy on the Irish Literary Theatre, Edward Dowden on Hamlet, and the 'Irish Literary Renaissance and the Irish language' by George Moore. Irish writers considered were Allingham, Ferguson, Goldsmith, Mangan, Moira O'Neill, Swift, and Canon Sheehan, and there was some original poetry by, for example, Eva Gore-Booth.[28]

Articles touching on politics received much notice, especially those by D.P. Moran. These included, as mentioned earlier, 'Is the Irish nation dying?' (December 1898), and 'The future of the Irish nation' (February 1899), but also 'The Pale and the Gael' (June 1899), 'Politics, nationality, and snobs' (November 1899), and 'The battle of two civilisations' (March 1900). This last, perhaps, caused the greatest stir. In it Moran delivered a scathing attack on the Anglo-Celtic school of writers in general, and on W.B. Yeats in particular, not excluding Mathew Arnold and George Moore. Irishmen were dropping the practice of reading, Moran averred, because they could find nothing that interested them. 'Practically no one in Ireland understands Mr Yeats and his school …' and 'if a literary man is not appreciated and cannot be understood, of what use is he?' Unfortunately, 'the Irish mind was wound down to such a low state that it was fit to be humbugged by such a school

... A muddled land which mistook politics for nationality was offered the services of a few mystics' to muddle her with more mysteries.²⁹

VIEWS ON THE STATE AND SOCIALISM

With respect to politics, it is convenient to note here that the nearest one gets to Finlay's political views is in passing remarks in articles with regard to the Irish parliament and free trade, and in his encouragement of self-reliance and co-operation. The State for him existed for the economic, moral, and social betterment of the people, and not to take over their lives. As a consequence, he considered it important to encourage people to be self-reliant and not dependant on an all-embracing system. He was particularly critical of the idea of the socialist state, and he tended to be sceptical about the lasting effect of programming and planning. A liberal humanist in his approach, he required that economics be made comprehensible to the general reader. Not surprisingly, John Stuart Mill was one of his favoured authors. Finlay, Horace Plunkett, and Finlay's successor, George O'Brien, would have agreed with Mills that

> The worth of the State, in the long run, is the worth of the individuals composing it, and a State which ... dwarfs its men, in order that they may be more docile instruments in its hands even for beneficial purposes, will find that with small men no really great thing can be accomplished; and that the perfection of machinery to which it has sacrificed anything, will in the end avail it nothing for want of the vital power which, in order that the machine might work more smoothly, it has preferred to banish.³⁰

JAMES CONNOLLY'S CHALLENGE

As might be expected, Finlay's views on socialism did not meet with the approval of James Connolly, the intellectual voice of socialism in Ireland. On 1 July 1899, Connolly replied carefully to an address by Finlay at Maynooth in the course of which the lecturer maintained that socialism had always broken down wherever it was tried because it violated man's right to do what he wished with what he had created by his labour. 'To forbid him the right to reserve it or use it as capital would be to deny him the right to possess property', and in this, and in other respects, socialism had 'much in common with slavery'. This address before the fourth annual general meeting of the Maynooth Union, Connolly observed, was deserving of more intelligent criticism than that afforded by capitalist contemporaries. 'We readily allow', he stated in unexpected tribute, 'that no man in Ireland within the clerical body, and few men in Ireland outside the ranks of the adherents of scientific socialism, can bring to bear upon questions of political economy, and the effect which theories of political economy have had upon the industrial life of the people, such a wealth of knowledge as the reverend gentleman whose paper we are now discussing. The feeble and ineffective efforts of the Home Rule pressmen to criticise the co-operative movement to which Father Finlay devotes so much of his energy and ability is in itself proof enough' that when it came 'to the intelligent discussion of the economic question' they were 'worse than useless'.

'The economic theories held by the non-socialist parties in Ireland today', Connolly continued, 'are in fact the theories which prevailed in England more than fifty years ago' during the agitation for free trade, and which now are considered 'outworn and obsolete' throughout the rest of the world. It was 'only in Ireland they survive', and in Ireland only among men who had 'failed to keep step with the intellectual march of the world'. He did not purpose to waste his readers time discussing the views of such people on economics, 'but the arguments of Father Finlay naturally carrying more weight, deserve, we repeat, a much more serious study'.

Connolly went on astutely to observe that Finlay in his address did not place before his hearers 'such a clear and definite idea of the true socialist position' as he possessed. Some years ago, in a lecture on the teachings of Karl Marx, delivered in Dublin before the Statistical Society, he gave 'an exposition of the evolutionary nature of the socialist doctrine, its historical derivation and materialistic base', which was not compatible with the 'crudely false conception of socialism' given by him at Maynooth. Socialism, in fact, had not 'broken down wherever it has been tried', 'because, being the fruit of an historical evolution yet to be completed, *it has never been tried*'. Father Finlay's 'statement was crudely false, mischievous, and misleading', and 'he would not risk his reputation by repeating it before any audience of scientists in the world. That he thought it quite safe to make such an utterance at Maynooth' was 'an interesting indication of the low estimate in which he held the intellectual grasp of his hearer on the thought of their generation'.[31] In typical apologist fashion, Connolly had not dealt with Finlay's main argument that socialism, as he defined it, could not succeed because it violated basic human freedom, but instead he had focussed on certain words of Finlay against which he could make a case. His respect for Finlay continued. Nine years later, in the *Harp* of October 1908, he remarked:

> I have read a good many scare fulminations against socialism from his Holiness down and I have never seen but one from such a source that showed any real knowledge of what socialism is.

The exception was Finlay.

The esteem in which he and his work was held by Connolly, by Moran of the *Leader*, and by Protestant and unionist colleagues in the co-operative movement, together with his active pursuit of a solution to the university question during the unionist period of government, almost inevitably prompted criticism of him by members of the Home Rule party. He also, as indicated earlier, occasioned criticism and opposition from the archbishop of Dublin. To understand the grounds for hostility and criticism it is necessary to recall the political and social background during the period 1890 to 1908.

6

Socio-political ambience, 1890–1908

In the 1880s and for much of the 1890s there was an attitude of neutrality towards politics in University College. A certain distance from political divisions went back to Newman's day and was linked to the avoidance of extremes, or of allegiances likely to weaken the case for a Catholic university. The beginning of the 1890s, however, brought the shock of the Parnell scandal and division in the Home Rule party. Peter Finlay, in the *Lyceum*, defended the bishops' criticism of Parnell, and Tom Finlay vigorously championed Tim Healy MP in his call for the deposition of the leader in the interests of moral standards in public life.[1] As a result, both brothers were viewed adversely by Parnellites, while Tom's friendship with Healy virtually guaranteed opposition from John Dillon and his supporters.

Meantime, the vehement and seemingly irreconcilable nature of the split generated a movement away from politics to wider interests. These included: interest in Irish history and archaeology, and, generally, a new openness to things Irish. A key development was the founding of the Gaelic League in 1893 to promote the Irish language and Irish music and dance. Significantly, it was founded by a Protestant, Douglas Hyde, and was quickly taken up by Catholic clergy who saw in Gaelic culture a bulwark against the materialism associated with British rule. A further interest in the lives of the people was provided by the Gaelic Athletic Association, which engaged large numbers of young men and youths in hurling, Gaelic football, athletics and cycling.

The interest in things Irish coincided with a new movement towards self-help and co-operation among Irish farmers. It was given life and force by the unionist, Horace Plunkett, assisted by some other Protestants, and by Finlay, who, as a Catholic priest, was able to assure Catholic farmers that it was all right to participate in an enterprise sponsored by Protestants and landlords. It became a highly successful venture and led to the establishment of a committee to plan the future of Irish agriculture, and this, in turn, resulted in the setting up of an Irish Department of Agriculture and Technical Instruction. In these advances, Finlay played a key role. He also furthered the co-operative cause by articles in the *Lyceum* and the *New Ireland Review,* lauding the movement for its encouragement of an independent spirit of self-help, and pride in nationhood, and providing an impetus to prosperity for the small farmer.

During these years, the sense of constitutional futility was heightened by the continuing presence of a Conservative government. The Tories were returned in 1895 and again in 1900. Intransigent on Home Rule, the government was prepared to make concessions in other areas in an effort to mollify the people. One of these areas promised to be the university question. William Delany, Tom Finlay, and some of the bishops, took steps to avail of this possibility, only to find themselves criticised by the Irish party and by a large section of the bishops under the aegis of the archbishop of Dublin. The Irish party viewed efforts to seek economic and educational support from a Tory administration as collusion with a hostile government that was determined to kill Home Rule with kindness; and Archbishop Walsh tended to agree with the party about deferring a decision on the university question until Home Rule was achieved, or until the British government granted equality with Trinity College by providing a fullequipped Catholic College in Dublin University.

As might be expected, the closing of the door on constitutional progress provided an opening for the militant minority in the Fenian tradition. The centenary of the 1798 rebellion offered this group an ideal opportunity. They worked actively with, and in, other organisations, and helped to colour the commemoration. It became not just an evocation of the rebellion, but an occasion to celebrate 'Irishness' and difference from Britain. It tapped into, and expanded, the growing sense of national pride, and promoted the spirit of self-help and self-confidence. These sentiments were given a strong public voice by Arthur Griffith through his *United Irishman*, which also gave expression to anti-Britain feeling by open support for the Boers during the Boer War. And, though D.P. Moran of the *Leader* had no time for nationalist rhetoric and flag waving, his fiery, original writing furthered the cause of an Irish-Ireland and its need to assert its distinctiveness from Britain. 'By treating the anti-Catholic bigotry, the snobbery, anti-nationalism, and political insincerities of the Irish people to a drum-fire of ridicule and criticism'[2] he stirred feeling, clarified thinking and motivation, especially among young people, and helped create a movement. In conjunction with other factors promoting things Irish, Moran helped make it a matter of honour to wear Irish clothes, to write on Irish paper, to smoke Irish tobacco, and to play hurling rather than soccer. This manifestation of 'Irish spirit' added to the spreading support for the Irish language, for Irish writing, music and sports, and for the exploration of Celtic and Gaelic themes in plays and poetry in the English language. The new 'Irishness', however, developed its own exclusivity and sensitivity. Yeat's evocation of Ireland in *Countess Cathleen* was strongly opposed by members of the central branch of the Gaelic League, by Cardinal Logue and some clergy, and by a number of vocal University College students. Finlay, however, and Dr William Barry, as noted, supported the play. Finlay's stance was a further indication of both his independence of spirit and his many-sided interests.

It is apposite to an understanding of his career to note that, as a priest and Jesuit, he consciously adapted his many talents to the needs and developments of the time with the apostolic intent of influencing and benefiting as many people as possible. In an age without radio or television, the way to influence was by the printed word, lectures, and informed conversation – a near art form highly valued among Dublin's more educated population. A priest working and moving in that *milieu*, and wishing to be influential in it, had to read widely in literature and history, be *au fait* with theatrical productions, and with new developments in science and psychology, be up to date on current national and international affairs, in addition to being well grounded in philosophy and in moral and dogmatic theology. William Delany's papers offer clear evidence of his labours in such fields in order to be effective in Dublin clubs and at exclusive dinner tables.[3] His efforts served him and university education well. Tom Finlay followed a similar line, though he was more directly concerned with social problems in Dublin, with economic policy, and the prosperity of the ordinary farmer. His interesting, wide-ranging conversation and obvious ability made him welcome at dinner-tables of nobility and governmental figures, his common touch rendered him at home with the farming population, irrespective of religion, while his strong social awareness won him the respect of both Horace Plunkett and James Connolly, and helped to impress on his students the importance of caring for the less well off, and of service to the wider community. His caustic wit, used at times against cronyism and corruption, was appreciated by his students, but not by the controllers of most public bodies, namely the Irish party.

In University College there was much criticism of the Irish party prior to 1905. In that year a revival in Liberal fortunes seemed likely and new horizons opened for John Redmond and his supporters. In January 1906, the Liberals gained a majority in the general election and returned to government.

Despite his formal avoidance of party allegiances, Tom Finlay was judged by John Dillon to be 'one of the damndest intriguers in Ireland',[4] a point of view strengthened by Finlay's friendship with T.M. Healy, whom Dillon detested, by his closeness to the unionist, Horace Plunkett, and his commitment to improving the lot of Irish farmers with the assistance of a Conservative government. Archbishop Walsh, as noted, also thought of Finlay as an intriguer: seeking through his *Lyceum* and his *New Ireland Review* to obtain a university settlement favourable to the Jesuit-run University College and the Royal University but at odds with 'the bishops' wishes', meaning Dr Walsh's. This negative image of Finlay was sufficiently current in certain quarters for Stanislaus Joyce, in *My Brother's Keeper*,[5] with reference to the protest of the university students at the performance of *Countess Cathleen*, in 1899, to make the 'untrue and wholly preposterous' statement that 'the budding mob-leaders among the students (were) egged on by a political intriguer, Father Finlay SJ.'[6]

The archbishop's suspicions and hostility were further fuelled in February 1896 by an article in the *New Ireland Review*, by William Magennis, entitled 'A layman's view of the University Question'. Having agreed that it was the bishops' right to approve or condemn 'the mode and character of the education supplied', Magennis discussed the three expedients that could meet the bishops' wishes for a university settlement. These were: an exclusively Catholic university, with suitably endowed Catholic colleges; in default of this, to have a distinct Catholic college, 'co-ordinate with Trinity College, within Dublin

University as a common university'; or, thirdly, to 'slightly modify the Royal University, and bestow suitable endowments and privileges on a distinctively Catholic college (or colleges) attached to it as a common university'. Magennis then commented on each of the three. The first arrangement was objected to by those 'to whom Catholicism is naturally distasteful', and by a section of Catholics. The second found 'considerable favour in the eyes of some representative Catholics who hail it as the ideal solution of the problem', though there were others who disliked 'communion with Dublin University as sharing in a prestige abhorrent to their religious and political sentiments'. Magennis pointedly went on to demonstrate why the Dublin University solution was not an appropriate solution for young Catholics, who had an 'imperfect grasp of principles, the lack of reflective habit and of rational convictions', and whose faith would be at risk in the non-Catholic environment of a university, where the professors were likely to be either zealous Protestants or agnostics. The third arrangement, which he judged to be the least demanding and most likely to gain government support, Magennis described as: 'Variously supported by those who consider an exclusively Catholic University objectionable or impracticable or ill-advised; by those, who, in the interests of Trinity College, dread any tampering with the administration of its university; and by those who desire the fulfilment of Lord Dufferin's hope, that the university of which he is chancellor 'may prove the nucleus of a National University of Ireland'.[7]

On the question of a suitable endowment for the Catholic college in the Royal University, Magennis proposed £30,000 a year in state grants, 'apart from allowances which will be requisite for building and equipment'. The case for an endowment for University College was deeply felt by the staff of the college. It was evident that too great a financial burden was being placed on the Irish Jesuit province, while no financial support came from the bishops who owned the college, and none from the government, apart from fellowships.

To make a proposal for an endowment in a public article, however, without first consulting the owners of the college, was likely to provoke opposition. The memory of opposition from Dr Walsh to articles in the *Lyceum*, in 1887, seems to have been forgotten.[8] Moreover, as Archbishop Walsh supported the proposal of a Catholic college in Dublin University, Magennis's case against Dublin University, and his support for the Royal University and a well-endowed Catholic college within it, seemed to him to point to a definite Jesuit intent to oppose his plan in favour of building up the Jesuit-run college and taking control of Catholic university education. He wrote a sharp public letter to the *Freeman's Journal*, on 2 March 1896, critical of Magennis's article and, on the same day, commented to Cardinal Michael Logue on the problems arising 'from religious bodies in the management of our public affairs'. As an illustration, he referred to the article in the *New Ireland Review*, a periodical that was 'simply "run" by Fr Finlay' and was 'being made use of altogether in the interests of schemes in which that body [the Jesuits] is interested'. He added:

There undoubtedly have been informal negotiations going on with a view to the settlement of the University Question by simply endowing the Stephen's Green establishment, removed, of course, to a more suitable site, leaving the Bishops simply on the shelf. I think the danger is now arrested for the present.[9]

Apart from a desire to receive additional endowments for University College, and to make a case for a solution based on the expansion of Royal University, there is no evidence of Magennis wishing to solve the University Question apart from the bishops; indeed the emphasis in the article was on the central position of the bishops. The practical nature of the solution proposed would probably have appealed to Finlay who, perhaps, had read the article before it was published, and may even have discussed it with Magennis, but to apply to him the motives ascribed by the archbishop seems unfair, taking no account of the periodical's policy to allow freedom to its writers and reflecting more his Grace's combined dislike of Finlay, the Royal University and the successful University College.

Magennis's article evoked not only a letter from the archbishop; it called forth criticism from Irish party interests in the form of an editorial comment in the *Freeman* of 3 February. Such reaction was not without effect on Finlay. The fact that he was known to be viewed unfavourably by the archbishop and the leaders of the Irish Party, and his reputation for independence, appear to have influenced the attitude towards him of authorities in Rome. In 1896, Fr Robert Carbery, the president of University College, 1888–97, was due to retire. In June 1896 the Jesuit provincial and his consultors, as was customary, sent to Rome three names, in order of preference, from which a replacement might be chosen. First on the list was Father Thomas A. Finlay. The Jesuit general, Luis Martin, refused to accept the province's choice. A second *terna* was requested, and Fr William Delany was recalled to the post he had vacated in 1888.[10]

TOWARDS A UNIVERSITY SOLUTION: SUCCESS AND REJECTION

In May 1905, frustrated at the lack of movement from the government on the university issue, Finlay captured the mood of the time with some dramatic proposals. 'Why wait any longer', he asked 'for England to do something about university education? Begging was neither dignified nor profitable. Ireland would probably be deceived again as in the past. Why not help herself? Why not revive Newman's Catholic University? The causes that had brought about its failure in 1854 no longer existed. Catholics could now obtain degrees (from the Royal University) without any sacrifice of principle and there was an abundance of good secondary teachers and university professors who were Catholics.' As mentioned in an earlier chapter, he set forth his scheme in considerable detail in the *New Ireland Review*. He had in mind simple, unpretentious structures built on to University College, and financed by parish contributions.

The proposals were received with interest. At a meeting organised by the Catholic Graduates and Under-Graduates Association, Patrick Pearse, and the principal speaker, Mrs Sophie Bryant, DSc, an English Protestant, spoke in its favour; and T.M. Kettle, in his paper, the *Nationist*, from September 1905 to January 1906, pressed the merits of the scheme. The intervention of a general election, however, with the possibility of a new government and new initiatives, suspended interest in the proposals. By October 1906 they were again in consideration. The demand for college places had advanced so considerably in response to scholarships offered by county councils that Fr Delany approached the archbishop for permission 'to erect on the grounds of the college a building of wood or iron' to house two or three small lecture rooms, and two or more larger rooms 'for scientific and chemical lectures'. His Grace approved. By the following May, the new buildings, known popularly as 'Fr Tom's tin university', in allusion to his proposals, were ready.[11]

The message to the new Liberal government and the chief secretary, Augustine Birrell, was clear. The latter, for his part, was determined to provide a solution to the university question during his administration. He did so in 1908 in the form of a National University embracing colleges in Dublin, Cork and Galway, and a separate university situated in Belfast. In the final stages all the main participants, Archbishop Walsh, the Irish Party, William Delany, and Augustine Birrell, worked amicably together. Birrell related well to unionists and nationalists, and made friends with a wide cross-section of people, among them Tom Finlay. When, however, the names of the members of the new governing bodies of the colleges of the university were announced on 9 May 1908, Finlay's name was not among them. His omission from the governing body of University College, Dublin, occasioned widespread surprise. As an educationalist and one of the best-known figures in the country his inclusion was taken for granted. William Delany was shocked. He wrote to John Redmond MP as leader of the party:

> It is widely current in Dublin that the exclusion of Fr Finlay's name from the list of members of the governing bodies of the new university and college in Dublin is due entirely to the intervention of a member of the Irish party, who is said to have strongly urged his exclusion on Mr Birrell ... Seeing that the very existence of this college is due entirely to the fact that Fr Finlay, with my other Jesuit colleagues, has devoted to its support and development, not merely what remained over beyond his personal maintenance of his salary from the Royal University, but all the gifts and *honoraria* which he received as a priest, and that he made himself jointly with me, responsible to the National Bank for a debt of £6,000 incurred in the early part of our administration – a debt of which £1,500 still remains – you can understand that I feel it a duty to my valued friend and colleague, and a duty also to the Catholic public, many of whom are shocked by such a rumour, to ask you frankly and simply, as leader of the

Irish party, whether any such action has taken place to your knowledge and with your approval, or with the knowledge and approval of the Irish party? And if so, on what grounds?[12]

What the letter was meant to achieve, beyond a pointed protest, is not clear. A political leader was unlikely to admit in writing to behind-the-scenes manoeuvring, least of all to a dialectician as sharp as Delany. Redmond replied three days later that he knew 'nothing whatever about the matter'. He took no part 'in the preparation of the list of members', he did not object to anyone, nor was he consulted. 'The Irish party took no action either'; and he knew of 'no action on the part of any member of the party', such as Delany had suggested, 'directed against Fr Finlay'.[13]

A further dimension to the exclusion was provided on 20 July when Edmund Talbot MP wrote to Delany from the House of Commons: 'I have not left Birrell alone about Fr Finlay, though he is still very obdurate. He makes out high ecclesiastical authority is the chief opposition ...'[14]

Finlay was appointed to neither the governing body of the college nor the senate of the university. On the day after the university bill was signed, Birrell acknowledged Delany's upset at the treatment accorded one of his closest colleagues.

> This was a painful business, and perhaps I ought to have been more adamantine than I was ... Then again, I had to conciliate certain high potentates, so that my path was perilous, and it was hard to say which of the perils were real perils, and which phantoms of the brain. To put it plainly, I am sorry that Fr F. was excluded, but I could not see my way to act otherwise.[15]

Despite this rejection, Finlay remained a figure of influence in University College, which he continued to view as a training ground for the future leaders of the country. A roll call of the small student body in the early years of the twentieth century, no more than 180 students, reveals a remarkable range of abilities and personalities.[16] So much so that W.P. Coyne, in 1900, assured a former colleague 'the real work for Ireland is being done over there', pointing to University College, and T.M. Kettle, in the *Nationist*, on 2 November 1905, proudly proclaimed the college as 'incontestably ... *the* university college of Ireland ... a centre of vital thought and culture'.[17] And with direct reference to Finlay's role, C.P. Curran noted:

> His teaching career covered three generations of college students. The first included William Magennis, W.P. Coyne and Bob Donovan, who as post-graduates first shared in the management of the *Lyceum*. The second, my own contemporaries, Tom Kettle, Hugh Kennedy, Arthur Clery, John Marcus O'Sullivan, Felix Hackett; the third, a notable pro-

portion of the men who, with some of their seniors, staffed our government after the Anglo-Irish treaty. These varying types, philosophers, economists, men of letters and of law, had one common denominator, an unselfish instinct for public service. They got their impetus in great measure from Finlay, and they had their baptism in ink in the papers Finlay founded, edited and in turn passed into their general control.[18]

As has been seen, many factors combined to forge Tom Finlay's remarkable impact on the student body of University College, and his influence among educationalists and literary figures. He was gifted intellectually, and an interesting teacher and independent thinker who mixed easily with young people, challenged them intellectually, socially, morally and politically, and fostered their skills as writers and public speakers. Moreover, as founder and editor of various periodicals he promoted interest in literary, social, moral and religious issues, and he raised his readers horizons above the political and economic events of the day. In education he was actively involved administratively at primary and secondary level and provided text-books in a variety of subjects, while at university level he had become a legend as a professor with wide-ranging interests, seemingly endless energy, and capacity for work. His contacts were manifold, and his open and amiable disposition drew people to him. All of these factors combined to make him widely known and respected in Dublin. What made him a household name through much of the country, however, was his work and leadership in the Irish Agricultural Co-operative Movement.

1 An early Foxford Mills school orchestra

Irish Agricultural Organisation Society, Ltd.

ANNUAL REPORT, 1895,
With Appendices.

President:
The Hon. HORACE PLUNKETT, M.P., 104 Mount St., London, W.

Vice-President:
The Right Hon. C.T. REDINGTON, Kilcornan, Cranmore, Co. Galway.

Committee:
The Most Rev. PATRICK O'DONNELL, D.D., Bishop of Raphoe, Letterkenny.
The Lord MONTEAGLE, K.P., Mount Trenchard, Foyne, Co. Limerick.
THOMAS SEXTON, Esq., M.P.
JOHN E. REDMOND, Esq., M.P.
Count ARTHUR MOORE, Mooresfort, Tipperary.
CHRISTOPHER DIGGES LA TOUCHE, Esq, James's Gate, Dublin.
The Rev. T.A. FINLAY, S.J., M.A., University College, Dublin.
Colonel GERALD R. DEASE, Clebridge, Co. Kildare.
GEORGE F. STEWART, Esq., 6 Leinster Street, Dublin.
Coroner JAMES BYRNE, J.P., Wallstown Castle, Castletownroche, Co. Cork.
WALTER McMORROGH KAVANAGH, Esq., D.L., Borris House, Borris, Co. Carlow.
JAMES MUSGRAVE, Esq., Drumglass House, Belfast.

Secretary:
R.A. ANDERSON (Organising Agent of the Co-operative Union, Ltd. in Ireland).

Bankers:
THE BANK OF IRELAND.

Solicitors:
Messers. D. & T. FITZGERALD, 20 St. Andrew's Street, Dublin.

Auditors:
Messers. CRAIG GARDNER & CO., Dame Street, Dublin
M.J. CLEARY, Esq., Mullingar.

Registered Offices:
2 STEPHEN'S GREEN, NORTH, DUBLIN.

Dublin:
PRINTED BY SEALY, BRYERS and WALKER
(A. THOM & Co. Ltd.)
94, 95 and 96 MIDDLE ABBEY STREET

1895

2 (above) Title page of the 1895 Annual Report of the IAOS
3 Preparing the wool at Foxford Mills
4 Foxford Mills interior

3

4

5 Lord Monteagle

6 Fr Joseph Darlington SJ

7 R.A. Anderson (portrait by Dermot O'Brien)

8 Thomas Kettle

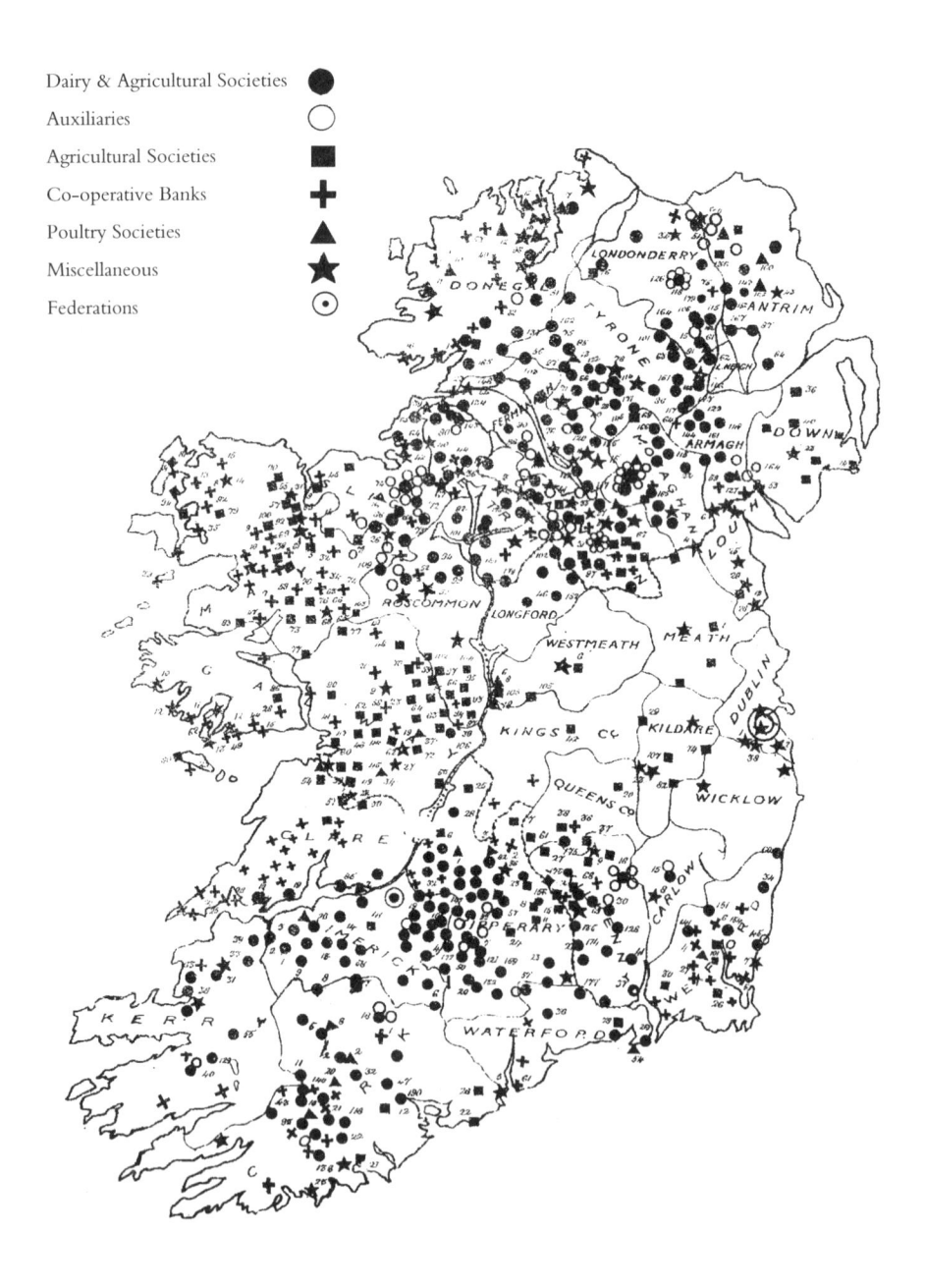

9 Map (above) showing the spread of cooperative societies by the end of 1902
10 T.M. Healy
11 Douglas Hyde
12 Eoin MacNeill
13 Fr Edward Coyne SJ, president of the IAOS

10

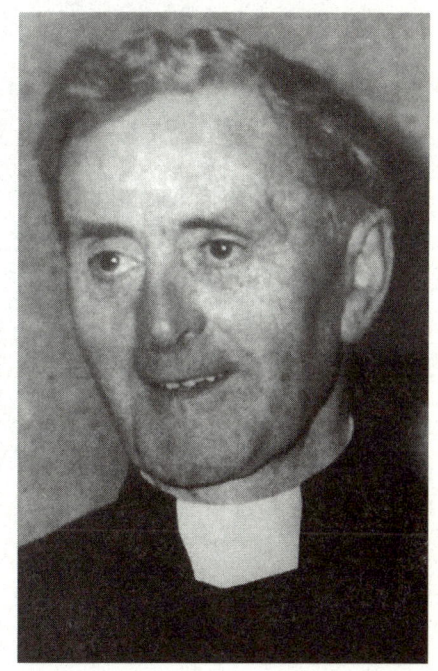

11

12

13

14 Fr William Delany SJ

15 Paddy 'the Cope' Gallagher

16 Dermot O'Brien, *Portrait of Sir Horace Plunkett*

17 Caravaggio, *The Taking of Christ* (1602)

18 University College Dublin at 86 St Stephen's Green

PART TWO

―――――――――――――――

The Irish co-operative movement, 1889–1932

7

The early years of co-operation

The Irish Agricultural Co-operative movement is indelibly linked to the name of Horace Plunkett. A member of an ancient Anglo-Irish family, his father a prominent Protestant landlord, Horace Plunkett viewed co-operation as the best means of improving the lot of Irish farmers. As a Protestant, educated in England, and the son of a landlord, he was not well placed to win the confidence of Catholic small farmers. This was to be part of Finlay's role. 'I began my Irish work in 1889,' Plunkett wrote later. 'I made a special speech to farmers in Munster upon co-operative dairying, which was reported in the press – probably my first platform effort to win that distinction. Father Finlay saw the report and took occasion to call on me and tell me that he was in entire sympathy with the views I had tried to express. I think I had heard of him, but that was all.'[1] At their meeting, as Plunkett recalled it, Finlay had told him that he 'had made some study of the support given by the clergy of his church to agricultural co-operative movements' on the continent, 'which appeared to him to be practically identical with that which I was advocating for Ireland'. Finlay also informed him 'of the appalling conditions of the Dublin slums, where some 20,000 families – perhaps 100,000 souls – were living in one-room tenements. It was clear from what he had said that much of his spare time was devoted to that baffling problem.'[2]

At that first meeting they exchanged views on what was possible in the way of reorganising Irish agriculture upon co-operative lines. It happened that the dairying industry of the south, just at that time, was being threatened with destruction owing to the invention of machinery and methods which made it possible for the first time to produce butter in quantity and in a uniform quality to meet the demand of the modern market. The Irish home-dairying was centuries old. In Munster, soil, climate, cattle and tradition favoured it. Now 'alien capitalists ... were beginning to erect creameries in the most favoured parts of Munster'. It was becoming clear that in the future the majority of dairy farmers would be faced with a stark choice: sell their milk to these new creameries which would then manufacture from it the butter which the markets demanded, or else combine together, as their competitors in continental countries were doing, and erect and operate creameries at their own risk and for their own profit. Moreover, they must arrange to sell their product without the intervention of middlemen, 'who would fleece producer and consumer alike'.[3] It was a formidable undertaking in a country with no tradition of such collaboration. At their meeting, Finlay informed Plunkett 'that, so far as his other duties permitted', he would do all in his power to be of assistance. 'That meeting', Plunkett added, 'led to his being the kindest and most loyal friend I have ever had in a work which has made my life worth living.'[4]

Something of the enthusiasm and growing friendship of the two men is indicated by entries in Plunkett's diary. On Monday, 1 February 1892, he noted: 'Had a long conversation with Rev. T. Finlay SJ, FRUI, on agricultural co-operation. He had studied in Germany and France and was quite an expert. He will attend the coming agricultural conference in Limerick.' On 10 February he went to Limerick to prepare for that conference (of creamery delegates). 'Met Bishop O'Dwyer who told me that he regretted my going into politics, (and) that Fr Finlay was the ablest man in Ireland.' Plunkett had been elected as Unionist member of parliament for South Dublin. A month later, 6 March, his entry read:

> Father Finlay came down for the day and I had very interesting talks with him. He (a nationalist) quite approves of my attitude in South Dublin. We talked cooperation all day and I have every hope we shall progress with our organisation rapidly now.

On 26 March he 'called on Fr Finlay and had a politico industrial talk with him. He told me the priests in Dublin had no political power. In the country they had and would have for many years to come as they were the only people who had any education and could be consulted about everything. The red-hot curate was getting less and less influence.'[5]

The work of co-operation began, in Plunkett's words, 'with a grandiose scheme for nothing less than a reorganisation upon co-operative lines of an industry upon which the prosperity of virtually every section of the people depended.'[6] A small band of practical idealists spread the message. It included Plunkett, R.A. Anderson, Tom Finlay, Thomas Spring Rice (Lord Monteagle of Mount Trenchard, Foynes). Indirect support soon became available from Bishop Edward Thomas O'Dwyer of Limerick, and from Patrick O'Donnell, bishop of Raphoe. 'We went about among the dairy farmers', Plunkett reported, 'holding meetings of them whenever we could get them to come and listen to our proposals. At first it was only when we had the support of a parish priest or curate that we could get a hearing.' Finlay, during his holiday periods, was in demand for retreats and missions throughout the country. At missions, or retreats for clergy, he encouraged the younger clergy to involve themselves in the social and economic betterment of their people, and he used relate how Catholic clergy in continental Europe supported agricultural and co-operative movements. 'We could always tell where he had introduced the subject', Plunkett related, even when he thought it prudent 'not to associate himself with our group, for we had aroused the bitterest opposition among certain traders', who did not neglect to call on the politicians 'to expose our insidious designs'.[7]

By March 1891, Plunkett and his followers were able to hold a conference of dairy co-operative societies in Newcastle West, County Limerick. In June, at Limerick city, there was a further conference attended by delegates from fifteen societies. The intention now was to form an agency for the joint marketing of creamery products. Eventually, in 1893, the Irish Co-operative Agency Society came into being. At that stage there were some thirty creamery societies with a turnover of about £150,000.[8] Realising that the agency was not going to solve all his problems, Plunkett, on 18 April, the following year, founded the Irish Agricultural Organisation Society. At the dinner for the press to mark the occasion, which was attended by some 250 people, Plunkett, not a good public speaker, surpassed himself with an address on the theme 'Better farming, better business, better living'. He set out clearly the objectives of the new society:

> To improve the condition of the agricultural population of Ireland by teaching them the methods and principles of co-operation as applicable to farming and the allied industries; to promote industrial organisation for any purpose which may appear beneficial; and generally to counsel and advise those engaged in agricultural pursuits ... (and to bring) to the help of those whose life is passed in the quiet of the field the experience which belongs to wider opportunities of observation and a larger acquaintance with commercial and industrial affairs.

Co-operative societies, he added, were the best channel for agricultural education, and the government would find their help invaluable. The Society, he went on, would be essentially propagandist but non-political, and its members must prepare themselves for years of apparently fruitless but beneficial toil.

The applause was prolonged. Lord Cloncurry was scarcely heard in putting the formal motion: 'That this meeting, having heard the principles of the Irish Agricultural Organisation Society, hereby approves of the same and resolves that immediate steps be taken to carry them into practical effect.'[9]

At the first ordinary general meeting of the Society on 10 May 1892 Plunkett was elected president. The membership of the committee was of critical importance. As a result, it was carefully balanced between conflicting parties, creeds and classes. The vice-president was Rt Hon. Christopher Talbot Reddington, the resident commissioner for National Education, whose presence on the committee suggested a measure of official approval for the new movement and its educational objectives. He was, however, an ardent co-operator in his own right, and was to become president of the agricultural bank founded in 1899 at Oranmore, County Galway, where he lived.[10] Other members of the committee were: the Catholic bishop of Raphoe, Patrick O'Donnell; Lord Monteagle, 'a quiet self-effacing man, popular with his peers and highly regarded by his tenants'[11]; Count Arthur Moore, Moorsfort, County Tipperary, a Catholic, who, influenced by Monteagle, founded a creamery in the Glen of Aherlow; Edward William O'Brien, a wealthy Protestant landowner, who, under the same influence, established a flourishing creamery at Ardagh, County Limerick; Christopher Digges La Touche; James Byrne, of Wallstown Castle, Castletownroche (near Doneraile), a farmer, a breeder of shorthorn cattle, and a strong nationalist, whose presence on the committee legitimised the co-operative movement in the eyes of many strong farmers; Major John Alexander, of Milford, County Sligo, another breeder of shorthorns; and Colonel Gerald R. Dease, of Celbridge, County Kildare, a member of a prominent, and highly respected Catholic landlord family. To represent the northern co-operators, Plunkett chose Jamie (later Sir James) Musgrave of Belfast, a shrewd Protestant businessman, chairman of the Belfast Harbour Commissioners, and patron of numerous charities. The secretary of the Society was R.A. Anderson, a blunt Cork Protestant, and an indefatigable worker for the movement. The names of nationalist members of parliament, John Redmond and Thomas Sexton, were added to the committee. Even though they never attended, it was politic to have both sides in the political 'split' represented.[12]

Into this mixture of backgrounds and allegiances, Tom Finlay appears to have fitted easily. Before the general meeting commenced, he was observed engaged 'in animated conversation with Christopher Digges la Touche, managing director of Guinness Brewery'.[13] R.A. Anderson in his *With Horace Plunkett in Ireland* observed that Christopher la Touche was one of the ablest and most charming man he had ever met, and that 'instinctively he and Father Finlay sought each other out, and when their wise heads were done with any puzzle, no matter how complicated, one might be sure it was solved'.[14]

It was 'his connection with the Society', Plunkett observed, 'which gave "Father Tom" (as he is affectionately but reverentially called by the thousands who knew his service to rural Ireland) his opportunity to drive home his social and economic principles for agricultural development … But his outstanding achievement in this field', Plunkett insisted, 'was the popular exposition of the co-operative idea' in the early years, 'the days of its struggle for existence.' He went on to give 'one or two illustrations' of Finlay's 'genius for probing and dealing with the extraordinary difficulties of the task we had undertaken'.[15]

One of the illustrations has appeared in different accounts of the Irish co-operative movement. The following account is a conflation of that given by R.A. Anderson[16] and that by Plunkett. Finlay's 'sense of humour was as great as his intellectual qualities were high', Anderson wrote, and none 'could tell a story better than he or enjoy a joke more heartily'. On one occasion he was asked to speak in a village on the borderland of Ulster, where the population were about equally divided between Protestants and Catholics. The member of the IAOS who was to have addressed the meeting was unable to be present. Finlay stepped into the breach even though it was close to the Twelfth of July when the battle of the Boyne was celebrated with militant band music, the banging of drums, and attitudes of coldness and even hostility to Catholic neighbours. The object of the meeting was to encourage the audience to start a co-operative creamery. Finlay found himself facing two hostile camps, the 'Papishes' on one side of the hall, the

'Prasbytarians' on the other. The mutual distrust was such that if one side supported the project, the other would have none of it. He began by explaining the accident of his presence, and he acknowledged the incongruity of they being addressed by a Catholic priest who was also a Jesuit. So far as he was concerned, however, he saw no reason why a Jesuit or an Orangeman should allow the events of two centuries ago to interfere with the practical affairs they had come together to discuss. He understood that considerable feeling was occasionally aroused over a battle fought on a famous river not far to the south of where he stood. But, he reminded them, that quarrel was not really one between Irishmen but between a Scotchman and a Dutchman, adding with a smile 'Surely we can now leave the old quarrel to be settled by those two gentlemen – that is, if too great a gulf does not divide them!' He then proceeded to make 'a luminous and convincing case for the immediate establishment of a creamery'. After he sat down, there was silence for some time. Then, an elderly, bewhiskered 'Prasbytarian' stood up slowly, looked around the room, and declared solemnly, 'Dod, but the mon's right.'[17] Plunkett later commented: 'No speech from the Irish co-operative platform was more fruitful in its result';[18] and H.F. Norman, a Theosophist and prominent promoter of the movement, retelling the story in his pamphlet, *Father Thomas Finlay, an Irish co-operative pioneer*, observed: 'Seldom can so notable a triumph over the handicap of a clerical collar and the letters "SJ" attached to its wearer's name have occurred amongst a more unpromising gathering.'[19]

Plunkett gave a further illustration of Finlay's successes in the borderland of Ulster. On this occasion he was the chief speaker. Again, the people of the district were about evenly divided, religiously and politically. Finlay, feeling he was among his own people, was unperturbed. 'I heard to my dismay', Plunkett declared, 'that the Orangemen and the Nationalists had both marched to the meeting with their flags and bands. I asked my friend if he did not scent trouble. "Not at all", he replied, "I must see the bandmasters." By tactful diplomacy, the most provocative air on either side was deleted from the programme. It was not quite so easy to secure an agreement that they should play alternately and not together; but even this concession was arranged', Plunkett concluded, 'and a pleasant and useful day was enjoyed by us both.'[20]

Another example illustrated Finlay's effectiveness as a speaker in the early years of the Society. The occasion was 'a creamery, in a most favoured district, over the starting of which Father Finlay had taken an infinite amount of trouble', that 'had come to grief owing to disregard of the non-political and non-sectarian rule in the constitution of all our societies. It was in the days of "the split", and the committee of the peccant society was evenly divided – perhaps necessarily so – between Parnellites and anti-Parnellites. Fr Finlay began by telling the story of their disastrous venture and used with wonderful success his inimitable power of so telling a tale that its moral will draw itself.' 'I could repeat this part of his speech almost verbatim', Plunkett went on, 'but will only give the last three sentences, leaving the reader to imagine the rest.' After telling the sorry tale of its final collapse, he concluded:

> Unhappily, when the crisis was imminent, someone raised the no doubt important question – 'Who ought to be the ruler of the Irish people at home and abroad?' That issue was debated at several successive meetings; no conclusion was reached, but bankruptcy ensued. I dare say every member of the committee felt himself competent to govern the country; all they collectively demonstrated was their incapacity to manage a churn.[21]

There was something of Finlay's Scottish forefathers' claymore in his powerful cuts, Anderson commented, but he succeeded because of his manner of delivery and his 'unrivalled knowledge of human nature'.[22]

In addition to his work for the Society by word and presence, he also, as noted previously, promoted it by means of his publications. As early as 1892 he printed in the *Lyceum* a lengthy article describing the aims of the movement, and its achievements thus far, and presenting a case for the establishment of an agricultural co-operative agency. It outlined the idea and purpose of co-operation, and explained its practical operation, in a manner understandable to the general reader. In that context, and as an illustration of Finlay's clarity of exposition, it is pertinent to summarise it here. He entitled it simply, 'Co-operation in Ireland'. It appeared in the issue of 15 March 1892.

CO-OPERATION IN IRELAND

Introducing the article, Finlay made it clear that co-operation, for him, was very much an aspect of 'social democracy', but not in the sense propounded by Karl Marx and Ferdinand Lassalle,[23] which envisaged 'a system of universal co-operation, promoted and controlled by state authority'. Such a system, he believed, could never be more than a 'utopian ideal' that testified 'to the philanthropic ambitions of its authors', but reflected 'upon their good sense'. It was out of touch with human nature and the selfishness and idleness inherent in it. The system, which he advocated, took account of self-interest, enabling workers, by means of co-operation, to become capitalists – 'to be owners of the wealth which assists labour, as well as furnishing the labour itself'. It extended, moreover, into trading capitalism. The producers of commodities and the consumers of products had reason to be dissatisfied with the trader, who acted as intermediary between them, and to a large extent controlled the market and was able 'to tax both for his own profit'. In the co-operative system, its members, who were producers and consumers, aimed to become their 'own agents for the sale and purchase of commodities' which they held, or which they needed, and thereby to 'secure for themselves the profits which now accrue to the trader'.

Rounding off the introduction, Finlay drew attention to the successes achieved by socialists in establishing co-operative institutions in places of large population such as Ghent, which conferred solid advantages on the working population. In several European countries, moreover, the concept of co-operation had spread from the towns to the rural population, and in Germany and France the farmers had greatly benefited from it. Having thus diverted attention away from the example of Britain to the patterns being set in Europe, he turned to the Irish scene.

In Ireland, he went on, the co-operative movement was beginning in the countryside, and would 'be carried thence to the towns, if it is to reach the towns at all'. He explained:

> Among the farmers of Limerick and the adjoining counties the first serious step has been taken in the establishment of a wide-reaching system of co-operation, and, so far, the enterprise has been attended with a distinctly satisfactory measure of success.

The first successes, however, had not been through distributive co-operation – that is, removing the middleman and establishing their own store to sell, 'distribute', their products. It was tried by the promoters of the movement at Doneraile, County Cork, but the stores there had a difficult struggle to survive, and only in the current year had they attained a 'safe financial position'. It took time and trouble 'to educate a rural community in the methods of distributive co-operation, and to create in them the mutual confidence which is necessary to secure its advantages'.

On the other hand, 'the methods of productive co-operation, as explained to the Limerick farmers,' had been 'quickly appreciated' and implemented. He explained the background and outcome. In Limerick and adjoining counties every farmer a few years ago had his own dairy, and produced butter for the market according to traditional methods. With the introduction of more sophisticated machinery in the manufacture of butter the dairies of the small farmers were at a disadvantage. In recent times butter factories, or creameries, were established widely throughout the south-western counties. The farmers were drawn away from making their own butter and, instead, focussed on producing the milk supply and selling the cream to the local creamery. 'The creameries, however, were the property of individual capitalists or joint-stock companies, which received the profits on the manufacture and sale of the butter', while 'the farmer had only the remuneration of (his) labour and capital' that was 'represented by the price paid for his milk'.

Then, Horace Plunkett arrived on the scene and set out to persuade farmers that there was no reason 'why the creamery should not be their property, and be worked in their sole interest, and the profits which flowed into the pockets of the capitalist or joint-stock company be theirs'. At first, Finlay conceded, the suggestion of co-operation was coldly received. 'The idea was new to the farmers, and, besides, they had not been accustomed to find friends and advisers in the class to which Mr Plunkett belonged. Eventually, however, they consented to discuss the proposal, and with discussion came an understanding of its merits. A co-operative creamery was established, and then another, and another, till the movement had grown to the dimensions it has now reached, when it counts sixteen fully equipped and successfully worked co-operative dairy societies, with about fourteen others in the course of formation.'

He went on to outline for the reader 'the plan on which one of these organisations is framed'.

> In a locality where, within a radius of three miles, there is to be found a number of farmers with an aggregate of 700 or 800 milch cows, a meeting is held and the scheme of a co-operative creamery laid before the assembled farmers. After much discussion and explanation, and weighing of details, the meeting resolves on the undertaking and, then, the first step is to subscribe the capital for the erection of buildings and the purchase of machinery. The farmers are required to take shares in proportion to the number of cows on their farms which will contribute milk to the creamery – a £1 share for each cow.
>
> The buildings and plant having been thus provided, and the requisite trained hands having been secured, the dairying operations begin. Each member of the society sends his milk-supply twice a day to the creamery. The cream is promptly separated, and the milk returned to him for feeding purposes, and he is paid for his cream at a rate fixed by the committee of the society, a rate which gives him little reason to envy his neighbour who may be selling to a joint-stock creamery. But it is not till the time comes for balancing the accounts and reckoning the profits that his advantages over his non-society neighbours become apparent. The creamery has manufactured large quantities of butter of the best quality that the technical skill of well-trained hands can produce, and this has been sold at a considerable profit. The profits thus secured are now divided among the members of the society. After paying the hands employed in the factory, 5 per cent is paid on the capital sunk in the buildings and machinery, and out of the remainder of the net profits a bonus is allotted to each member of the society proportionate to the quantity of cream he has contributed to the factory operations during the period.
>
> This system secures for the farmer all the profits which, under the joint-stock arrangement, or that of individual ownership of the creamery, should necessarily pass to others.' It is not surprising, Finlay commented, 'once the system's successful working is seen by farmers, the demand for its extension taxes the energy and resources of the promoters.

The advantages of the system, if well worked, were obvious, but the difficulty was to work it well. The system of account-keeping in the creamery, he warned, had to be 'rigorously exact'. The inspector or organiser charged with the general superintendence of the societies had to have 'the gifts of a quick-eyed accountant, in addition to his skill in dairying'. In Limerick they were fortunate to have a man who had been trained in the best dairies of Sweden, and also had 'the trained habits of an inflexibly accurate book-keeper'. But an organiser could only advise and inspect, the work of book-keeping had to be done by the farmers' committee, and this was a task for which they had to be trained. Besides, a high degree of technical skill was required by the workers if they were to compete with the pre-eminent Scandinavian dairies. This increase in technical knowledge, however, 'should extend not merely to the hands employed in the creamery' but also to the farmer. 'There is an art', he explained,

> in the raising of stock and in the feeding of milk-giving cows, on which the richness of the milk in great measure depends. In this art the farmers who supported the co-operative creamery required instruction – an instruction which could be efficiently imparted to them only by some skilled adviser, who would visit their farms, point out to them the defects of their methods, and guide them in their attempts at improvement.

'Instruction of this kind was undertaken by the promoters of the co-operative movement. They secured the services of the most competent instructor they could find, and set him to visit not merely the working creameries, but the farms which supplied them as well in order to point out the way of progress to the factory hand and the farmer alike.'

But the resources available for co-operation in Ireland were limited. They could not provide technical instruction of this eminently practical kind on an adequate scale. The commissioners of education, Finlay suggested, had it in their competence 'to contribute efficiently to this development of genuine technical instruction'.

He went on to make a plea for a central agency. The creameries thus far in operation had been 'successful without exception' They had been operating independently of each other, 'each manufacturing for itself and then selling its products through the usual agencies'. The next step was to establish 'a common central agency ... maintained by the combined societies, and through which all their produce' would 'be sold'. The output of the Irish co-operative creameries for the coming year would reach an estimated total value of £200,000. 'Why should not the sale of this large butter-supply be effected by the combined societies, and the profits of the sales secured for the members?' It would ensure the procuring of expert assistance in dairy farming and butter manufacture. It would lead, moreover, to an expansion of the dairy industry that would have widespread effects. To utilise the central agency to the full it would be necessary to introduce winter dairying on a large scale. This 'would demand a considerable modification of the existing system of dairy farming. It would be necessary to raise feeding stuffs in large quantity, not depend merely on the summer grass supply. The cultivation of these feeding stuffs would mean a return to tillage, and to an increase in the labour demand on all sides – a result which we cannot contemplate without satisfaction ... Again, the central agency, once established, would become a medium not merely for the sale of commodities, but for their purchase also.' The societies, as was the practice on the Continent, might 'buy through their agent as well as sell through him. And buying through him, they could obtain their agricultural commodities, machines, artificial manures, feeding stuffs, and the rest, not merely at wholesale prices, but at especially favourable wholesale prices. Their societies' agent would represent not an individual or a firm, but the consumers of a county or a province, and a manufacturing firm, dealing with a county or province, could afford to offer better terms than to individuals or even a trading house.

Concluding his article, Finlay observed: 'We have been dwelling on what are the material advantages of the co-operative system as applied to the dairy industry in Limerick and the neighbouring counties. We have not taken account of the mental and moral improvement which the system must promote – and which, in the long run, must also issue in material well-being, though, of course, it has a higher and better effect also. To carry out successfully the co-operative scheme in any of its applications, business capacity, an understanding of the ways and means of commerce, a rigid observance of business rules, a knowledge of the right method of expending money as well as of saving it, a capacity to test things by their practical results, patience and perseverance to enable these results to exhibit themselves – all this is demanded from the members as well as from the promoters of co-operative societies. And further, there is required from all concerned, the faculty of working in harmony with others, of making allowance for their views and even for their prejudices, a disposition to join together in a strong and earnest effort for the common good; and these, it seems to us, are points of popular education, on which such object lessons as the southern creameries furnish will not, in our actual circumstances, be amiss.'[24] Clearly, his enthusiasm for co-operation did not lead to any watering-down of the demands and standards required for success!

His belief in the value and importance of the co-operative movement was to be mirrored in an active commitment to the Irish Agricultural Organisation Society for more than forty years. He played a key role, moreover, in the setting up of the celebrated Recess Committee, which led to the establishment in 1900 of an Irish Department of Agriculture and Technical Instruction.

8

The Recess Committee; growth and difficulties

The State, in the second half of the nineteenth century, was playing an increasing role in economic development. The Danish co-operative movement swept across Denmark with government support. English economic opinion, however, adhered to a non-intervention policy. Plunkett determined to change this. He went about it after the general election of 1895, in which he was returned with an increased majority by the Unionist electors of South Dublin. He described how it happened:

> One evening in 1895 while I was coming to Dublin in a badly lit railway carriage, I wrote a letter inviting all interested in the material progress of Ireland, to a non-party conference for the purpose of formulating a demand for the kind of State assistance we needed both for agriculture and other industries. Next day I showed the letter to Father Finlay, who advised me to send it to the press ...[1]

He forwarded his 'proposal affecting the general welfare of Ireland' to the papers on 27 August. The proposal urged that as Home Rule was in abeyance so long as the Unionist government was in power, the Irish, instead of dissipating their energies by fighting about the issue, should unite for the purpose of promoting useful legislation that all parties agreed upon. He cited two objectives: a board of agriculture for Ireland, and a technical education bill; and then added what he termed a 'crude, informal and unconventional' proposal that the various party leaders should each nominate a few members of parliament to form the nucleus of a committee, which then would co-opt by unanimous agreement representatives of the agricultural, industrial, commercial and professional interests of north and south. Seeking to raise thoughts above the political slough, he pronounced:

> We Unionists, without abating one jot of our unionism, and the Nationalists, without abating one jot of their nationalism, can each show our faith in the cause for which we have fought so bitterly and so long, by sinking our party differences for our country's good.

He was astonished by the result. Although the leader of the largest nationalist party, Justin McCarthy, refused to become involved, stating that this was just another unionist ploy to find a substitute for Home Rule, public support for Plunkett's initiative was widespread. The Parnellite leader, John Redmond, agreed to join the committee, as did T.C. Harrington, John Parnell, William Field, Richard Dane, and Sir Thomas Lee, all members of parliament. Among the prominent figures co-opted were: R.F. McCoy (lord mayor of Dublin), Monsignor Gerald Molloy, Mr Justice Ross, Lords Mayo and Monteagle (Unionist peers), Sir John Arnott (representing southern commerce), Thomas Andrews (a Belfast merchant), Prof. H. Brougham Leech, Thomas Sinclair (a leading Liberal Unionist), the O'Conor Don, and C. Litton Falkiner. The members of the co-operative movement on the committee were: T.A. Finlay, Count Arthur Moore, and James Musgrave. The latter was appointed chairman of a special consultative body for Ulster. Plunkett was made chairman of the main committee, termed at first the Round Table, and then, as its meetings were held during the parliamentary recess, the Recess Committee. As secretary, he chose a Catholic and well-known nationalist, the efficient and influential Thomas P. Gill.[2]

The first conference was held at the Mansion House, Dublin, in September 1895. On 23 September, Plunkett noted in his diary: 'Came to Dublin – saw Fr Finlay, the Lord Mayor, and (Thomas) Sexton about the Recess Committee. The two latter admitted that the nationalist objection was that I was killing Home Rule by kindness.' His vast nervous energy was being devoted to preparations for the committee meetings. Nevertheless, on Saturday 26 October, he found time to go with Finlay to the Loreto convent, Dalkey, County Dublin, 'to help to start a co-operative embroidery society'.[3] Two days later the preliminary business meetings of the committee took place. Finlay was among those invited to join the preliminary meetings on 30 October.[4] The committee then adjourned, and a period of research intervened. This was conducted at Plunkett's expense. He despatched investigators to study and report on agricultural departments, technical instruction, and co-operation in several European countries. Gill was sent to Denmark and France, Michael Mullhall, an eminent statistician, was commissioned to visit Belgium, Holland, Bavaria, Wurttemberg, Austria, Hungary and Switzerland. Submissions were sought and received from Mons. E. Tisserand, the French director-general of agriculture, who, in Plunkett's view was 'probably the greatest living authority on state-aid to agriculture'.[5]

Finlay attended meetings of the committee on 21 and 29 January 1896, and on the latter date he and Plunkett 'were appointed to a sub-committee ... for procuring information respecting State aid to agriculture in Continental countries, other than those visited by Mr Gill'.[6] Plunkett and he were empowered to co-opt members. On 31 January the committee resolved 'that for the encouragement of agriculture and other industries, and the promotion of technical education in connection with the same, a joint department or board of Agricultural Industry should be constructed for Ireland'. Finlay was present at subsequent meetings of the committee on 4 and 7 February, 12–13 March, and 22, 27, 29

May. On that last date the committee urged that the report, in regard to technical education, should recommend the provision of 'a system of state-aided technical and agricultural education which shall include secondary schools and superior colleges', and that 'schools for technical and agricultural instruction should be established under the control of the new department'.[7] Thereafter, the chairman pressed ahead with the collation of the research with a view to an early report from the committee. The committee was an unofficial one and had to work without the secretarial service and civil service support available to a Royal Commission; but Plunkett recruited and personally remunerated an excellent staff. The material was collected, condensed, clarified and collated skilfully and with remarkable speed.[8] Plunkett prepared a draft report on the basis of the material collected and the various resolutions passed in the Recess committee meetings. The draft was submitted to each member for comment. Many suggestions were received. All was then considered by a sub-committee consisting of Plunkett, Finlay, Professor Leech, T.P. Gill, and C. Litton Falkiner. On 1 August 1896 the unanimously agreed report was forwarded to Gerald W. Balfour, chief secretary of Ireland.

The Recess Report, a remarkable document of 418 tightly-written pages, began baldly:

> We have in Ireland a poor country, practically without manufactures— except for the linen and ship-building of the North and the brewing and distilling of Dublin – dependant upon agriculture with its soil imperfectly tilled, its area under cultivation decreasing, and a diminishing population without industrial habits or skills.

It contained five well-defined sections: Part 1, The past action of the State in Ireland, and its effect upon the economy and habits of the people; Part 2, The available resources of Ireland (agricultural and industrial) and the possibilities of development; Part 3, How resources were being developed in other countries through the action of (a) the people themselves, and (b) the State; Part 4, How similar methods might be adopted with profit in Ireland – (a) Recommendations for the promotion of agriculture, (b) Recommendations for the promotion of industry, (c) Recommendations for the promotion of both agriculture and industry by means of practical (technical) education; Part 5, The constitution of the new proposed Department of Agriculture and Industries.[9]

The committee had analysed every aspect of the Irish economy, and every development proposal – even to categories of cottage industries said to be flourishing in the province of Moscow. There were numerous suggestions and recommendations, and some hard-hitting criticism of the government's past performance.

The Report had a dramatic effect. An important Irish issue had been dealt with outside the British parliament, and had united representatives of different parties, religions, and affiliations in a clear, well researched demand for control of the administration of their major industry. Press comment on both sides of the Irish Sea was largely favourable. The *Freeman's Journal*, however, as might be expected, denounced the Committee's proposals as a 'burlesque substitute for Home Rule'.[10] Plunkett, stirred up correspondence in the newspapers to ensure the Report would not be pigeon-holed and left to gather dust as had happened to many royal commission reports. On 25 August 1896, T.P. Gill sent a long typed letter to Gladstone accompanying a copy of the Report. He drew attention to the fact that the Report had been signed unanimously by representatives of all political parties in Ireland, from Ulster as well from the South and West, and by representatives of industrial interests. After this sweeping claim, he endeavoured to substantiate it by naming individuals. The O'Conor Don and John Redmond represented the Financial Relations Commission. Justice Ross was representative of the legal profession, Thomas Sinclair was leader of the Ulster Liberal Unionists and their parliamentary representative, and there was Sir Thomas Lea, the nationalist lord mayor of Dublin, Sir John Arnott, the proprietor of the *Irish Times*, and Lords Mayo and Monteagle. The wealth and industry of Belfast was represented by James Musgrave, Thomas Andrews, Sir William Ewart, and Sir Daniel Dixon, as well as by Thomas Sinclair. Gill went on to fill an obvious gap in the representatives with a startling attribution. Efforts to obtain a member of parliament from Mr Dillon's nationalist party had failed, Gill acknowledged, and then added:

> The party, however, is well represented by the Rev. Thomas Finlay, SJ, Fellow of the Royal University, who is distinguished in Ireland for his earnestness as a nationalist as he is for his high position and his zeal as an educationalist.

'Need I emphasise', Gill added, 'the importance of the fact that there sat side by side in friendly conference with this gentleman, and with another Catholic dignitary, the Rt. Rev. Monsignor Molloy, D.D., and joined with them in making a common recommendation for legislation, the Rev. R.R. Kane, D.D., of Belfast, Grand Master of the Orange Society.'[11]

In April 1897, Gerald Balfour, chief secretary, introduced the Agriculture and Industries (Ireland) Bill, acknowledging that it was based on the report of the Recess Committee. The queen's speech at the opening of parliament had promised a board of agriculture for Ireland. Balfour's bill, however, was deficient in two aspects: the financial provision was inadequate, and there was no reference to technical education. The bill was withdrawn a month later pending the introduction of the Irish Local Government Bill. Plunkett, anxious lest the agricultural bill be left in abeyance, promoted the demand for it through the various IAOS organisations throughout the country. Balfour responded by redrafting his Agriculture and Industries Bill to embrace technical education and presented it for its first reading in the House of Commons on 9 May 1899. He aimed to push it though quickly before the summer recess. Suggestions and amendments put forward by Dillon, Moore, Davitt, and Redmond received short shrift. Balfour availed of the technique of challenging objectors to put themselves on record as opposing 'this measure of great and far-reaching import to the material interest of Ireland', and he taunted Dillon, in Alexander Pope's words, as being 'willing to wound but afraid to strike'. The bill was through the House by the end of July 1889, and Lord Ashbourne guided it speedily through the House of Lords. It appeared in the statute book as 'an Act establishing a Department of Agriculture and other Industries and Technical Instruction in Ireland and for other purposes connected therewith'.[12] The new department was to have the chief secretary as president, and for its practical operation and direction a vice-president, assisted by a secretary and two assistant secretaries together with a number of inspectors, instructors, officers and servants. Plunkett was appointed the vice-president, and took up his post on 2 November 1899. T.P. Gill was appointed secretary. The broad functions designated for the department under the act followed the lines of the Recess Report, namely, 'aiding, improving and developing the agriculture, fisheries and other industries of Ireland in so far as may be proper to such a department and in such a manner as to stimulate and strengthen the self-reliance of the people'.

A Board of Agriculture was established to discuss and advise on policy and organisation. It had the power to veto expenditure from the department's endowment fund, and generally played a role similar to that of a board of directors of a business enterprise. It had fourteen members, including the president and vice-president of the department. There was also a Council of Agriculture, a more innovative development. Plunkett conceived of it as a way of bringing the people, through their elected representatives, close to government. The council, elected every three years, was built on the newly established local government system, and consisted of 104 members. Of these, 68 were elected by county councils and 34 were nominated by the department. Considerable status and effectiveness accrued to the council through its statutory right to elect eight members of the 14-member Board of Agriculture, and through its right, together with the county councils and urban councils, to elect the majority of the 23 members of the Board of Technical Instruction, which advised the department on education and technical training. The department was not legally bound to accept the advice of the council, but its recommendations, when backed by a strong majority, could not easily be ignored.[13]

Plunkett, at the age of forty-five, had achieved the opportunity, denied to most people, of being charged to carry out a policy which he himself had conceived and had long advocated. Yet, speaking of the Recess Committee, 'a then wholly unprecedented union of Irishmen outside of politics or religion', he remarked:

> It is not generally known that it was Father Finlay who guided the propagandist work which was needed to get this remarkable body to come together for one of the greatest politico-economic achievements in Irish history.[14]

Regarding Finlay's role in 'propagandist work', one can only surmise, in the light of the limited information available. As an editor he reached a certain public. He also had an obvious opportunity to speak to colleagues in the university, and to students past and current, about the proposal for a special conference devoted to the general welfare of Ireland. There was also the more likely audience provided by local farmers at co-operative meetings around the country, whose innate conservatism and nationalism were likely to be influenced by his being both a priest and a noted nationalist. And, of course, there were the clergy, whose influence in country areas was of major importance.

Plunkett, as noticed earlier, testified to Finlay's impact on the clergy in many parishes. In his *Ireland in the New Century*, he observed regarding co-operative societies organised by the IAOS, 'there are no fewer than 331 societies of which the local priests are the chairmen', and 'during the summer and autumn of 1902, as many as 50,000 persons from all parts of Ireland were personally conducted over the exhibits of the Department of Agriculture and Technical Instruction, at the Cork Exhibition, by their local clergy'.[15] Moreover, Bishops Patrick O'Donnell of Raphoe, and Edward Thomas O'Dwyer of Limerick, were enthusiastic supporters of the co-operative movement, as, for a while, was Cardinal Michael Logue. That being said, it is necessary to be circumspect, as Finlay had to be, as regards clerical enthusiasm for the movement.

THE CLERGY AND THE CO-OPERATIVE MOVEMENT

One has to recall that there were three major elements in the co-operative movement. They were, by and large, the credit system societies, the creamery system, and the agricultural store societies. The first of these appears to have posed least problem for the local clergy, the second could at times be controversial but was generally acceptable, the third was largely unwelcome.[16] This was not surprising. The co-operative store created problems for local traders. The local priests may have been related to the town or village trader or traders, and, in any event, as pastors, they could not afford to be opposed to such an influential business figure. The shopkeepers as a body, moreover, were among the largest contributors to the Irish party, and many of the clergy themselves were active supporters of the party, and the highly organised Irish party system, which stretched into local areas throughout the country, was actively opposed to the co-operative movement. Significantly, Bishop O'Donnell of Raphoe cautioned, shortly after the movement began, that while 'co-operation was in itself a sound and healthy plant', care had to be taken not to protrude its roots 'under the foundation of the shops of the country', and 'as a friend of the movement he would warn its promoters to beware of promoting throughout Ireland any general system of co-operative stores'. To do so would, he emphasised, 'alienate from the movement the sympathy of the clergy …'[17]

Despite Plunkett's enthusiastic depiction of clerical support, some studies suggest that the Catholic clergy generally were slow to promote the co-operative movement in any form. Only two priests were among the 60 delegates who attended the first general conference of the co-operative dairy and agricultural societies in September 1895, and only 15, or 4 per cent, were among the subscribers. Attendance at general conferences is not a necessary barometer of interest, and it was early days as regards subscribers. A decade later the number of subscribers had risen to 13 per cent, but by 1915 it had declined to just 6 per cent of total subscribers. It is difficult to know what conclusion to draw from these figures, given the uneven spread of the co-operative movement across the country and the business and political hostility to it. It seems safe to assume, however, that over a considerable part of Ireland there was not a marked enthusiasm for the co-operative movement among the clergy.[18] Margaret Digby, indeed, in her *Horace Plunkett*, commented that Finlay 'was one of the few Catholic clergy of high standing who from first to last gave Plunkett active support and valuable counsel'.[19] As regards 'active support' this comment is quite exaggerated, but the situation was such, *vis-à-vis* fellow clergy, that Finlay walked a careful path in promoting co-operative ideals and practice. He had little sympathy for many of the local traders, but he was fortunate, where the clergy were concerned, that he was particularly identified with the least objectionable part of co-operation, from their point of view, the credit system.

THE RAIFFEISEN CREDIT SYSTEM

Finlay was a strong proponent of the Raiffeisen credit model, which he had first come across in Prussia. Friedrich Wilhelm Raiffeisen (1818–88), a German civil servant, was credited with being the founder, in 1849, of the credit union movement. Concerned at the way in which the rural populations was being made desperate by remorseless usury, he set out to help the people to help themselves. He established his first people's bank near Coblenz in 1865. Satisfying the people's money needs, however, was but a means towards inculcating a spirit of self-help and self-responsibility, and educating them towards better living. Raiffeisen lived to see his movement spread to Austria, Switzerland, and Italy. Impressed by the operation of the system in Prussia, Finlay introduced it to Ireland, and by 1908 there were to be 268 agricultural credit societies, popularly known as village banks, set up throughout the country and not dissimilar to the Raiffeisen's people's banks in Germany.

Finlay's belief in the system marked a difference in emphasis from Plunkett, though this was never allowed to interfere with their work or their friendship. According to H.F. Norman, Plunkett viewed 'small cultivators as essential wealth-producers in an impoverished rural community' and aimed 'at enriching production'. Finlay, on the other hand, viewed them 'as the embarrassed debtors of middle-men, themselves indebted for their own livelihood to the risky but often extortionate triple profits accruing from a form of barter that kept their farmer-customers permanently "on their books".' The shopkeeper charged the farmer maximal prices for the necessaries of life, credited him at minimal rates for farm produce taken over the counter as a set off against his debts, and added a good percentage for the absence of coin in the exchange of goods. Finlay believed, Norman explained, 'that agricultural co-operation can be more firmly established by starting with co-operative credit, and building thereon a system of sale, purchase, and finally production as in Germany'. He 'believed and remained an adherent of the Raiffeisen model, and Plunkett, later in his career, expressed the opinion that a more rapid understanding of the co-operative movement might have accrued if he had followed the Raiffeisen model'.[20]

But to return to 'propagandising' in preparation for the Recess Committee and his role as editor with regard to co-operation.

'PROPAGANDISING' THROUGH PUBLICATIONS, ESPECIALLY THE 'IRISH HOMESTEAD'

In the *Lyceum*, as instanced earlier, and also in the *New Ireland Review*, he wrote on different aspects of co-operation and on improving standards of agriculture. Not content with this partial treatment, however, he launched a publication devoted to the co-operative movement, with finance obtained by Plunkett. The first edition of the *Irish Homestead* appeared on 9 March 1895, before the Recess proposal had been thought of. 'Not to have a publication is to be in danger of being thought insignificant', Finlay stated in the first editorial. The paper was to prove a significant venture. Its success under the distinctive editorship of Æ (George Russell) is generally acknowledged, the fact that it ran successfully for ten years before that is seldom adverted to. Finlay was to be the active editor for the first two years of the paper, the years in which the Recess proposal came to fruition. He outlined the aim and hopes of the publication in the first issue.

Under the heading 'Our programme', he commented on an awakening of farmers, over a large area of Ireland, 'to the new needs of their industry which the changing conditions of modern social and commercial life' had 'brought about'. With the awakening had come 'a demand for the information which men who take up these new methods must possess'. The *Irish Homestead* sought to be the necessary medium of communication of this necessary information. As an earnest of this, the issue of 9 March 1895 carried information under such headings as 'Dairy, Live Stock – Sheep, Cattle, Poultry', and also news from R.A. Anderson on developments in the co-operative movement. A column headed 'Fireside Section' dealt with aspects of life in the home, and with education. A further dimension was provided by a short story, 'Dora', from the German, and an appreciation of Christina Rossetti – 'one of the most remarkable women of the present century …' Subsequent issues continued to raise the cultural level by means of selections of poetry, while also appealing to a more popular clientele with a column of 'Wit and Humour' of an obvious nature, and by providing, under 'Country Sport', pieces on 'angling' and 'fresh water fisheries'. Women's activities received frequent mention, and women writers were urged to contribute.[21]

In May 1896, in the preface to the bound volume encompassing the issues of the first year of the *Irish Homestead*, the editor felt able to make the claim:

> The *Homestead* records from week to week the progress of agricultural co-operation in Ireland, and these, we believe, are chapters of the economic history of Ireland which will grow in importance as the years go by. In the next place, our treatment of current agricultural and economic questions has been, we trust, of more than ephemeral interest. The principles and rules which concern poultry-raising for instance, do not change from year to year, and these we have discussed with a fullness and a detail worthy of the importance of the subject and of the interests which – especially in the case of our smaller farmers – are involved in it. We are confident our first volume will furnish one of the best treatises which has yet appeared on this important question.

In its first two years, Finlay's experienced editorship gave a stamp to the paper that was to continue, with a variety of emphasis, under his successors. Always there was the promotion of co-operative principles, of practical farming knowledge, of education, and of interest in books and poetry. In 1897, confident that the publication was soundly established, Finlay passed on the editorship. J.K. Montgomery took up the task and almost immediately, in January 1898, wrote of 'the steady progress' of the movement, its 'increasing popularity and strength' throughout the four provinces, and that its most striking feature 'is the spirit of union and mutual confidence' it promotes 'irrespective of class, creed, or section'. By 15 October the same confident voice proclaimed that the *Homestead* had gradually developed until it had become 'an organ of which no movement need to be ashamed'. Montgomery carried on the promotion of poetry and the habit of reading. The issue of 20 January 1899 included 'a list of one hundred books towards the formation of a village library'. This emphasis was continued under H.F. Norman, who succeeded as editor in 1900. On 16 November 1901, he announced that the *Homestead* would 'keep abreast of the literary movement in Ireland' as 'business alone can neither make a nation great nor a newspaper attractive. Besides business, there must be imagination, beauty and humour'. It was very much in the spirit of Finlay, whom Norman would later describe as 'initiator, office boy and first editor as well as contributor for more than thirty years'.[23] The character of the paper was well set when Æ took over in 1905.

From early on, too, the *Irish Homestead* defended Horace Plunkett and the cause of the co-operative societies from attack, especially from the *Freeman* and the Irish party. The 'Notes of the week', in the issue of 6 August 1898, commented caustically on the 'sickly tone' of the *Freeman's* editorial two days previously which had announced 'there are only two hundred and forty-three societies organised' in the co-operative movement. In other words, the *Homestead* wryly observed, 'only about thirty thousand have joined the movement. This is delightful from the *Freeman* to whom an audience of a couple of hundred constitutes a magnificent demonstration when it is gathered in support of its own policy. But to seriously examine its criticism would be a waste of time. It is determined to see no patriotism beyond that which Mr Dillon advocates.'

THE INJUDICIOUS SIDE TO PLUNKETT

Supporting Horace Plunkett by word and pen, however, was not always easy. He had a tendency to indulge whims, and give expression to criticisms that made enemies for himself and for the co-operative movement. Even in the Recess Report, without consultation with anyone, he included a passage critical of the prestigious Royal Dublin Society, claiming that despite its ample funds, and a government subsidy, it had not effected any marked improvement in the methods of the Irish farmer. This led to a pamphlet critical of the Recess Committee and to a recommendation, to Plunkett's annoyance, that the Irish board of agriculture be simply a branch of the English board. Plunkett availed of two of Finlay's publications to reply. In the sixth issue of the *New Ireland Review* for 1897 he added to the acrimony with 'The apologia of the Royal Dublin Society', and he resorted to an unsigned article in the *Irish Homestead*, 2 January 1897, on 'The Royal Dublin and the Recess Committee'.[24]

The use of his publications by Plunkett, and their defence of the co-operative movement against the Irish party, exposed Finlay to criticism from both angry unionists and ardent nationalists. Sadly, Plunkett's *penchant* for injudicious, headstrong action, was eventually to tarnish his reputation and obscure his magnificent contribution to Irish life. The instrument was his *Ireland in the New Century*, published in February 1904. It provided an economic and moral analysis of Ireland's problems but, in the process, placed emphasis on the lack of moral courage among Irish people and on the extravagance of the Catholic clergy in building large churches while their people lived in poverty. His commentary gave rise to *Catholicity and Progress in Ireland* (London 1905), a 500-page rebuttal by Monsignor Michael O'Riordan, rector of the Irish College, Rome, and to his book being banned by county councils and public bodies, and subjected to virulent censure from the *Freeman's Journal* and provincial newspapers. Cardinal Logue, without reading the book, joined in the chorus, as did many clergy. Bishop O'Dwyer of Limerick, however, declined to criticise, while he congratulated Monsignor O'Riordan, who was a priest of his diocese. Finlay also refused to criticise, even though he and R.A. Anderson had cautioned Plunkett against his tendentious observations. Anderson had been given the opportunity of reading the chapter on the Catholic Church. He informed Plunkett that if such a chapter had to be written, its author should be a Catholic and not a Protestant, and he reminded him that Protestants had possession of the two great cathedrals in Dublin, 'both of which had been churches of the ancient faith, and that, only on rare occasions, were we able to fill one of them with a congregation'. The book did not make the task of the IAOS organisers any easier, but, Anderson added, 'it speaks volumes for the tolerance and co-operative spirit of many Catholic priests, who had taken a prominent part in promoting the movement, that it alienated none of them'.[25] The decline in his popularity, however, and nationalist pressure, constrained Plunkett to resign from his cherished and influential position of vice-president of the Department of Agriculture and Technical Instruction. The department missed his creative drive, and it became less supportive of the IAOS and heavily bureaucratic, but it continued, under its secretary, the cautious but hard-working T.P. Gill, to make a major contribution to Irish life.[26]

Meantime, the *Homestead* of 2 June 1900 had noted that Finlay was elected to represent Leinster on the Board of Technical Instruction and that he had a particular interest in the application of science to agriculture. He also had a particular interest, as his publications made evident, in the development of Irish industries, and in the Gaelic League, not only for its promotion of the Irish language, but also for its emphasis on self-help and its encouragement of Irish business ventures.

THE GAELIC LEAGUE AND IRISH INDUSTRIES

By 1906 the promotion of Irish industries had become part of the official programme of the Gaelic League. It turned to Finlay and other prominent supporters of native enterprise and self-help. Its involvement, given its wide influence, was important. Eugene Sheerin, about to commence a pottery industry in Dublin, acknowledged this in a letter to Eoin MacNeill on 2 July 1906.

> Seeing the strong pronouncement of Dr Hyde on the importance which attaches to the industrial activities of the League in the eyes of our American supporters, and considering, also, that the same consideration at home is winning for it the public approval of those who were formerly neutral, if not opposing forces, I am very hopeful that you, and the prominent Gaels will accord my proposal your warm support.[27]

A high-powered 'Industrial Committee' was nominated by the League. At a meeting on 1 August 1907 the members present were: 'Rev. T.A. Finlay, MA (in the chair), Count Plunkett, Messrs. John Sweetman, Arthur Griffith, D.P. Moran, R. Hazelton RDC, Geo. W. Russell'. 'Draft schemes of work and instructions for local committees, prepared by the Rev. Chairman and Mr Sweetman, were discussed,' and certain matters were agreed which would be issued as a pamphlet if approved by the *Coisde Gnotha* or general council.[28] The *Coisde* approved, and various steps were recommended:

1. That the branches of the League form industrial committees.
2. That such committees support 'such industries as exist in its neighbourhood, and encourage every effort to develop such industries ... and make their products known'.
3. That local committees use Irish goods in their works and urge their members to ask for Irish goods in the shops.
4. That the local committees 'keep before the minds of our farmers and labourers that an excellent market for the produce of their farms and gardens is in their own homes, and that the more largely they support themselves out of their own produce, which they have first cost, and the less they substitute imported goods, the better for themselves and for the country'.
5. That the local committee should induce shopkeepers to put up the names of their establishments in Irish as well as in England.

In these and other ways the local committees were urged 'to develop the industrial energies of the people', and the central committee, chaired by Finlay, was prepared to receive reports from the local committees of the schemes they might frame, 'and to advise them as to the best methods to be adopted'.[29]

Thus, Finlay was centrally involved with two of the major popular movements in the country, influencing each by his economic and social knowledge, and that combination of idealism and practical common sense, matched to clarity of exposition and a lightness of touch, that made him the most popular speaker at the annual conference of the Irish Agricultural Organisation Society.

9

Vice-president of IAOS; speeches and the course of the movement

'The general meeting of the IAOS,' Plunkett observed, 'was always the most important occasion of the year for the advancement of the movement, and Father Finlay's speech never failed to say just what was wanted to clear up misunderstandings, which were the inevitable result of speeches in the country made by less clear exponents of the principles for which we stood, I myself, it must be confessed, too often being the worst offender.'[1] R.A. Anderson concurred: 'Of all our leaders, not even excepting Horace Plunkett ... none was so thoroughly imbued with the true co-operative spirit.' It would repay any student of agricultural co-operation in Ireland, or indeed in any country, he claimed, 'to read the reports of the speeches which he delivered at our annual general meetings and conferences, all of which are published fully in the reports of the IAOS. Plunkett's speeches at these meetings always seemed to me too long ... I fancy he felt it himself, for when he sat down he would turn to Father Finlay and whisper, "Father Tom, I think they'd like a little emphasis." And they usually got it!' 'I have never listened to a more telling speaker,' Anderson added. 'Father Finlay's voice was clear and incisive. He wasted no words; he got straight to the points he wished to make and then drove them home with irresistible force ... When the cause of co-operation was assailed it had no more valiant and skilful defender than he. He alone seemed to recognise that our somewhat sluggish people wanted shaking up if they were to make a success of the work which lay in their hands. And to him, alone, was given the power to dispel apathy and to turn a seemingly placid audience into a concourse of enthusiastic applauders.'[2]

It was necessary, indeed, to stimulate and encourage Irish farmers who were inherently conservative, and who, especially the dairy farmers, were constantly reminded of the easier life of those who adhered to grazing, engaging in what Plunkett cuttingly called 'their lotus-eating occupation of opening and shutting gates'.[3]

For the best part of thirty years at IAOS conferences, Finlay's speech as vice-president was eagerly awaited. The substance of most of them has been recorded, as Anderson noted, in the official reports of the annual general meetings, but the written word fails to convey the presence and spark that gave the speeches life.

Early on, at the third annual conference of delegates from the Irish co-operative societies, on 4 November 1897, Finlay's address dealt frankly with his own role in the organisation, and underlined his vision of the co-operative movement. Published in the *Irish Homestead*, it was reprinted as a pamphlet under the title *Co-operation and the Saving of the Celt*. It announced a personal *credo*, a vital expression of belief.

In appearing before another conference as vice-president, he felt, he declared, an explanation was due as to why he, a priest, occupied that office. As a priest he was supposed to have other ideals before him than the mere making of money for himself or others, and he agreed that if the co-operative organisation was concerned with the application of economic laws merely to create and accumulate wealth, he should be singularly out of place in the position he occupied. 'But', he insisted,

> we have to do here with something more than the mere creation of wealth, with interests infinitely more sacred, with interests which appeal to everyone who is concerned for the welfare – I would almost say for the existence – of the Irishman in Ireland (Applause).

'And', he went on, 'when an issue of this magnitude is involved there is no one who recognises the claims of humanity and patriotism who will not feel justified in helping practically to its favourable solution. (Hear, hear)'

It had been abundantly demonstrated, he continued, 'that the principles of co-operation intelligently applied to the industry of agriculture' were 'capable of giving life and development to that industry'. They had done so to the agricultural industry of Belgium, France, Germany, Holland, Denmark and Italy. Why should they not do so in Ireland? Indeed, the need was pressing to introduce 'these better methods of industry' in Ireland and to pursue them with vigour straightway. 'We cannot afford to wait much longer for our industrial regeneration. The outflow of our population – of its best and healthiest elements – is continuous.' Other remedies had been recommended as a cure for this evil, namely a political solution and the settlement of the land question. Their importance and benefit were undoubted, but despite the great activities in these areas over many years the deadly drain upon the life of the people had not been appreciably affected. 'The largest yearly exodus of the population' had taken place 'thirteen years after the beginning of the land legislation.' 'This suggests', Finlay observed, 'that the evil in its present stage, whatever may have been its origin, is chiefly economic. If so, it is to be met by economic remedies.' 'Looking at the world as it is', he went on,

> I feel justified in asserting that the main hope for our agricultural industry, and for the people dependant on it, lies in the policy of co-operation among the people, backed and sustained by the resources of the government.

'Furthermore, I find myself justified in taking a place in the ranks of our practical co-operators, by the fact that co-operation *goes to the root of the poor man's poverty*, and is of all methods that which most directly and immediately tends to lift him to a higher plane.' 'The principles of co-operation', he insisted with strong social emphasis, 'are democratic in the best sense of the word – democratic as no other system can be. It puts rich and poor, high and low, on a level of equality in a way which no other form of social alliance can attain. If the rich man, the man of education and position, chooses to become a co-operator – and many of them I am glad to say are amongst us – there is one condition to which he must submit. He must *come down from his eminence of wealth or social standing*. He must consent to enter the organisation with exactly the same rights and principles as his humblest neighbour ... He cannot claim for himself any superior authority. Here, at least, it is 'one man one vote' in the most thoroughgoing sense of the phrase.' This form of association of great and lowly 'on terms of friendly and helpful equality' was of benefit to both, but was especially elevating for the poor man. The 'frank and full recognition of a man's own qualities – his honesty, his industry, his capacity – as the one title to influence or distinction cannot but lift and ennoble the man whose only shortcoming is his poverty. (Applause)'

Having offered these and other considerations in justification of his part in the movement, and in support of other priests, Finlay went on to draw his audience's attention to practical obstacles to progress in Ireland. Their task was harder than that which faced the pioneers of co-operation among the peasants of Belgium or Germany.

> We have to do with people who are imperfectly educated in the ways of higher industry, and with whom the habits of punctuality, perfection of work, and steady perseverance in the face of difficulties – qualities essential to success in co-operative undertakings – are not traditional.

'The explanation of this' he added, 'is not far to seek – the causes will suggest themselves without further reference by me. As a consequence of these causes we must be prepared to find the people unskilful, and, it may be, apathetic and inert at the start.' Unfortunately, some members of the press had added to this condition by dismissing home-grown co-operative ventures and praising 'the vast and potent organisation' of the English Co-operative Wholesale Society, to which many Irish societies had 'surrendered the ownership and control of their own industry', thereby voluntarily surrendering ownership and control 'to the foreign invader'. Finlay viewed 'a disaster of this sort' with 'a poignant feeling of humiliation'. On the other hand, the true expression of the business capacity of the Irish farmer was represented by the healthy and vigorous life of the 166 societies represented at the conference. Here, there were the marks of education 'in the higher methods of industry', there was a harmony in their councils, where interests were debated with keen intelligence and practical measures adopted, and, as a result, there was 'the ever-increasing extension of our societies through the length and breadth of the land'. In all this, he concluded confidently, 'I discern the growth of a new spirit which will make Irish agriculture live with a new life, fortify it against every rivalry by which it may be assailed, and falsify every prediction which assigns to it a future of disaster. (Loud applause)'

The vice-president's address followed that of the president's report to the meeting and seconded the report. Sometimes, Finlay repeated the main burden of the report, emphasising particular aspects, sometimes he focussed his audience's attention on just one feature or drew attention to a current national or international problem affecting the movement. Always, however, the approach was business-like, the words prompting efficiency while promoting confidence and animation. In March 1901, for example, he reminded the annual general meeting 'that a meeting of co-operative societies was for purposes of business. Its purpose was to discuss their progress, and ... to examine what was defective in their methods, with a view to correcting the defects.' 'Frank but friendly criticism was a service to their cause' as much as enlightened suggestions on how to overcome shortcomings. He then put before them 'a view of the business significance of the operations in which they were engaged'. Their co-operative societies now numbered about 500 with a total membership of 50,000. Most of these were heads of families. Allowing four persons to each family, the interests, therefore, of some 200,000 people were intimately connected with the future of the co-operative movement in Ireland. They had a capital of £300,000 invested in the businesses they were variously carrying on. This had given them a four-fold increase. This material benefit, of course, was not regarded by the members, Finlay emphasised, 'as the most valuable reward of their efforts. For them the improved industrial habits of the Irish farmer, his elevation in the economic order, his wider knowledge, his increased self-reliance and self-respect, were much more important than mere additions to his material wealth (applause)'. 'These products of their work', he went on perceptively, 'were beyond reach of the accidents which affect the mere money market; they have a guarantee for national prosperity which could not be shaken by any fluctuations in the value of marketable securities. It has been said that the most productive investment of capital was to be made in the character, the business qualities, and social virtues of human beings. Tested by this standard, the investments of the Irish Agricultural Organisation Society have yielded a rich return to its founders and supporters.'[4]

The address almost modelled most of his other speeches as vice-president: A comment on progress, a mention of one particular feature, and finally an appeal to the high ideals of the co-operative movement, drawing his listeners beyond their own particular units to the overall values and needs of the movement, constantly reiterating the importance of their corporate union, constantly endeavouring to emphasise the benefits of co-operation and to build up confidence and morale, while, at the same time, striving to transcend, overcome, the human selfishness that undermined unity. It was a complex task.

In 1902 he made one of his most stimulating addresses: an apologia for the Co-operative Society that also answered its critics, to the delight of his audience. He had been asked to speak to the proposal 'That this conference commends to the thoughtful consideration of all patriotic Irishmen, irrespective of creed, party, or class, the appeal for financial aid which the IAOS has made to the public and the grounds upon which this appeal is made'.

He commenced with a word of gratitude to Plunkett, who, as vice-president of the new Department of Agriculture, had to surrender his presidency of the IAOS, but 'whose genius planned, and whose self-sacrifice made feasible, the work we have accomplished (applause)'. Then, turning to the annual report and its evidence of further expansion, and referring to the country-wide map of the Society's outlets which was before the conference, he remarked: 'We notice a network of some 650 co-operative associations with a total number of 65,000 individuals. We are glad to notice', moreover, 'that the tissues of the net are densest in the poorest and most neglected parts of Ireland, for we believe that in these co-operative societies the poverty of Ireland will ultimately find its most effective remedy (applause).' He reminded his listeners, however, that without a central co-ordinating agency the movement as a whole 'would speedily dissolve into an aggregate of powerless individual units'. 'Critics of Ireland', he continued, 'expressed surprise that so large a movement was possible', given the country's reputation for discord and dissension. They asked by what magic this phenomenon had been brought about. 'We can give no other reply than this', Finlay declared, 'it has been accomplished by the familiar magic of common sense. We have not put before the people any utopian schemes', any golden dreams to be created by act of parliament. 'We have told them that Ireland and her fortunes would be exactly what the Irish people themselves chose to make them (hear, hear).' 'We assured them – and we assure them still

> that their fortunes are absolutely in their own hands, that by their own energy they must rise, or by want of energy they must fall; and we pointed out to them that as things now stand in the world ... men and nations live by industry alone. It is on the industry of a nation that its life is based; on this its public institutions rest, by this its literature, its art, its science, and every other development of social life are made possible. A nation that has not industry, and will not acquire it, is either dead or on the road to death (applause).

'By industry,' he explained, 'we mean the ordered control of nature, the labour which is expended, not in taking the place of beasts of burden – of that we have had enough in Ireland – but the labour which, guided by knowledge, subordinates material forces to men's control (applause), the labour which substitutes clearness of thought for mere physical strength, and in which method is much more than muscle. It is by that industry that modern nations live; it is by that their prosperity has been attained, and it is by industry of this kind that the prosperity of Ireland is to come, if it comes at all (applause).'

There were many obstacles in their path of progress, he went on. There were hindrances and difficulties which were 'legacies of a dismal history: our education is defective, there is amongst us a want of business traditions, our system of land tenure is chaotic, and … we are told that it is useless to strive against difficulties of this kind, that circumstances are hopelessly against us.' 'Our answer to that', Finlay asserted, 'is: a resolute man is above his circumstances (applause). We say it is the business and the duty of the man of courage and resolution to conquer his circumstances and not to sit down and wail and groan under them (applause).' All through Ireland, even under the gloomiest circumstances, there were to be found 'the individual known as the "strong farmer". He became strong in spite of his circumstances, by intelligent and methodical industry. The aim of our Association is to make every farmer in Ireland strong.' 'We maintain', he added, that 'if under present circumstances hundreds of men have become strong, the application of the same means can raise thousands to the same condition (hear, hear).'

Moving on, Finlay pointed out that the Society's programme and policy had commended themselves not only because they were practical, 'but also because people realised that their effect was immediate'. 'We begin', he asserted, 'with the evils at our door, and strive to redress them. Foremost among the depressing misfortunes to which our nation is subject … is the constant stream of emigration from Ireland.' The IAOS did not just deplore that misfortune, 'we have set ourselves to stop it, and we claim the merit of having kept in Ireland not one but hundreds of emigrants'.

In support of this striking assertion, he described the concrete impact on emigration by the founding of a local co-operative society in the north of Ireland.

> Last September I had the privilege of presiding at the founding of a cooperative society for the girls of a populous parish in the county of Tyrone – a parish in which the drain of emigration had already set in. Every spring dozens of healthy, vigorous girls, daughters of the small farmers of the parish, emigrated to America, and the usual heartbreaking scenes took place at the railway stations. The society was formed last September; 170 girls joined on the day it was founded, and set to work at the industries we recommended with true northern vigour. I had the satisfaction of receiving a few weeks ago, a letter from the priest of the parish stating that this year not a single girl had emigrated from the locality (applause).

'I could quote instances of the same kind from the neighbouring counties of Fermanagh and Monaghan', Finlay added. He was not acquainted with results in other counties, but he was confident that if the Society had the means to carry out its schemes throughout Ireland, and received in every parish 'that vigorous local support' received in Tyrone, he would venture to prophecy 'that within ten years abnormal emigration would have ceased in Ireland (applause)'.

Following on this seemingly overdrawn presentation, he addressed himself to criticisms levelled at the Society of being, it seems, nationally and socially divisive and of undermining certain Irish businesses. 'Not only are we practical, and aim at immediate results, and thus secure favour from the thinking public, we are also, in the truest and best sense of the word, nationalists. We aim at the well being of every man and every class in this country. There is nothing sectional about us ... We invite into our association the members of every class, on this condition, however, that no matter what their rank may be, when they enter our organisation, they shall stand on the same footing of authority and control as the poorest member of the association (applause).'

Warming to his defence of the Society, he dealt brusquely, even harshly, with the criticisms of industries and traders.

> It has been urged against us that we have interfered by our methods with certain existing industries in the country. Gentlemen, wherever progress is made, that result is unavoidable. It is incidental to every sphere of industrial effort. For instance, you could not introduce locomotives into a country without interfering with the industry of stage-coach making (laughter). You cannot introduce power-looms into a country without dislocating in some way the industry of those who make spinning-wheels and hand-looms, and you cannot introduce creameries into a country and set up the machinery of the creameries, driven by steam-engines, without interfering in some way or other with the manufacture of antique urns.

Turning to the further criticism, 'that by teaching the farmers to combine and purchase in common the requirements of their industry, we have interfered with what is called the "legitimate trader",' he asked: 'Who is the legitimate trader? (applause)' And he pressed on unremittingly:

> In a country where free trade is supposed to prevail, is it not open to every man, woman, and child, to become traders if they feel so disposed? (Hear, hear). The law, as it has so far been expounded, has not reserved the privilege of trading to any section or any class. It does not readily appear why there should be a legitimate trader any more than there should be a legitimate farmer. And if it is true that a trader in the town has the right, and sometimes exercises it also, of taking a farm in the neighbourhood, and working thereon for his profit or pleasure, why should it be a crime for the farmer, if he feels so disposed, to engage for his advancement or even for his amusement in the occupation of trade (applause).

'As for *combination* in these trading operations,' he queried sardonically, 'are not the Irish farmers just as free to combine as a railway company, or a brewing company, or a mining company? The privileges of the law are open to them as to their richer neighbours, and the fact that they are, as a rule, poor men is no reason why they should not use any advantage which the law creates while they are pursuing their industry honestly. In the fullness of this liberty we have acted hitherto, in the exercise of the same freedom we propose to continue (applause).'

Having generated and sustained enthusiasm, Finlay reminded his listeners of the purpose of his talk, namely, to show that the IAOS merited public support, and also merited improved financial support from themselves. 'The economic results obtained by the Irish Agricultural Organisation Society', he observed, 'have not been secured without a large expenditure of money by the few amongst us who are rich men, notably by your late president, to whom every form of self-sacrifice is familiar, and expenditure of time and thought and labour by those who could give little more.' The question had been raised: 'Why is this trading society, which has a turnover of one and a half millions, not self-supporting?' 'The answer is: Because it is *not* a trading society. The Irish Agricultural Organisation Society, as its name implies, teaches the methods of profitable industry to others, but it does not pursue them for its own gain. It cannot possibly make an income out of its operations. Its function is teaching, and teaching, you may take it as proved, is not a lucrative position when it is wholly supported by the pupils.' The annual report had demonstrated that the expenditure had been spent wisely and fruitfully. But the sources of income had been limited. 'We have had to choose', he emphasised in conclusion, 'between restricting our work, or appealing to those outside our ranks who share with us the belief that the life of the Irish people depends on the industry of Ireland ... We believe we have established a claim on the support of those friends of Ireland who hold to practical ends by practical methods, and we bespeak their aid for a movement which must, we are convinced, have a decisive bearing on the issue of that struggle for life in which the Irish race in Ireland is involved (Loud and sustained applause).'

The following year he did not attend the general meeting. He, Plunkett, Lord Monteagle, and a Mr Tisdall, were in North America appealing for the financial aid mentioned the previous year. The visit was not particularly successful. It was not assisted, it would appear, by the presence of William Butler Yeats seeking funding at the same time. Professor Roy Foster's biography of Yeats refers to Finlay 'sniping' at the poet during the American tour. The sole source appears to be a letter from Æ to the American supporter of Irish causes, John Quinn, in January 1904, which makes the most unlikely of comments, namely, that Finlay's dislike of Yeats arose from 'a fear that mysticism would destroy Jesuit education'! It is not clear that Finlay disliked Yeats, or, indeed, that he was estranged from Æ, which is also alleged in the same biography.[5]

At the AGM for 1904, Finlay reminded the members that 'they had arrived at a turning point in the history of the co-operative movement', that in the past the organisation had been conceived and virtually financed by one man but now its maintenance was thrown on themselves. The task before them was to build up 'a comprehensive and solid system of finance' by means of trading. That year the IAOS had revised its rules in order to turn over control of the organisation to the member societies, of which there were now nearly 900 compared to 63 when the Society was founded in 1894. A new central committee was formed and the societies were asked to pay a special capitation contribution, in addition to affiliation fees. The response was poor, and the IAOS, in 1906, reported that the organisation was still 'mainly dependant upon the Department of Agriculture for its income'.[6] The subsidy had been introduced by Plunkett as vice-president of the Department, an initiative not favoured by Finlay and a number of other exponents of self-help. By 1906 challenges were being made within the Council of Agriculture to the subsidy. That year, Finlay re-emphasised the need for corporate trading, summarising what was required in clear and timeless terms.

> *The trade side of the movement would make or mar it.* They should, therefore, concentrate their efforts on the development of the trade organisation of the movement, and by bringing the various societies into some system of combination enable them to bulk their produce in larger consignments, to grade them, and to have some mark which would safeguard them from the operation of fraudulent rivals, and which would secure for Irish products a better reputation and a better place in the English markets (applause).

The following year, the Department of Agriculture used its position to dictate terms. Henceforth, the IAOS was required to confine its work to organisation and auditing. Its organisers were not to give technical advice except with Departmental approval, and salary scales and the expenses and allowances of IAOS officials would be subject to the scrutiny and approval of the Department's officials. That year, following a barrage of attacks on Plunkett in the House of Commons, led aggressively by John Dillon, Plunkett resigned from the Department and was succeeded by Thomas Wallace Russell, who had been born in Scotland and, according to Tim Healy, was 'devoid of the geniality and humour of his race'. Russell had no time for the co-operative movement and in autumn 1907 withdrew all financial aid from the Irish Agricultural Organisation Society.[7] Plunkett, meanwhile, was received back with acclaim as president of the IAOS.

In his vice-presidential address in 1907, Finlay set out to build up morale in the membership. Referring to the attitude of the Department of Agriculture, he announced that many in the Society held the view that it was 'a radical mistake to have entered into such an alliance with any government department'. A subsidy brought control with it. Liberty of action had been restricted. 'Their movement began as a self-help movement, and many of them believed that its prospects and fortunes would have been brighter, even if its resources had been more restricted, if it had remained perseveringly and unfailingly a self-help movement (hear, hear).' Under the arrangement with the Department the number of societies had certainly increased, but there had also come about 'a condition of paralysis'. 'When men come to think and believe that the work in which they are engaged had been taken up by the State, they considered themselves absolved from vigorous activity in prosecuting it.' 'They were now returning to the condition in which they must rely upon themselves. They might have to face difficulties, but for himself he looked forward with confidence to the future (applause).' When the movement began their resources were very limited and 'they had to depend upon the enthusiasm and self-sacrifice of men who believed in the system'. These were the most effective resources. 'He looked forward with hope to the time when they should have to fall back entirely upon those forces (hear, hear) ... He believed that a small number of societies, properly organised, and imbued with the proper spirit – the spirit of co-operation applied on the scale on which federations were built up – would do better work than a large number would do, in whose members the spirit of co-operation was defective (applause).'

The rhetoric of independence expressed by Finlay and other prominent members of the movement seemed hollow at first sight, but affiliation fees and subscriptions increased and signalling the new spirit of independence was the co-operators' gift to Plunkett of a large house in Merrion Square to enable him to carry on his work. The annual report for 1909, however, pointed out that while dues and subscriptions from the societies had increased, many societies contributed little and others nothing at all. From 1909 to 1913 the IAOS was dependant on it own resources and was kept going, in effect, by the generosity of Plunkett and his friends. Nevertheless, despite the financial strictures, it was a period of considerable progress. The number of co-operatives grew from 881 in 1908 to 985 in 1913; the Society's trade turnover increased from £2.2 million to £3.3 million; the Irish co-operative movement was evoking international interest, and students from abroad were coming to study its organisation and methods.[8]

In these years, Finlay continued to be the encouraging, and chiding voice, building confidence, fostering morale, in the face of external critics and of ineffective local societies and selfish successful ones. In 1913, however, an external occurrence called for special comment.

1913: THE GREAT STRIKE/LOCK-OUT IN DUBLIN

The expansion of the IAOS in spite of financial constraints, led Finlay to proclaim in his vice-presidential address: 'We have now resources sufficient to justify us in extending our work, in widening our field of organisation ... We are warranted in anticipating that our movement will spread over a larger and larger area ... We might even venture on the hope that it will so largely permeate the economic life of the nation that we may see realised amongst us the ideal which is described as "the co-operative commonwealth" (applause).' His use of the phrase 'co-operative commonwealth' was a deliberate attempt to assure conservative farmers that their 'co-operative commonwealth' was very different from James Connolly's 'Co-operative Commonwealth', which Connolly viewed as the goal 'common now to the militant workers of the world',[9] and which, in the intense feeling generated by the Dublin strike/lock out, the press linked to socialism, meaning for many 'the red flag of anarchy'.[10] However sympathetic Finlay may have been to the workers' cause, however much he respected Connolly, his task in the IAOS was to clarify the difference between its use of the phrase and that associated with socialism. 'Let us make clear to ourselves and make plain to others', he stated, 'what we mean by this term. You will have noticed that it is currently used in a sense widely different from that in which we employ it (hear, hear). Like the terms Liberty, Equality, Fraternity, it may have different meanings in the mouths of different men, and as a formula of different parties. For the socialist the term "co-operative commonwealth" stands for one form of economic and social organisation; as we employ it, it has quite another signification. We have little or nothing in common with the ideas and ideals of socialism (applause); the "co-operative commonwealth" that we would willingly see established is profoundly and radically different from that for which the socialist strives.' Having thus assured his audience, and conscious that the enemies of the co-operative movement might avail of the confusion, he went on: 'To prevent a confusion in the public mind which might be to our prejudice, it is worth while to delay for a moment to define our position in this connection.'

'THE CO-OPERATIVE COMMONWEALTH'

In the course of his explanation, Finlay, as will appear, also expressed his dislike of 'the tyranny of a so-called democratic majority', a tyranny which had been accentuated for the IAOS by the Council of Agriculture's rescinding of its previous resolutions by voting to withhold all financial aid from the IAOS after 1908.[11] His definition of the Society's position on the co-operative commonwealth was

> one in which groups of humble men combine their efforts, and to some extent their resources, in order to secure for themselves those advantages in industry which the masters of capital derive from the organisation of labour, from the use of costly machinery, and from the economies of business when done on a large scale. They apply in their industry the methods by which the magnates in commerce and manufacture are made. With this difference, however, that the gains from the better methods are shared equitably among all who are engaged in industry; they are not reserved for an individual who controls it, or for the body of shareholders who are not actively involved in the operations.

But how is this form of association different from that of the socialists? He proceeded to explain in a more ample manner than in previous addresses, with the echo of Dublin's disturbances in the background:

> In the first place it is wholly voluntary. It is not forced upon anyone by State authority; it is not imposed by the vote of any majority (hear, hear) – we are democratic, but we know nothing of that most odious form of tyranny, the tyranny of a democratic majority. Our combination is free – free in each of its members, free in each of the societies established within the system. In the second place it is not in its character, or its aim, hostile to any class or to any interest. We make no war upon capital or capitalists (applause). We aim at being capitalists ourselves, at amassing for the group which works co-operatively the capital necessary to the operations carried on for the common benefit. But with us the individual and the society alike obtain capital by work not by plunder (applause). In doing so we concede the same right to every one who chooses to enter the field of industry in which we are occupied. We do not bar competition, we welcome it … The idea of a war of classes is wholly alien to our movement, which, of its nature, makes for social and economic peace (hear, hear). It brings capital and labour into harmonious combination, gives them a common interest in the wealth-producing undertakings to which both contribute, and in distributing the resulting products provides equitably for their several claims (applause).

Finally, he drew attention to the most fundamental of all the differences between the aims of the IAOS and 'those which the preachers of socialism profess'. 'Our co-operative combination, with its common fund of capital, its common use of machinery and agricultural implements, its common marketing agencies – whether for sale or purchase – and whatever else is held for the common service, has for its ultimate object to enhance the wealth and increase the property of the individual; by no means to use the individual to create property for the community. Briefly:

> with us community of effort is directed to give property to the individual; with the socialist the effort of the individual would be directed to create property for the community (applause). Herein lies the profound and radical difference which separates irreconcilably our scheme of industry from every programme of revolution or reform – call it as you will – to which the designation socialist applies.

'So long as this distinction is kept clearly in mind', he added, 'we may speak of our ideal as that of a co-operative commonwealth'. By it was envisaged, in short, 'an Ireland in whose industries men will group themselves for mutual assistance, realising that in helping others each man is most effectively helping himself; that the poor man is economically strong only in association with his fellows, and that the diffusion of property and the consequent economic strength of the masses is the assured basis of the social order (applause).' One can almost imagine James Connolly, too, applauding that final paragraph!

Moving on to internal developments since the last general meeting, he acknowledged assistance from the State through the Development Commissioners to the amount of £4000 in aid. Seeking to combine this with his previous emphasis on self-help and independence of the State, he informed his audience that being recipients of public funds made a new demand on them for energy in propagating the co-operative movement, 'and for vigour in maintaining within it the true co-operative spirit'. 'We have now to submit our work and its results', he pointed out, 'to other eyes and other judgments than our own. We have to justify the actions of those who have endowed us with public money, and to do this we must spread wider the network of our societies, and see to it that the principles they profess are realised in their operations (hear, hear).'

As always, there was need to warn against abuses of the movement. One such was monopoly. 'Co-operation is not planned to create small groups of capitalists to control the industry of the masses, it is designed to give all alike, the few and the many, not merely an interest in the industry, but also a voice in its control (hear, hear).' He referred to men of vision, who had been founders of creameries in their area, and who 'feeling that the success has been mainly due to their enterprise, now refuse to admit as shareholders those who declined the first invitation and the new suppliers who have since come in.' 'I can understand this attitude', Finlay proclaimed, 'but, as a co-operator, I cannot justify it (hear, hear).'

Concluding this historic address, the last in an era of peace, he looked back over the quarter of a century since the Society was founded, hailed its achievements, and looked forward to its future with no foreboding of the World War that would alter its world.

> It is now a quarter of a century since the first co-operative society was established on behalf of the farmers of this country. It is impossible to estimate accurately ... (how much) the movement has since contributed to the welfare of the class in whose interests it was initiated. Other causes – notably the changes in our system of land tenure – have contributed to the growing prosperity of the Irish farmer. But side by side with those other causes, the co-operative movement has had a large share in increasing the resources, and brightening the lives, of that class in the community on which the prosperity of our country mainly depends. That it has achieved so much is more than a reward for those who in this long period have been striving to promote it, with no interest in its success beyond the good it would confer on others (applause). In the new conditions now created for us we may look forward with confident expectation to its extension over broader fields, and its efficacy for larger benefits.

And in a resounding diapason, he dared to hope that the example and teaching of the IAOS might present a way forward to the antagonists in Dublin and to the growing divisions among Irish people, north and south. 'Is it vain to hope', he asked, 'that its influence may extend beyond our ranks, that our teaching and our practice may affect the stormy antagonisms which disturb public life in other spheres, that all our countrymen may learn from our experience the virtue of peaceful combination for the common good, be won to the truth of which we have convinced ourselves – that in kindly good feeling and mutual helpfulness are to be found the most trustworthy foundations of a national economy and the most assured guarantee of a nation's development? (applause).[12] This hope to some extent reflected the optimism demonstrated in a memorandum prepared for the visit of an American Commission that year. The IAOS expressed the view that 'rural Ireland is ready to be completely organised. We believe that in less than 20 years even urban Ireland will recognise how much it owed to this movement among the farmers.'[13]

THE WAR YEARS

The war years brought a period of increasing prosperity for the Irish farmer. Many new societies were formed and the trade turnover of co-operatives rose from three and a half million sterling in 1914 to over fourteen and a half million in 1920.[14]

In 1914, Plunkett, with characteristic enthusiasm, outlined to the annual general meeting 'the opportunities' the war would offer them, and the services it would demand from them. Finlay, by contrast, sought to prepare his audience 'for the difficult time when the ruined industries of Europe come to be rebuilt and the hideous waste of war to be repaired'. Like many, he evidently expected a short but disastrous war. He feared, however, that the central agency of the IAOS, and the unity of the organisation, could be damaged by the profits and strain of wartime. As a result, much of his talk was devoted to praising the importance of the central agency. It reminded societies of 'the fundamental principle of mutual help' in which they were founded, and of the need to avoid competitive methods towards each other. There were examples of these competitive methods, Finlay stated, 'in the case of creameries under-selling one another in the market, and outbidding one another for milk supplies'. Moreover, where interests had thus become antagonistic, the central agency performed the necessary role of mediating impartially on the points of dispute. It's one concern was the common good. It also served as 'a central intelligence department' which helped farmers look beyond their local horizons to changes abroad and how these might influence, favourably or unfavourably, the Irish farmer's prospects. Again, the agency served as a defensive instrument when co-operative societies were attacked.

In his concern for the leadership and staff of the IAOS, he went on to draw together and emphasise the central functions it provided.

> As a bond of union, as the guarantee of harmony and peace among the societies, as the intelligence agency of the movement, as the champion

> of its rights, as its defence against hostile attacks, the IAOS has borne a part in our agricultural co-operative movement which all who know its history must recognise as indispensable. In addition to the tasks thus discharged, it has been the educational agency by which the farmers have been instructed in co-operative methods, by which new additions have been made to the societies already created, and by which, in virtue of this extension, added economic strength has been given to every existing society in the organisation. To all it has been an advisory body in their difficulties, saving many from the consequences of their mistakes, helping them to repair disasters, encouraging the active and the strenuous, and stimulating the listless and the apathetic with energetic business vitality.

He followed this encomium, with a reminder of the agency's need of financial assistance. The time had come, he observed, 'when we should provide at our own cost the services which the IAOS can render'; and all needed to remember that even 'the most vigorous constitutions are liable to sudden ailments, and in their ailments they need assistance from someone who takes an interest in their well being'. And with the 'most vigorous' in mind, he stated baldly: 'There can be selfishness in corporate bodies as well as in individuals, and it is no more admirable in the one case than the other.'[15]

In 1915, he placed particular emphasis on the importance of organisation. Farmers would not be taken seriously by the government until their voices were heard in the councils of State through members of their own class. 'The artisans, the dockers and the miners are wiser in their generation than the toilers upon the land. They have chosen from their own ranks their spokesmen in parliament ... We have a trades union party in the House of Commons: when shall we have a farmers' party? We have a trades union minister in the cabinet: when shall we have a working farmer in the ministry?'

'The answer to these questions' was 'when agriculturalists are organised as are the artisans.' Organisation, he insisted, would be essential at the end of the war.

> Peace, when it comes, will bring with it conditions which will try our powers of endurance to the utmost. However we may be spared the devastation which will face the tillers of the land over which the hosts of Europe have trampled and fought, the burden of exorbitant taxation will have to be met, and that out of prices which will have fallen much below the normal level. Money will be scarce and credit will not be obtainable on the easy terms of better times. The farmers' money income will be seriously reduced, and the demands upon that income will increase beyond anything of which this generation has had experience.

'The circumstances of the present and the prospects of the future', he concluded, 'call for a new development of the co-operative spirit in our societies, for closer union among their members, and for ... a more determined support of the central body in which they are united.'[16]

The following year the sombre picture of life after the war no longer seemed relevant. No end was in sight. The conflict had entered its most devastating stage. Finlay concentrated on the spirit of the movement. The increased trade brought by the war was having an undermining effect. Sixty-two branches had been cut off, and had been replaced 'by 30 living and energetic offshoots'. 'What makes for the strength of any organisation', he once more reminded his hearers, 'is the degree in which its members are bound together, and pursue their common end unitedly (applause)'. Weakness, on the other hand, 'finds its expression in three ways: first, in individualism; secondly in particularism; and thirdly, in capitalism'. Finlay explained each in turn. Individualism was present when members 'join a society not to promote their ultimate well-being by making the organisation efficient, but to secure at once their own benefit, whether it accords with the welfare and progress of the society, or whether it does not (hear, hear)'. Particularism referred to individuals or societies that restricted their concern 'to the locality in which they' were 'resident' and did not 'take a wider view embracing the whole movement'. He pointed to societies that had drawn on the services of the central body, but which when they 'thought themselves sufficiently strong, left the IAOS and took care only of their own interests'. Capitalism tended to break out when societies became prosperous. In Ireland, Finlay pointed out, there were 'societies extending their business without taking in new members, establishing what is really a capitalist system, and refusing to admit any others. These men are capitalists in the strict sense of the word … These men have to be resisted; they must recognise that co-operation is not for the benefit of speculators and investors but for the benefit of the workers as a whole and for the welfare of the nation (hear, hear).'[17]

In 1917, at the age of sixty-nine, Finlay's work load was further extended. Plunkett explained the circumstances in his address to that year's annual congress. 'My neglect of your affairs has, as you know, been due to circumstances beyond my own control. I was ill for a large portion of last year, and I had hardly got well again and resumed my ordinary business when I was diverted to another occupation (applause).' On top of his illness, Anderson, the indefatigable secretary of the society, had been gravely ill, and the chief auditor, in Plunkett's phrase, 'thought it his duty to serve his country in another capacity'. In this critical situation, Plunkett added,

> An old friend of ours, Father Finlay, stepped into the breach (applause). He is not, as you know, an idle man. He has clerical and academic duties, and by consenting to work for fourteen or fifteen hours a day he managed to do not only his own work, but a great part of Mr Anderson's, and the whole of mine

Plunkett's mention of his being 'diverted to another occupation' referred to his appointment as chairman of the National Convention set up by Lloyd George with the ostensible purpose of enabling Irish people to arrive at an agreement about Home Rule which would satisfy the northern unionists and prevent partition. On 16 May 1917, the prime minister outlined the purpose of the Convention in a letter to John Redmond to the effect 'that Irishmen of all creeds and parties ... meet together in a Convention for the purpose of drafting a constitution for their own country which would secure a just balance of all the opposing interests ...' Lloyd George, in effect, was playing for time, seeking to placate American public opinion at a difficult time in the war. He had privately assured the Ulster unionists that their position would not be interfered with by the deliberations of the Convention. Sinn Féin, suspicious of the prime minister, refused to attend. The Conservative Party, moreover, announced that they would not be bound by the decisions of the Convention.[18] In the circumstances there was little prospect of success.

Finlay strongly advised Plunkett against participating, presumably because he saw it as involvement in a political process, which was contrary to IAOS policy, and also, perhaps, as a fruitless endeavour. In his diary for 16 July 1917, Plunkett noted: 'Father Finlay is very much annoyed at my touching the Convention. He thinks the Co-operative Movement the only thing worth fighting for in Ireland at the present time.'[19] Plunkett, over-sanguine and wilful in political matters, ignored the advice. Despite his comment that Finlay saw the co-operative movement as the only thing worth fighting for, the latter's known nationalist spirit led William Martin Murphy, owner of *Independent* newspapers, and the strongest national voice in the Convention, to invite him, towards the end of May 1917, to attend a select meeting at his house to meet with the chief secretary for Ireland, H.E. Duke, who was known to be opposed to both conscription and partition.[20]

Finlay's own speech at the 1917 annual general meeting referred as usual to current problems and future possibilities and requirements, but it gave particular intention to farmers' grievances against the government. 'We are still in the throes of a disastrous war', he remarked, and the 'shortage of the necessaries of life are inflicting increasing hardships on everybody and aggravated misery on the poor.' It was only after two years, when 'the dearth of food supplies from abroad began to be acutely felt', that the government 'called on their own farmers ... to feed the people. The venerable dogmas of Free Trade were flung to the winds. Prices were guaranteed, the extension of tillage was made compulsory, and the government took into its own hands the control of distribution'. The government officials appointed to carry out these measures, however, had no practical acquaintance 'with the details of the farmer's industry', could not see things 'from the farmer's point of view, or gauge, as he could, the effect of their multitudinous regulations. As a result, mistakes were inevitable, and discontent followed on the mistakes.'

With the public reporting of his speech in mind, it would seem, Finlay declared that from his own knowledge, and from what he gathered from members of the IAOS central staff, who knew the country as no others did, he could state 'that over a large part of Ireland the farmers are profoundly dissatisfied with the administration of the schemes for increased production. Whether it be the complicated and ever-changing regulations with which they are bewildered, or the unsatisfactory prices fixed for their produce, or the contrast between their gains and those of the traders who traffic in the fruits of their toil; whatever be the cause, their discontent is widespread and profound. Responsible officials cannot too soon or too earnestly give attention to this state of things. A failure to furnish the town populations with a sufficiency of essential foodstuffs, or with the raw material of their industry, could not fail to have disastrous consequences.' The government would be 'likely to have occupation for their troops elsewhere than in Flanders'. To obviate such dangers, there was 'but one course to follow:

> The farmer must be dealt with sympathetically and intelligently. He must be consulted before the regulations, which are intended to control his industry, are issued and before final decision is taken, as to the price at which his produce is to be sold, and as to the methods by which it is to be distributed. He will not be found unreasonable, but, like other men, he wishes to have a voice in the affairs that are peculiarly his own.

'Our difficulties will not end with the war', Finlay continued, warning of the disorganised industries that would have to be re-established. Where the co-operative movement was concerned, the best preparation for the future would be found, he declared, following a familiar line, 'in the strengthening and perfection of the organisation, the efficacy of which has been so convincingly demonstrated ... Put new life into the local societies and bind them closer to the central body – that is the watchword which the circumstances of the moment and the prospects of the future dictate to us.'[21]

The organisation's policy of avoiding political involvement meant that the annual conferences made no reference to political developments, not to the 1916 insurrection, not to conscription, nor to the growth of Sinn Féin, nor, except in a passing way, to the later attacks on the creameries by crown forces.

In 1919 Horace Plunkett was absent from the annual general meeting and Finlay acted as chairman. He gave the presidential address. It was brief. His belief in the merits of the co-operative system was made very clear. 'The industrial world, in all directions, was unsettled. The chasm between labour and capital seemed to be widening', but, 'notwithstanding a disturbance, political and social, which had convulsed the world, one class of institution had escaped the general convulsion', even in Russia. 'That class of social institution was the co-operative society.'

Finlay's faith in the co-operative society as the way forward, seems strangely naïve in the capitalist oriented twenty-first century. Yet, at the end of the First World War numerous writers and thinkers searched for alternatives to capitalism, which was seen as the vehicle of injustice, greed, and war. The alternatives seemed to be a socialist or a co-operative society. Even in the United States of America the debate was waged. In September 1920, Professor John A. Ryan, of the Catholic University of America, Washington, gave as his considered opinion: 'Our industrial system as now constituted is well-night bankrupt ... There are only two conceivable alternatives: one is socialism; the other is co-operative control and ownership by the workers of the greater part of industry.'[22] He strongly favoured the co-operative alternative. 'Co-operative ownership and management would end the unnatural divorce that now exists between the owners of capital on the one hand and the users of it on the other. It would be the most effective obstacle to and preventive of Socialism.' Both were concerned with ownership, but the difference between them was 'the difference between a man's proprietorship of his front lawn and his interest in a public park'.[23]

Finlay concluded his presidential address with a suggestion 'for the happiness of the health of the nation' which, to some extent, still has relevance. Manufactures should be brought to the country, and located 'in the immediate neighbourhood of the people themselves, instead of carrying people from the land to the towns'; and, 'in a district where there was a large number of small farmers', it was appropriate to 'have an industry in which the surplus labour could find employment in the season when it was not wanted for agricultural purposes. If that were done, the homes of the people would not be broken up, and they could live under far happier conditions than they could possibly do in crowded cities (hear, hear).'[24] In some ways, Finlay appears to have held views similar to those of M. Paul Dubois in *L'Irlande Contemporaire* (Paris, 1907), who looked for the prosperity of Ireland to progressive agriculture, and the smaller rural industries that come naturally to cluster around it.[25]

THE TROUBLED YEARS: 1919–22

The years 1919 and 1920, as the struggle intensified between Sinn Fein and the forces of the British government, brought tension to the IAOS, straining the links between landlords and the small farmers. Plunkett acknowledged it in his presidential address in 1920. 'It would be foolish to ignore the fact that our non-sectarian and non-political pledge has been more severely tested of late than at any time since the foundation of the movement.' Moreover, there was the prospect of political partition. 'It is common knowledge', Plunkett stated, 'that the government are about to propose ... a political settlement which will involve the division of our country for purposes of legislation and administration. My view is that, whether there be one, two, or twenty Irelands in other departments of Irish life, in the basic industry which we have been trying to re-mould through the life of a generation, there need be – there can be – but one Ireland.' Rather than awaiting the possible split in the movement, he urged members to work for further growth. In the past the benefit of co-operation had not been extended to farm labourers, 'largely due to the restriction by which we were debarred from encouraging co-operation in the supply of domestic commodities'. It was now clear 'that the restriction had no justification in principle' so that 'the benefits of co-operation' may be extended 'to those who need them most'.

Following the president's powerful speech, Finlay emphasised the self-supporting tradition of the movement, and the desirability of a 'co-operative propaganda' extended to Ireland as a whole. Then, seeking to counter political and social division, he underlined that they were 'all for each', and pressed on:

> If we can extend this movement in Ireland so as to include in it every man engaged in agricultural interests, be he landless or otherwise, if we can bring them all in and harmonise their interests in combination, as Sir Horace Plunkett proposed in his address, then we shall have made of the Irish agricultural community a power which will dominate this land and dominate it for its safety and salvation. If this work of spreading throughout Ireland a spirit of harmony and legal co-operation in the agricultural community be achieved, we shall have solved one of Ireland's gravest problems, and saved it from disasters that will overtake lands, perhaps not so fortunate as ours.

In 1921 he was happy to hail the marvel that the movement had avoided the antagonism and discordance so evident in other spheres. There had been damage to property, to 'creamery and other societies', but these, 'being merely material losses' were 'temporary'. There was before them, however, 'a division of a political kind, a division of the country into two areas, and it would be … a matter of supreme misfortune that any division of that kind should be introduced into, or effect, the co-operative movement'. The government could 'impose such a measure … upon the country at large', but, Finlay insisted, 'within the co-operative movement nobody could impose such a division upon us if we refuse to impose it upon ourselves. Co-operators are masters of their own destiny'. Therefore, he would plead that every effort be made 'to secure the cohesion of the Society as a whole'. 'I believe', he concluded, 'that in maintaining within the co-operative movement the spirit of cordial unity and friendly co-operation for the common welfare of our country we shall do a great deal to maintain a feeling in Ireland of common interests and common purposes, and eventually lay the foundation of a union that will make Ireland prosperous as a whole, and unite all her people for the benefit of the nation.'[26]

His plea and hope had no chance of immediate success. Co-operators could not be 'masters of their own destiny'. The North of Ireland administration was already in operation. The Irish Free State was established on 31 March 1922. Thereafter the two parts of the island had separate departments of agriculture, separate currency, and separate systems of taxation and subsidy. Moreover, the political divisions in the south over the Anglo-Irish treaty, the outbreak of civil war in June 1922, and unionist fears and hostility in the north, killed the immediate prospect of harmony between the two governments. The IAOS suffered. Addressing the general meeting in 1922, Finlay noted 'the number of societies that made no contribution to the body that created them was unpleasantly considerable'.[27] That year, too, the inevitable split occurred. The Ulster Agricultural Organisation was formed. A former active promoter in the north of the country, Harold Barbour, was appointed its president. That ensured some continuity of good-will and understanding in the co-operative movement. Fifteen years later, on 15 April 1937, when he was due to receive a special presentation from the northern prime minister, Lord Craigavon, he invited a number of members from the IAOS to the ceremony. Tom Finlay, seriously ill and now aged eighty-nine years, was unable to attend, but he sent his apologies and good wishes. Barbour, reflecting the spirit of good will that had been preserved in the movement, publicly acknowledged his indebtedness to his southern friends.

> I had the good fortune to have been taught and trained by Sir Horace Plunkett, Father Finlay, and R.A. Anderson, and the devoted band of workers whom they had attracted around them ... In 1922, of necessity, the Ulster Agricultural Organisation was formed ... To the IAOS, our old parent body, I would say we have tried to keep the faith.[28]

The fact that friendship survived and that the ideals of the original movement were maintained, despite political partition and bitterness, was a testimony to the training, idealism, and hard work of Plunkett, Finlay and Anderson; and the greatest of these three, when it came to rhetoric and the creation of a climate of hope, harmony, and self-discipline, was Finlay, as the other two acknowledged. After the horrors of the civil war, the task of recreating unity fell ever more heavily on Finlay. Plunkett, having had his house burned down by anti-government forces, left Ireland. He retained his interest in the IAOS, corresponding from time to time with Finlay, but never returned to live in a homeland to which he had given so much but in which his house had been burned as if he were an enemy.

The Irish Agricultural Co-operative Society, and University College Dublin, absorbed a great deal of Finlay's time and energy, but he still found time for other work and interests. These occupy the final section of this biography.

PART THREE

The priest, his commitments and friends; the final years

10

The priest and preacher

In his public career, Finlay served God through the service of others in education and in rural and social life, but behind that very active existence was a man who was punctilious about his morning meditation, his Mass, and his 'Divine Office'. Indeed, as the *Anglo-Celt*, the paper of his native county, commented after his death: 'Father Tom was, first and last, a priest. He had given more retreats to the Irish clergy than almost any priest in Ireland. He knew their life, and felt that he was working with them for the good of the people whom they served.'[1] He had visited every diocese in Ireland, both as retreat director and preacher and on co-operative business, travelling thousands of miles by side-car, and was known, as a result, to most parish priests and to every bishop. For a number of the hierarchy he was the chosen preacher at their consecration, and he, for his part, was ready to respond, even to the point, on one occasion in 1892, of standing in, at very short notice, for the intended preacher at the consecration of John Conmy, as bishop of Killala in County Mayo. Finlay had, as a fellow Jesuit observed, 'a wonderful ability for speaking with ease at a moment's notice' and 'a great power of explaining philosophical questions so that ordinary people could understand'[2] Combined with these gifts was a 'deep faith and simple piety' which, with his approachability and humour, made him sought after as a retreat director in convents throughout the country.[3]

Unfortunately, the paucity of written material, and the absence of living witnesses, make it difficult to convey in any adequate way this very important aspect of Finlay's life. All that remains to represent the preacher are a few sermon and spiritual lecture notes, and a few pamphlets based on sermons or talks he had given. Among the sermon notes, one entitled 'Duties to our enemies' provides an insight into his rational way of treating a topic concerned with moral behaviour.

> It is laid down by Our Lord in his moral code that we shall *love* our enemies. Let us try to understand clearly the precept … The law that obliges us to love our neighbour … is but the expression of an obligation laid upon us by the natural law. Every man is an image of the Creator, a something in the scale of created good which we are bound to esteem.

Furthermore, he is 'a member of society, of a confederation into which we are born and in which we are forced to live, and to the members of which, by virtue of our natural condition, we are bound to render the services which make social order a possibility. Now a man who has offended us does not thereby lose his dignity as a man or his rights as a social being, nor do our correlative obligations cease ... Therefore we still owe him the reverence due to every being that has human shape. We have no permission to express contempt for him: and every external manifestation of positive contempt and hatred, as well as every such positive contempt deliberately entertained in our heart is a violation of natural as well as of divine law.

'But over and above these claims upon us, what about things to which we are not obliged ?' Friendship is one. Friendship is 'a relation which we enter into freely with our fellow creatures ... If friendship becomes a burden, if we judge that the person we have chosen for a friend is unworthy of our affection, nothing forbids us to separate from him. With the dissolution of our friendship will naturally disappear the amenities of affectionate interchange ... You are allowed put him back into the common category of men and to restrict your good offices to those which you owe to all.' What, then, if 'you have been betrayed by a person whom you made your friend?' You are not obliged to speak to him. 'The law of God does not oblige you to speak to all men whom you meet in the street ... you may pass him by as if he were a stranger, but your manner must not express contempt.' But, if the person 'who showed himself unworthy of your friendship addresses you, are you bound to answer? ... If a stranger spoke to you, you are obliged to reply. It is an insulting expression of contempt to refuse. You must, therefore, make to your enemy at least the same reply you would make to an utter stranger who asked a question.'[4]

On a more scriptural theme, Finlay's style tended to be quite different. This is illustrated in a published sermon dealing with the living presence of Jesus Christ, entitled 'The Name of Jesus'.[5] 'Fame after death has been the ambition of most men who have done great things during life', he commences, and comments on its unwisdom. For 'what is he – the living, personal, conscious creature that once was Socrates, or Caesar, or Dante, or Napoleon? A little insensate clay, and a soul which, whether happy or miserable, is at all events beyond reach of the emotions that the world's praise or censure provokes. His name still haunts the earth, but it is only as the ghost of his former life.' 'One name there is, however,' the preacher went on, 'round which no mist of time has gathered, and which has nothing hollow or ghost-like in its sound, ... it has been active in this world for nineteen centuries.' Finlay then recounted the significance of the name of Jesus, the symbol of the living Christ, for the early Christians, their belief that 'He is very near us still, dwelling in us with the Father, if we be not unworthy'. 'This enduring, energising, personal presence of Christ', he added,

> is the essence of the Christian system. This it is which makes of Christianity a living power, which saves it from being a mere scheme or

morality or school of doctrine; this it is which gives the warmth of vitality to our faith, which infuses the sense of contact with a living soul into our devotion to the Gospel.

Moving from the witness to Christ in the early Christian centuries, he recalled instances from the Middle Ages and more recent times, including in his examples Ignatius Loyola and his followers, thereby revealing a key feature of his own life. The secret of their well-doing, he declared, was to be sought in 'the living presence of the Jesus of Faith'. In calling themselves the Society, or Company, of Jesus,

> they took His name as the pledge of a direct personal allegiance to Him, and the fundamental law laid down for the guidance of their lives was, that they should identify themselves wholly and absolutely with Him. What dress they wore, what language they spoke, what air they breathed, how else they lived, or how else they died, were matters of small moment, provided only they were one with Jesus Christ. If they have served the Church not indifferently, that is the secret of their usefulness; where they have blundered or failed, they will be found to have departed from this plan of action.

Drawing to a close, the homilist explained that he had selected the examples before the congregation 'with the purpose of showing that, where the Church has triumphed over adverse social institutions, or hostile military power, or perverted intellectual systems, she has owed her victory to vital faith in Jesus'. Christians are called to stake their present and their future on Him. 'The final reward of Christian fidelity is to know Jesus as He is ... for "this is eternal life, to know Thee, the one true God, and Jesus Christ whom Thou hast sent".'[6]

Finlay's reputation as a lecturer and preacher, and his links with various social works, led to his being invited to speak to a variety of gatherings. One such invitation was to Leighlinbridge, County Carlow, on the occasion, in 1907, of the founding of a branch of the Anti-Treating League. His address, entitled 'The drunkard in Ireland', pleased the organisers sufficiently for them to have it printed in pamphlet form. It was a subject of which he had experience from an early age in his family's public house, quite apart from what he had seen and heard in his travels throughout Ireland.

'There is not', he stated, 'any libel involved in the charge that one in every forty-five of the population of the country is a drunkard, an offender who has been arrested, or has deserved arrest, for over-indulgence in intoxicating drink.'[7] The amount spent on drink in Ireland, he continued, was computed at £13 million sterling. This, in an agricultural country where the total yearly value of the produce of the land was estimated at under 40 million. Hence, 'an amount equal to one-third of this sum' was 'squandered upon drink!' 'We complain bitterly of our poverty', Finlay commented, but 'can we be otherwise than poor while we waste our substance in this criminal fashion? We are loud in our denunciation of those who, we think, take from us an undue part of the wealth produced by our labour. We condemn in fiery language what we call the rapacities of landlordism. Have we no words of condemnation for those who draw from the poor total of our national earnings a sum equal to one and a half times the total rental of the country and spend it on a useless and demoralising luxury?' The evil, however, did not stop with the mere waste of money. 'Indulgence in drink paralyses the working energies of the nation; it demoralises and degrades the worker; it blasts the happiness of the home which he is bound to support; it prepares for the generations that are to come hereditary tendencies to vice; it deprives the growing children of opportunities of education and blights their prospects for life.'

Going to the causes promoting 'this distressing drink evil', Finlay chose three. 'In the first place, the multiplication of licences is multiplying for us the sources of temptation.' At present there was one seller of intoxicating liquor for every 174 inhabitants in Ireland, and popular magistrates were granting increases in the issue of licences 'at an unheard of rate'. The second cause was 'the easy tolerance which public opinion extends to the drunkard's offence'. A pickpocket or burglar was deemed a criminal and shunned, whereas the drunkard was absolved by the familiar – 'Poor fellow, he is nobody's enemy but his own'. Indignant at this attitude to what he considered quite unacceptable behaviour, Finlay expressed vigorous disapproval.

> Nobody's enemy but his own! Who has done so much as the drunkard amongst us to demoralise our people, and to make our country a byeword amongst the nations? Who has done so much to fill our jails, our asylums, and our workhouses? Who has pulled down so many roof-trees, and extinguished the fires in so many hearths? Who has made so many women weep, and so many children wail? Who has brought so many families to destitution, and scattered their members in beggary or exile?[8]

The deliverance from the condoning of the drunkard and his/her damage to society, Finlay stated, can only be brought about 'by a reformed and determined opinion'.

A third cause of 'the woeful prevalence of intemperance amongst us', he declared, 'is the custom known as "treating".' This is the practice of one person pressurising others to join him for a drink, then, he having bought the round of drinks for those he invited, they, in turn, were expected to 'treat' the others, buying drinks for them. 'To refuse to share in a "round" is to offer an indignity to the person who pays for it; not to insist on paying for a "round" is to incur the reproach of meanness and want of spirit.' 'And it is all done,' Finlay added, 'in the name of good fellowship, of that generous, large-handed hospitality which is a vaunted characteristic of our nation.' But, he insisted, 'to call generous the man who has received a week's wages of eighteen or twenty shillings, on which a wife and children must live, and out of which house rent must be paid, and who spends a quarter of the sum on himself and a circle of drinking companions, is to profane a word which language has devoted to noble use. This is not generosity; it is selfishness carried to extravagance.'[9]

Drawing to a close, the speaker summarised the main points in his address. 'The evils which I have now enumerated call loudly for a remedy. But the remedy we cannot, in every case, apply at once.

> We cannot change the licensing laws in a moment, nor can we prevent the increasing issue of licences if the magistrates will insist on granting them. We cannot reform immediately the public opinion which extends such a large tolerance to the drunkard, and deals so leniently with his offences – though we all have it in our power to do something towards this end. But the gigantic mischief of the 'treating' system we need not tolerate for another day.

'The Anti-Treating League, for which I seek your support', he concluded, 'is an association formed to suppress this source of waste and demoralisation amongst us. It calls for no heroic sacrifice, imposes no grievous restrictions. It does not oblige its members to abstinence, total or partial. It binds them to no more than this: that they shall not give or accept a "treat" in a public house.'[10]

His presence and a prepared speech in a worthy cause, in a small rural area, seems to have been characteristic of Father Finlay. 'He was always ready,' the *Anglo-Celt*, the paper of his native county, remarked, 'to give a hand in any reconstructive work for the prosperity of the country, and his voice was heard on many platforms, often in most remote districts.'[11] It was all part of his identification, as a priest and Jesuit, with the person and values of the living Christ, who came 'not to be served but to serve'.

Finlay's life can fairly be described as one of service, a service made more attractive by his approachable manner, his readiness to listen, and his humanity, so that a wide range of people were drawn to him who might otherwise be reluctant to approach a priest. Despite the absence of personal papers, an indication of this attraction to others is instanced in the writing and behaviour of George Moore, and in his friendship with people as diverse as John O'Leary, the old Fenian, Christopher Digges La Touche, managing director of Guinness, and Paddy the Cope Gallagher from Donegal. He had, it has been said, 'a quiet charm' and 'a genius for making friends',[12] so that very often those whom he assisted became friends for life. Examples of this are many and varied, and constitute some of the more colourful occurrences in his long life. They are worth considering separately.

11

A range of friends and services; introducing Caravaggio and Paddy the Cope

Horace Plunkett's zest for living was inexhaustible. He revelled in playing host to numerous people, especially people of influence and of literary repute. The guest book at Kilteragh, his large house in Foxrock, County Dublin, from 1906 to 1921, provides a remarkable record of distinguished visitors. They include across the years, from England – Gerald Balfour, Lords Londonderry, Milner, and Grey, G.K. Chesterton, and H.G. Wells; from America – Laurence Lowell, president of Harvard, and Charles McCarthy of Wisconsin; as well as all the main Irish literary figures, including George Bernard Shaw, and political personages from Redmond and Dillon to Casement and Michael Collins. The house had a railway station nearby, and Plunkett, besides, had his di Dion Bouton, one of the first automobiles in Ireland. The furnishing at Kilteragh had been arranged by Plunkett's close friend, Elizabeth, countess of Fingall, who frequently acted as hostess to the distinguished guests. The visitors to the house greatly increased in number and quality in the three years before the outbreak of war. The ever-active Plunkett had purchased land around the house to be used for practical agricultural instruction under an experienced instructor, Thomas Wibberley. Before long, Foxrock station witnessed almost every Sunday the arrival of farmers, who travelled at their own expense from Clare and Kerry, from Wexford and Donegal, to see new ideas put into practice.[1]

In addition to all the foregoing, there were the 'regulars', the irrepressible Lady Fingall, Tom Finlay, R.A. Anderson, and Æ. Elizabeth Fingall, frequently known as Daisy, described Finlay as 'Horace's greatest adherent', and added:

> When Horace Plunkett first met Father Finlay, he told me that he had at last found a man who had been thinking on the same lines as himself long before they met. It was like the meeting of two fires. In those days it was still a brave thing for the Jesuit to join the Protestant Unionist M.P. Father Finlay brought varied gifts to the work. An extremely good business man, he had the deep knowledge of human nature which belongs to the best type of Catholic priest. He had the wisdom of the serpent and the gentleness of the dove. Also a rich sense of humour – perhaps that the greatest gift of all.[2]

The countess and Plunkett enjoyed Finlay's company. He became close to them both. They set out in Plunkett's car to visit various co-operative ventures throughout the country. Recalling those experiences, with an excitement and humour undimmed by time, Daisy Fingall represented Plunkett driving 'about the quiet lanes at the terrifying speed of ten or twelve miles an hour, being frequently stopped for furious driving by an apologetic RIC man.' 'I have some old photographs of this first motor car,' she added. 'One of Horace in it, and one with myself, Lady Mayo and Father Finlay as passengers. Our hats, including Father Finlay's clerical one, are tied with enormous veils! We are all just about to start on one of our expeditions. We shall rattle over the bad roads, terrifying the donkeys and cows who graze on the strip of grass by the roadside and who have never before seen such a contraption as ours. Hens and chickens will fly before us and we shall have a sensation of moving at desperate speed through space. We are going (at twelve miles an hour!) to wake up the Irish countryside, to visit some budding industry or to try to start others. What adventures we had on those tours of ours!' She told of a hotel in Mullingar where the condition of the beds obliged them to sleep in their dressing-gowns, and the windows could not be kept open unless propped up by the water-jug; and of their expedition 'to Foxford in the County Mayo, for the Connacht Exhibition, organised by that great woman and wonderful Sister of Charity, Mother Morrogh Bernard'.[3]

When a fine Georgian house, at 84 Merrion Square, Dublin, was presented to Plunkett in 1908, it, too, became a focal point for visitors. George O'Brien, then a lecturer at University College, under Finlay, became a regular visitor to Kilteragh and to Plunkett House, Merrion Square.[4] He later recalled the buzz of activity in Plunkett House, which seemed to him like a court in which Sir Horace was king. His close friendship with Finlay made him welcome at both houses. On one visit to Kilteragh, probably in 1919, there was something of a crisis in which Finlay played a characteristic part.

> There was the case of the cabinet minister who came over to study Anglo-Irish relations in the months before the fighting started. He was not of the first rank in the cabinet, but it was necessary that he should be well informed before he went back on the mail-boat. Unfortunately, a crisis arose on the very morning of the day that he was due for dinner; the cook informed Sir Horace that she was leaving the house on the spot. This was no matter of a wage dispute. She had surprised Sir Horace's then secretary in an act of love with the youth who was deputising for the regular postman. She would not remain under the same roof. The crisis was solved by recourse to the one person in Ireland who could be trusted to handle delicate affairs of high or low degree. Father Finlay was rung up at 35 Lower Leeson Street. He walked around to Harcourt Street station and caught one of the then frequent trains. He pointed out to the cook that the minister's visit might turn out to be of enormous benefit to

Ireland and that her well-justified anger should not be pressed to the point of hazarding the future of the country. The cook was mollified and discharged her duties like a culinary Joan of Arc. The dinner was a great success, though the Irish Question remained unsolved.[5]

George O'Brien's depiction of Finlay's role on this occasion corroborates the latter's reputation for resourcefulness in the co-operative movement. Many years after his death, it was recalled, in the centenary publication of the Irish Co-operative Organisation Society, 1894–1994, that 'throughout every crisis in the IAOS (and there were many) Father Tom Finlay was at once the moral mentor, the Mr Fixit (when he could) and the unfailing purveyor of good cheer'! The anonymous author added informatively:

> His influence in government circles was enormous. He was appointed a Commissioner of National Education, a trustee of the National Library, and a member of various Royal Commissions … He was the prime mover in the establishment of co-operative village banks and was vice-president of IAOS from 1896 until his death in 1940, always refusing to accept the highest office … In the North he was at his best – an Ulsterman among Ulstermen – at co-operative gatherings … His relationship with the Reverend Edward Fitzharding Campbell, chairman of Killyman co-operative creamery and chaplain to the Orange order, was a remarkable one. While openly abhorring each other's heresy they managed to be great personal friends.[6]

Elizabeth Fingall's reference to their visit to 'that great and wonderful Sister of Charity, Mothor Morrogh Bernard' of Foxford, County Mayo, introduces one of the most successful ventures assisted by Finlay and about which, after his retirement from the University, he published a pamphlet. *Foxford and the Providence Woollen Mills: Story of an Irish Industry*, appeared in Dublin, in 1932.

THE FOXFORD WOOLLEN MILLS

He commenced his story with an account of the desolate landscape surrounding the village of Foxford and its rushing river Moy, and of the poverty of some 1,500 inhabitants within five miles of the village. It was poverty which was, in his words, 'at once repulsive and pitiable, … a poverty in which privation dulls the higher sensibilities and self-respect seems extinguished, in which rags and squalor are acquiesced in, apparently without a sense of their deformities or any effort to abate their offensiveness'.[7] To this setting came the Irish Sisters of Charity, led by Sr Morrogh Bernard. With dedication and industry they established a school and helped to change much of the rural scene within a few years. Their school was attractive to its pupils.

It offered the comfort of clean, warm, and well-lighted rooms for five hours daily in relief from the cold and darkness of a squalid hovel; it gave prizes of decent clothes and other luxuries for regular attendance, and it provided a nutritive morning meal of hot porridge and milk for famished little scholars who had trudged to school on a scanty breakfast; too often without any breakfast at all. The school roll filled rapidly, and the diffusion of a knowledge of the three Rs among the rising generation was assured. Other knowledge, equally essential, was also imparted: needlework, dressmaking, knitting, and such elements of cookery and laundry-work as suited the home conditions of the pupils, were included in the school programme.

The Sisters spread their instruction to the parents, calling to the homes to minister to the sick and dying, and thereafter addressing themselves to introducing new standards of sanitation and house-keeping. Animals were no longer given 'the run of the house', windows were made to open and chimneys to draw, sleeping areas were divided by partitions, and the manure heap was removed from the front door. It was a struggle against apathy and traditional prejudice, but eventually the Sisters won out with nearly all the residents. There still remained, however, the men's seasonal migration to England and Scotland, and the emigration to America of boys and girls when they had reached working age. Reflecting on this, and on the need for local employment to keep people at home, Sr Agnes considered the idly rushing river and evolved the project of a woollen factory. She was clear about what she wanted, and was enthusiastic and determined, but she had no business experience and no knowledge of wool making. She sought guidance from Mr J.C. Smith, proprietor of the Caledon Woollen Mills, County Tyrone. A surprised Mr Smith is reputed to have replied 'Madam! Are you aware that you have written to a Protestant and a Freemason?' Whatever the exchange, the Protestant and Freemason travelled to Foxford, was met at the station by the parish priest and his curate and accompanied to the convent. 'Having surveyed the proposed site and gone into other details, he advised Agnes Morrogh Bernard to abandon her scheme. When that had no effect, he placed himself 'and his twenty years experience at her disposal'.[8] 'He advised in the construction of the first buildings, selected the first plant, and furnished from his mill the first manager.'[9]

The building and plant were completed by the beginning of May 1892. Horace Plunkett and Mr Charles Kennedy, as members of the Congested Districts Board, set the first looms in motion. By the time Finlay was writing his pamphlet, 1932, the year in which Sr Agnes Morrogh Bernard died, he could state 'the mill now employs 200 hands' and

> the latest Foxford balance sheet shows that, within the year, £18,000 had been paid in wages, and £14,000 in local purchases of wool. It may be added that the workers out of their savings have invested £14,000 in the

factory, on which they receive an interest of £5 per cent. The schools educate 200 children. Sixty neat cottages have been built for the families wholly dependent on the mills. A spacious hall has been erected, in which the mills orchestra and dramatic society entertain their friends. Accommodation for men's and women's clubs has also been provided. The wood and iron structure which served the purpose of a chapel has been replaced by a concrete building. The workers have themselves established a co-operative store for the supply of their requirements.[10]

The factory, moreover, had become celebrated for its textile fabrics. 'Its flannels, friezes, tweeds, clerical cloths, shawls, blankets and rugs won prizes at various exhibitions and carried off, year after year, the prizes of the Royal Dublin Society's shows.'[11]

The countess of Fingall, referring to their expedition to the 'Connacht Exhibition', explained: 'The exhibition was designed primarily to advertise the woollen goods being purchased at the Foxford mills. But the side sections indicated the width and imagination of Mother Morrogh Bernard's work in her district for the better living towards which we were all, in our different ways, trying to help the people. There were prizes for gardening, domestic science, poultry, dairy products, even for the most humble and necessary trade of mending. The great business woman, who was responsible for all this, forgot nothing, organised everything. And then, when the grand party of influential people, whom she had collected about her, travelled to the County Mayo for the Exhibition, she hid herself away as she always did on such occasions.'[12]

Finlay's account of the Providence Mills makes no reference to his own contribution to the enterprise. Yet the *Anglo-Celt*, owned by the O'Hanlon family, who were related by marriage to Finlay, commented: 'He was, perhaps, more proud of his work for the Providence Mills at Foxford, which had been established by the Irish Sisters of Charity, than of any other work in his life.'[13] Aubrey Gwynn, moreover, writing Finlay's obituary in the Irish Jesuit *Province News*, noted that 'he took a leading part in the establishment of the Providence Mills' and that his memory was 'most cherished in Foxford'. He added:

> During his last illness two of the workers in the Mills were married in Foxford. They were old friends of Father Tom, and they were not satisfied until they had travelled to Dublin, in one of the lorries owned by the Mills, to get the old priest's blessing on their married life. When news of his death reached Foxford ... telegrams of condolence were sent by the staff as a whole, and by some of his personal friends in the Foxford Mills.[14]

Commenting on the significance of the Foxford development, Finlay raised a recurring theme. 'We cannot do without manufactures, but is it not possible to establish them in rural districts, where labour is abundant, and where it can be employed without breaking up rural homes or drawing the people off the land? The Foxford Mills stand proof that it can be done, and the results in Foxford demonstrate the advantages of the policy.'[15] He conceded, however, with his usual realism, that the personality, business ability and determination of Morrogh Bernard were key factors in the success.

> The story of the Foxford industry is the story of a prolonged struggle against singularly adverse conditions, a struggle in which success was achieved by ability which, in its own order, might be characterised as genius, and by a resolute, systematic, and persevering fortitude which fell little short of heroism.

Finlay's admiration for Morrogh Bernard, and his ability to work with her, was replicated in his work with many women.

WOMEN AND WORK

Plunkett and Finlay exhibited a common concern for women, especially for those tied to drudgery and toil on farms. In 1910, in conjunction with Elizabeth Fingall, his cousin Emily Lawless, and other prominent women co-operators, Plunkett founded the United Irishwomen, later to be known as the Irish Countrywomen's Association. In his address to the annual general meeting of IAOS, on 29 November 1910, he announced: 'Long ago we should ... have appealed to leading women within our movement to try and organise their sex for three purposes –

> Firstly, to attend to women's business in the life of a community which no man, least of all an old bachelor like myself, can understand; secondly, to see that the farmers attend better to the business of their organisation ...; and thirdly, to encourage Irish women to take up their rightful part in the building up of a rural civilisation in Ireland.[16]

The organisation, in fact, was already in operation before its official foundation. Following a talk by Æ on 'The Building Up of a Rural Civilisation', in December 1909, a number of women were sufficiently impressed to embark immediately on the work of organising. Mrs Ellice Pilkington (sister of Sir Thomas Esmonde, a member of the IAOS committee from 1898–1906 and a close friend of Finlay) was appointed first honorary organiser. Another Wexford women, Mrs Harold Lett, of Enniscorthy, formed the first branch on 15 June 1910, and shortly afterwards was elected first president of the national organisation. The United Irishwomen was registered as a co-operative society, in 1910, and was invited to hold its meetings in Plunkett House. Mrs Pilkington displayed her enthusiasm as an organiser almost immediately. Shortly before Christmas 1910, she travelled to Dungloe, County Donegal, heralded by a letter from Father Finlay and carrying an introduction in Irish from Douglas Hyde, president of the Gaelic League. 'On arrival', she recounted vividly, 'I found an independent, capable community, a flourishing co-operative society with a manager who not only knew his work, but held the confidence of his people, a knitting industry in the hands of the women and girls, and all round them great possibilities for cottage gardening, dairying, and jam-making; a village hall for social meetings, a fine healthy race of men and women, bilingual, capable of enjoying intellectual pursuits and not ashamed to use their hands. And yet there was a silent sorrow here, for the curse of emigration was upon them.' With the help of the manager, Patrick Gallagher (the Cope) of the Templecrone co-operative, her proposal to start a branch of the United Irishwomen 'was welcomed enthusiastically and the men promised to safeguard the interests of the sister society'. Less than a year later there was a busy branch of the United Irishwomen in Dungloe with over 200 members. In January, Ellice Pilkington visited Wicklow and Wexford and inaugurated branches, at Davidstown, Oylegate, Glenbrien, and Coolgreaney, before starting on a tour through Waterford, Tipperary, Cork and Clare which resulted in the establishment of the first Munster branch at Kilkee, County Clare.[17]

In addition to his links with the United Irishwomen, most of whose first provisional committee were known to him, Finlay was also actively involved in Plunkett's Home Improvement Scheme, which pre-dated the United Irishwomen. In a letter to Lord Monteagle, on 16 March 1911, Plunkett mentioned that the Home Improvement Scheme was 'doing really good work in several districts' and that its committee consisted of 'Father Finlay, Ladies Mayo, Fingall and Arnott, Dr Smith and myself'.[18]

The development of the United Irishwomen was not welcomed universally by women. Lady Aberdeen and her Women's National Health Association were quite critical at first, because the United Irishwomen included nursing in its remit.[19] Writing again to Monteagle, on 29 March 1911, Plunkett explained, with regard to a letter of his in that day's *Irish Times*, that, between the lines, 'I was trying to defend the United Irishwomen from what I am afraid is an organised attack upon them by Lady Aberdeen and her entourage of worshippers and office seekers'.[20] Plunkett and Finlay, however, took great care not to fall out with her ladyship, who had energy as well as influence and did a great deal of good in matters of health and in support of Irish industries. Finlay willingly involved himself in her campaign to counter tuberculosis, and he and Plunkett were conscious of the importance of her support to such bodies as the Irish Industries League and the Royal Industries Association, organisations which promoted the co-operative societies catering for home industry – societies mainly of women, formed according to R.A. Anderson, in his report to the general meeting in 1898, 'not so much to provide a living wage for the workers, but to find them pleasant and profitable employment in their own homes, and to supplement such scanty and precarious earnings or income as the population in poor districts have hitherto been forced to subsist upon.'[21] The majority of these societies were concerned with what were termed 'feminine crafts' – lace, crochet and knitting.

'In those Victorian days', the historian of the *Irish Co-operative Movement*, Patrick Bolger, observed, 'the ladies still considered it advisable to have some men on the committee of management, particularly to guide them in organisational and business matters'.[22] Finlay seems to have been in demand in such roles. One extant indication is provided by the minutes of the committee of the Dublin Food Supply Society Ltd. The minutes are in three volumes for respectively, 1916–17, 1918–21, 1921–5. The object of the society, as indicated in volume 2, is 'the supply of cheap food to the poor of Dublin in difficulties due to either the Great War or the local Irish situation'.[23] Already, in April of 1916, during the Rising, Finlay had made his way through many back streets carrying food to people in distress. He was left unharmed, he believed, out of respect for his clerical collar.[24] The first meeting of the Dublin Food Society took place on 8 December 1916. They met at Lincoln Place. Lady Frances Moloney was in the chair, and present were Mrs O'Brien, Cogan, Wilson, and Messrs Ryan, Dermod O'Brien, Cruise O'Brien, secretary, and Fr T.A. Finlay. The latter, who attended almost every meeting, occupied a specific financial-business role. There is extant a notebook of his dealing with receipts and expenditure for the Dublin Food Supply Society Ltd for 1917 covering such items as potatoes, coal (coal tickets) and carriage of same, and milk; also work on roofs, and other contractor services.[26] There are also extant conveyances in his name on behalf of the society. One such, in May 1924, was between Finlay and Rev. George Redington Roche SJ, and others, assigning the use of certain premises to the Dublin Food Supply Committee Ltd with a view to carrying on a business 'solely for the purpose of supplying the poor all or any manner of household supplies at such a price, and no greater over and above the wholesale price, as will cover rents, rates, and other costs of distribution and provide such reserves as may, in the opinion of the trustees, be necessary to meet any sudden or abnormal rise in the wholesale price of the goods to the company business firm or society aforesaid'.[27]

The committee operated during difficult years. The annual report for 1919, presented by the then chairperson, Marie P. Wilson, conveyed something of the problems presented by the disturbed state of the country.

> The interruption of railway traffic deprived our depots of their milk supply for fully five months of the year ... Our depot in North Kings Street was closed, the remaining six depots were maintained in the hope that the restoration of railway facilities would enable us to continue our services to the poor. That expectation was realised. But the losses sustained during the period of depression was very serious ... During the months of the year in which a shortage of coal intensified the hardships of the poor, the Committee strove to relieve this added distress by procuring supplies from the available stocks and distributing them at prices much below those of the street hawkers. In this task they were aided by a free grant of 35 tons from a generous benefactor

'Notwithstanding the difficulties experienced during the year', Mrs Wilson concluded, the Committee estimates that in their total sales 'they have secured a saving to the poor, which they serve, of close on £6000 – a result, which they submit, amply justifies the work of the Society.'[28]

FR FINLAY AND CARAVAGGIO

Finlay had another, even closer friend, called Mrs Wilson. Lea Wilson was the wife of a British officer, who had dealt with the Irish prisoners at the surrender of the insurgents in 1916 and had humiliated the elderly Tom Clarke, the senior signatory of the 1916 proclamation. This was remembered, and he was subsequently shot by members of the Irish republican army. In his loss, his wife found support and spiritual guidance from Fr Finlay. Encouraged by him, she took up the study of medicine and became a prominent consultant on children's illnesses. Finlay, because of his friendship with her, became involved in efforts to provide proper hospital care for children, and with proposals for the reorganisation of the Irish hospitals.[29] As late as 1935, when he was eighty-seven years of age, he received the following letter from Dr J. Stafford Johnson:

> Dr Lea Wilson asked a few days ago to call on you with reference to the Hospital situation ... I enclose you a summary of the position which was drafted some months ago, it is therefore not up to date as regards the recent events in the matter of the children's hospitals ... Dr Wilson, no doubt, has put you in touch with most recent happenings so that you will understand in what directions the summary needs alteration.[30]

Lea Wilson's regard for her friend and spiritual guide had been expressed earlier by a significant gift. She presented his Jesuit community at Leeson Street, Dublin, with a valuable painting, believed to be by the Dutch artist, Honthorst. A dark canvas depicting the arrest of Jesus in the Garden and the kiss of Judas, it had been bought many years previously by her husband who was interested in art. It was to hang in the Jesuit parlour, and subsequently in the community refectory, for almost sixty years before it was discovered, in 1990, to be a virtually priceless work by Michelangelo da Marisi, called Caravaggio, who became famous in Rome around 1600 and was an originator of the Baroque style.[31]

MEN AND WORK

In addition to these instances of Finlay's friendship with a number of women, many examples of his male friends have been mentioned in previous chapters. They covered a wide range. The most obvious ones were Horace Plunkett, R.A. Anderson, H.F. Norman, Professors George O'Brien and William Magennis, all of whom wrote about him, but also such contrasting figures as Christopher Digges La Touche, managing director of Guinness, Sir Thomas Esmonde, the Revd Edward Fitzharding Campbell, chaplain to the Orange Order, and Patrick (the Cope) Gallagher from Donegal. The last, fortunately, has told at some length the rather dramatic circumstances of his first meeting with Father Finlay.

The story of Paddy the Cope
The most persistent critics of Plunkett and the co-operative movement were traders. Instances of their vigorous opposition to co-operative initiatives in County Donegal brought Finlay into a new and colourful relationship.

Patrick Gallagher, known locally as 'Paddy the Cope', recounted in *My Story* (London, 1939) how his co-operative near Dungloe was accused by traders as a venture subsidised by Orange lodges in order to split the nationalist Home Rule movement in Donegal. As a result of this campaign, only four families in Dungloe would speak to him. He and his supporters managed to get a grant to build a hall for education and recreation purposes. When it was completed, they found next morning a large notice plastered across the door with 'The New Orange Hall' in large letters. At the next meeting, a member read from the *Irish Homestead* 'a speech made by Father T.A. Finlay SJ, on a co-operative society in the south of Ireland. When he had finished reading, we all began cheering.' It was decided to invite Fr Finlay to open the new hall. Finlay agreed. Posters were prepared announcing his arrival, and were attached to traders' doors. 'They retaliated by circulating that Father Finlay was an Orange priest; the last place he was seen was in Lisburn with a Mr Harold Barbour, who had an Orange co-operative society right in the centre of the town.'[32] Barbour, as has been seen, was a key promoter in Ulster, and another friend of Finlay.

At the public meeting on his arrival, Finlay was puzzled by Paddy the Cope's bald introduction:

> Men and women of the Rosses, I am very glad to see such a big gathering here to day to welcome Father Finlay. Look at this man; surely none of you are in doubt now that he is anything but a real Catholic priest, and not an Orange priest.

Finlay looked at him in some embarrassment. A member of the crowd explained that their opponents had been circulating the story for some weeks that he was not a Catholic priest but an Orange priest, and that 'none of the real Catholics of the Rosses' believed a word of it. 'Father Finlay got up with a smile on his face, and said, "I hope I have discharged my duties this morning as a Catholic priest by saying Holy Mass in your church. I can assure you that I consider helping the farmers of Ireland to join together for their mutual advantage, let them be Catholic, Protestant, or Orangemen, is in keeping with the teaching of the Church." Then, he went on to explain the objects of the co-operative movement, and said in his opinion Sir Horace Plunkett was one of the greatest

Irishmen of his day, and that he, Father Finlay, was glad "to have the privilege of working with Sir Horace". The meeting was one of the most successful ever held in Dungloe.' Gallagher added, however: 'All the Cope members were delighted, yet the Dungloe people, with a few honourable exceptions, continued to call our hall the Orange Hall'.33

A rather different account of the meeting came from an unusual location, from Mountjoy prison. Peadar O'Donnell in his book *The Gates Flew Open*, pp 207–9, described an unexpected aspect as he recalled the meeting in detailed, perhaps exaggerated clarity, in the course of a 41-day hunger strike in 1923. The scene came before him as he reflected on his dislike of people who used religion as a pretext to conceal their self-interest. He wondered if his distaste arose from his memory of the first public meeting he ever attended, 'as a bare-footed youth'. He wrote in his diary:

> Rev. T.A. Finlay was the principal speaker, for it was a co-operative meeting, but before the speaker could get down to his subject he had to face the rumours that he was no priest at all but a blackguard that had stolen a priest's clothes and was gadding around with a 'widow woman' from America. Father Finlay explained who he was and described his ordination, smiling every now and then. His smile revealed tobacco-stained teeth. I have never seen him since, and yet I can recall those tobacco-stained teeth and I squirmed, for I was on his side and I knew these tobacco-stained teeth would ruin us. And sure enough on the way home all the talk broke out anew – those who didn't agree with the co-operative were more emphatic than ever he was no priest for didn't the world know that no priest would either smoke or chew tobacco.

'And those of us who were co-operators', O'Donnell continued, forgetting that he was conveying the views of a young boy, 'backed him lustily because in our hearts we didn't care a hoot whether he was a priest or not (and these teeth had rocked his claim even in my mind).'

Matters subsequently, in fact, became more serious when the traders and local priests opposed the hall and built an opposition structure which they called the Parochial Hall. Then it was announced from the pulpit that no dances were to be held in the co-operative hall without the consent of the priests. Depressed, Gallagher contemplated returning to Galway with his family. His resolution was fortified, however, when he attended a mission at Dungloe, informed one of the visiting missioners of his problem, and questioned whether he should leave. He was told: 'Fight your corner. God bless you!'34

At the next county council election, Paddy the Cope was nominated but the local traders combined against him by warning traders outside the Dungloe area that he would crush them by opening a store at each shopkeeper's door. Then they visited everyone who owed them money and informed them that they would have to pay the amount due before the election if they planned to vote for Paddy the Cope. A few weeks later he was summoned by traders for allegedly stating in public 'the traders were a pack of gombeen men' and would be 'the ruin of the country' and that 'he would kill gombeenism in the Rosses before long'. After consideration by the magistrates, the resident magistrate announced that the magistrates by a majority had decided, 'to ask Mr Gallagher to apologise to the traders', and that if he did so they would 'give his case most consideration'. 'Let there be no mistake', he added, this was not a unanimous but a majority decision. Gallagher refused to apologise. He had stated what he believed to be true. The magistrates then put him under bail of ten pounds to be of good behaviour for twelve months, especially towards the Rosses traders. Gallagher refused the bail. After long consultation, the resident magistrate announced: 'By a majority of the magistrates the verdict is that Mr Gallagher goes to Derry jail for one calendar month. In making this announcement I wish to say that I am doing so as presiding chairman. I do not agree with the decision.'[35]

After his conviction, Gallagher wrote to Finlay to the effect that the local magistrates had sentenced him to a month in Derry jail because he would not go under a rule of bail to be of good behaviour. He expressed the hope that by going to jail for a month he would not bring any disgrace on the co-operative movement.'[36]

'At the time, Father Finlay was on holiday in Doochary,' Paddy the Cope explained, 'and the day I was arrested he was out fishing. Miss Brady, from Castletownroche, County Cork, who was teaching domestic economy, under the United Irishwomen, in Dungloe, left her class and cycled to Doochary; she went up the river where the priest was and told him I was in Derry jail. He rolled up his line, and went back to the hotel. He was too late for the train at Fintown. On Thursday he went back to Dublin. After my conviction on Tuesday, a report of the trial had appeared in the *Derry Journal* on Wednesday, and in large type it had shown that the Resident Magistrate was against the conviction. Father Finlay got a copy of the paper.' Some time later, at Dungloe, he informed Gallagher of what he had then done, perhaps exaggerating ironically for his benefit. As presented, it conveys something of Finlay's readiness to help a friend, his social standing, and his ability to tell a story.

> I went up to Dublin Castle and asked for the Lord Lieutenant. I was told he was not in. I then asked when he would be in, handing my card to the porter. He took it and came back in about five minutes. He said that the Lord Lieutenant was in London. I asked him, ' Who rules Ireland in his absence?' He went inside again, and when he returned, he said, 'The Lords Justice.' I said, 'I want to see them.' He told me they did not sit on Fridays, but that they would be there at ten o'clock the following morning. I left the Castle very much annoyed.

'The next morning', Finlay went on, 'the porter was waiting for me to arrive, and immediately brought me into a great big room. There was a young man there sitting at a desk; he got up and knocked at a door, walked inside, came out instantly, and beckoned me to follow him. There were four men sitting around a table. They were the Lords Justices. One of them said, "Well, Father Finlay, what can we do for you?" and I asked him release Patrick Gallagher JP, manager of the Templecrone Co-operative Society Ltd, Dungloe, from Derry jail immediately. "Here is the report of his unjust conviction, and here is his letter to me. You must release him. I came from Donegal on Wednesday, but I could not see you yesterday."' 'Each of them read the report in the paper, and your letter to me; they then held a short consultation and one of them rang a bell. The young man came in, and the Justice who rang the bell said, "Take down this – To the Governor, Derry Jail. Release Patrick Gallagher of Dungloe immediately. By order of the Lords Justices".'[37]

After three days in jail, Gallagher was summoned by the governor, who read the lord justices' letter to him and congratulated him on his release.[38] Among those who met him on his release was Mrs Gardiner, the wife of the local doctor. As a result, Gallagher declared, 'the gombeen men held a meeting the following day and decided to boycott Dr Gardiner'. They brought a new doctor into the district. 'I think,' Gallagher concluded bitterly, 'of all the lousy tricks they did the boycotting of Dr Gardiner was the lousiest.'[39]

Finlay continued his interest in the Co-operative Society at Templecrone, rejoiced at its success, and paid a visit every year as long as his health permitted.[40] No correspondence is extant in his papers, however, relating to Templecrone or to his friendship with Paddy the Cope. Indeed, the only correspondence that has survived is in connection with but three of his numerous friends. The three were: the chief secretary, Augustine Birrell, Horace Plunkett, and T.M. Healy, governor general of the Irish Free State.

EXTANT LETTERS OF FRIENDS: BIRRELL AND PLUNKETT

Finlay's Jesuit obituarist, Professor Aubrey Gwynn, wrote of his friendship with Birrell.[41] But the extant indications of friendship are quite indirect. They are but two letters from the chief secretary, dated respectively 21 February and 5 March 1915. They reflect Birrell's efforts to respond to Finlay's concern, as chairman of the trustees of the National Library of Ireland, regarding the wartime stoppage of grants to the library. On 5 March, Birrell reported that he had 'spoken to the Financial Secretary of the Treasury about it and found him sympathetic on the point of securing the government for the *maintenance* of the Library', but as he, Birrell, was unable to attend the House of Commons just then, it was difficult 'to find out precisely what is happening'.[42]

Plunkett's last letters were also concerned with business. After the burning of his house by Irregular forces in January 1923, he had moved his headquarters and the co-operative reference library from Merrion Square to London. He carried on his co-operative crusade from there. On 10 April 1926, he wrote, from a sick bed, a long letter on co-operation in India, and how Ireland, by means of the co-operative movement, might help 'to solve the otherwise insoluble problem of some 250 millions of peasants ever on the verge of starvation'. He had offered 'to have a few (Indian) organisers trained in the theoretical part of the work in the Co-operative Reference Library, ... and then to get them instructed by H.F. Norman (in Ireland) for their field work'. Now he had learned that some Indians, who had come to look at the work of co-operation in Ireland, had occasioned local suspicions. He had no particulars, but there was evidently an 'absurd misunderstanding' which Finlay 'would be able to deal with'. 'It would be deplorable', he concluded, 'if we lost the chance of earning the gratitude for the real service of these millions of peasants on account of an extravagant and absurd fable started by people who have nothing else to do.' He envisaged no more than ten Indian students, who would be trained how to set up a training system of their own in India, but it would be a service 'in which we should do good to ourselves by helping others'.[43]

No further information on the Indian scheme occurs in the correspondence. The next letter was from Finlay on 14 June 1928. He commented on a letter of Plunkett's in the *Times*, which he thought excellent but which required more detailed treatment to enable the public to understand the question at issue. He expressed the hope that Plunkett could find time for a paper on 'The place of the small farmer in a rural economy'. 'It would be helpful to us in Ireland', he added, 'and would not be without value to students of this agricultural problem in England.'[44] Three days later, Plunkett replied from his family base, Killeen Castle, Dunsany, County Meath, with another ambitious scheme to redress injustice and poverty. 'I have come down here', he announced, 'in hopes of completing four articles upon "The wider aspects of English agriculture". They will be addressed to the non-agricultural majority, who, in existing circumstances, will decide absolutely the agricultural policy of the government. The subject will be treated from a new point of view and I will certainly get your assistance in presenting it.' With the general election looming, 'all three political parties were grovelling to the National Farmers Union', which had a hundred thousand members, all large farmers. 'I am going behind their backs to appeal to the general public to insist upon an agricultural policy which has some regard for the interests of the labourers and small cultivators.'[45]

The remaining extant letter between Plunkett and Finlay was written by the former less than three months before his death. It marked his final message to an annual general meeting of the IAOS, and to the end it was imbued with enthusiasm for the organisation and with plans for the future. His doctor refused to allow him attend the AGM to be held on Tuesday next, he informed Finlay on 10 January 1932. In his place he was sending a letter which Finlay, if he saw fit, might read to the meeting. Following a comment on the Report which Finlay would ask the meeting to adopt, he looked ahead to an international event, the Eucharistic Congress, scheduled for Ireland, which he was not destined to see, and pointed to the opportunity it offered Irish agricultural co-operation. 'In the summer there come to Ireland from all over the world tens of thousands of Irishmen and friends of Ireland. Most of them', he continued with characteristic optimism, 'will have heard of the Irish idea for a new rural civilisation, and will be anxious to discover how far they have been fruitful in Ireland.' He had particularly in mind visitors from France, where 41 per cent of the population were enagaged in agriculture. 'Might it not be well for you', he suggested to Finlay, 'to tell the country, as, alas! only you and R.A. Anderson will be able to do at first hand, that our movement was in its origin a practical protest against the neglect of *our* agriculture by a country which had persistently subordinated its basic industry to manufacturing and commercial interests. We were, in effect, laying the foundations upon which, so soon as our political, economic, and social destinies were transferred to Irish hands, the new rural civilisation we had conceived could be built.'

Plunkett went on to acknowledge that the Irish government had 'accepted as far as possible the principles of our movement in framing their agricultural policy' and had 'recognised to the full the necessity of having the farmers organised, and organised on the co-operative plan'. Emphasising yet again the need for organisation, he pointed out that world conditions were 'compelling every people to re-adjust its economic life' and that 'everywhere that re-adjustment' was 'taking the form of more effective organisation'.

He had intended 'enlarging on this subject', Plunkett concluded, 'as well as on that wider aspect of our movement to which I attach *paramount importance*, namely, the *threefold approach* to our problem of developing *better farming, better business, and better living*, an approach which bids us treat agriculture as an industry, as a business, and as a life. This is the aspect which distinguishes the Irish idea of agricultural development from the idea of any other country that I know.' His intention of enlarging on these topics, however, had been foiled by his doctor who had forbidden him 'to do any more writing'.[46]

In many ways it was a fitting final message to a General Meeting of the Society, reiterating his emphasis on highly organised co-operation and his distinctive three fold aim of developing, through organised co-operation, 'better farming, better business, better living'. And it was fitting, too, that he chose to have it presented by the one he termed 'the kindest and most loyal friend I have ever had in a work which has made my life worth living'.[47]

Finlay's friendship with Horace Plunkett was linked to their common interest, his equally long friendship with T.M. Healy MP, and later Governor General, was equally warm but probably more expressive.

CORRESPONDENCE AND FRIENDSHIP WITH TIM HEALY AND FAMILY

Finlay's link with T.M. Healy went back, at the least, to the 1890s. He appears to have admired Healy's courage in standing up to Parnell, and he could not but have enjoyed his quickness and the salty wit that remarked of a number of nationalist members in the House of Commons: 'Some of these fellows are a standing argument against an Irish parliament. It would pay Ireland to employ them at a high salary to stay at home'.[48]

He was also conscious of a deeply spiritual side to Healy, a side too frequently veiled by his acerbic comments. He viewed his celebrated speech on the Education Bill of 1906 as a genuine expression of religious belief, not just rhetoric to make an impression. Healy had questioned the government benches – 'Why do you propose to put under proscription our thousands of Catholic schools?' And then, declaring that he did not wish to indulge in emotional language or to make a religion protestation, he proclaimed:

> But I will say this. I would rather have my children learn to say 'Our Father' than learn the use of globes. I would rather they understood their religion in preparation for the eternity that is to come, than that they become rich and prosperous in this world. I cannot spell myself; I cannot parse a sentence; I cannot do the rule of three; I am supposed to know a little law but I think that is a mistake (loud laughter). But if there is one thing that I and mine have got a grip of, it is a belief in the infinite Christ to come, it is the conviction that our children, whatever may be their distresses, whatever may be their misfortunes in this world, will reap a rich reward in putting into practice the lessons of Christianity which they have learned in the Catholic schools.[49]

Commenting on the speech in *Studies*, Professor Tim Corcoran observed: 'To pass from high seriousness to sheer comedy, and then again in one moment to attain a seriousness not only high but sublime ... is rare if not unexampled in modern oratory.'[50]

Finlay and Healy exchanged visits during much of their lives. When Healy became governor general (1922–7), Finlay was a regular guest at the governor's residence in the Phoenix Park, was taken on drives in his excellency's motor car, and remained a close friend to the family, which consisted of three daughters and three sons. The daughters were Elizabeth (Liz), Maev, and Erina, the sons, Joseph, Paul, and Timothy. Liz resided with Healy at the Viceregal Lodge, cared for her ill mother, and assisted Healy in carrying out the social functions of his office. Finlay was available to them all in times both of jubilation and of grief. On 8 July 1927, he comforted his friend after his wife, Erina Sullivan, died after an illness of more than five years;[51] and he was at hand again just two days later when news came of the murder of Kevin O'Higgins, a relation on the Sullivan side, to whom Healy was deeply attached. Three years on, there was rejoicing at the ordination of Healy's son, Paul, as a Jesuit priest, and also at the close of that year, December 1930, when Finlay's retirement from University College, Dublin, was marked by a presentation ceremony, which Healy and his daughter, Liz, attended. Later that night, Healy penned a letter to Finlay that mirrored the depth of their friendship:

> My dear Fr Tom,
> I enjoyed tonight so much (as did Liz) it can do no harm to assail your humility with a compliment. You did admirably. Best token of all your labour, was the loyalty and organisation of the young men. May grace descend on them, and dear friend, on you, tho' you may well be spared my invocations.
> Not a day passed that I don't think fondly of you..
> M'Onam thu!
> Tim Healy.[52]

Three months later, 26 March 1931, T. M. Healy died. His son, Paul, assisted in the administration of the sacrament of Extreme Unction. It was the anniversary of Paul's ordination. One daughter, Erina, who had become a member of the Ursuline religious congregation as Sister Bernard, was not permitted to attend her father's final illness. On 29 March, Finlay took care to send her a consoling, if somewhat stylised, account of her father's death and funeral.

> It was my privilege – for which I thank God gratefully – that in the afternoon of Wednesday, the day before his death, I spent with the invalid as much time as his strength would allow. Throughout the interview he held my hand – we had been close and intimate friends for forty years. It was to me a supreme consolation to observe that the unquestioning faith that had been characteristic of him during life was his assured support as death approached. He awaited the summons of the Master with a serene confidence possible only to a soul at perfect peace with God ...
> Next day as I knelt beside his body ... I thought of the storms of that life now ended in great calm. I remembered how fearlessly and uncompromisingly he had, in memorable scenes of political strife, professed devotion to Christ as his first allegiance, and the prayer came to my lips: 'Lord, he professed Thee before men, remember it for him before thy Father who is in heaven.'
> Yesterday he was laid to rest in Glasnevin. The funeral was as he wished it – without pomp of Church or State ceremonial. The archbishop attended the Mass in the cathedral, but he knelt by the altar as a worshipper, he did not occupy the throne. The ministers of State were present, and with them a crowd of men eminent in public life, but these, too, were silent worshippers; all seemed to feel that the most fitting tribute to the man they wished to honour was prayer, not parade. In Glasnevin the ceremony was of the same simple character; the archbishop blessed the grave, and, in the falling rain, waited to recite the *De Profundis* when it was filled in. All must have felt as they left the cemetery that they had been doing homage not to that career which had secured a foremost place in Irish history, but to a life which had won a high place in heaven.[53]

In the years of activity remaining to him, Finlay endeavoured to be as firm a friend to the Healy family as he had been to their father.

12

The final decades

In the 1920s, under the government of the Irish Free State, Tom Finlay continued to serve on a number of public bodies, as well as to work for the co-operative movement, and to lecture at University College. A foundation member of the Central Savings Committee, he was one of the first to be consulted by the government on the establishment of the Irish Savings movement in 1923. Apart from his public activities, he was reputed to have been called on 'to give counsel and advice to many men of great public influence' who had recourse to him 'for trustworthy guidance'.[1] He remained gifted with strength and good health in his stocky frame so that, for example, during his long years as chairman of the Board of Trustees of the National Library of Ireland he never missed a meeting,[2] and in UCD, it was his boast that during his forty-seven years' teaching he had never omitted a lecture for ill-health or any other reason.[3] He was eighty-two when he retired from the College. As a former Fellow of the Royal University, he was not required to retire at a fixed age.

STRONGLY CRITICISED

Finlay had been a brilliant, stimulating lecturer as a young man. What was he like in his final decade in the classroom? The only comment known to the author is highly, even harshly, critical.

C.S. (Todd) Andrews, in his autobiography, *Man of No Property*,[4] was indiscriminate in his criticism. He first found fault with Finlay's appearance, commenting that he had a long upper lip such as was often ridiculed in *Punch* cartoons, and then continued:

> Father Finlay was an old man who spoke with an old man's voice and it was difficult to follow his lectures. But that was not really necessary because he lectured straight from the textbook – Gide's *Principles of Political Economy*. Indeed, attendance at his lectures could have been dispensed with altogether except to discover, for examination purposes, whatever topic interested him particularly ... He felt clearly no obligation to keep abreast of developments in economic theory. The name of Keynes was never mentioned even though the *Economic Consequences of the Peace* had

been long since published. The first edition of Gide's textbook came out in 1889, and the version we were using had been published before the 1914 war after which economics were never the same again.

Andrews' criticism is credible with respect to almost any lecturer who had been lecturing for more than forty years. Its very harshness, however, has to be seen in the context of his comments about all his lecturers. All were found inadequate on one ground or another. The personal nature of his remarks about Finlay may also reflect a hostility generated by Andrews association with the anti-Treaty forces in the civil war and Finlay's links with many on the government side. There was, moreover, no awareness on Andrews part of the particular relevance of Charles Gide for Finlay. The Paris professor's combination of Christian asceticism and socialist idealism, his standing as the virtual 'founder of modern cooperative doctrine', and his 'moral even religious inspiration', drew Finlay to him and encouraged him to make Gide's teaching known both to his students and to farmers in small groups throughout Ireland.[5] The book was to remain highly regarded in UCD long after Finlay's departure. Finally, there is an element of reading back into history on Andrews's part, as Keynes did not become a figure of note until the later 1930s; and ironically, when a series of public lectures was introduced to honour Finlay, after his retirement, the lecturer chosen to commence the series in his honour was John Maynard Keynes![6]

RECOGNITION AND HONOUR

In the Catholic newspaper, the *Universe*, on 2 January 1931, it was remarked that neither of the brothers, Tom and Peter Finlay, 'ever cared a straw for publicity, and so their eminent value is best known to but a few'. In the years 1929 and 1930, however, Tom's life and work was acknowledged with public praise and presentations.

The *Anglo-Celt*, which was run by John F. and Edward O'Hanlon, relations-in-law to Finlay, reported, on 6 April 1929, of a remarkable gathering of Finlay's friends and admirers in his native Cavan. A memorial was presented to him, and speaker after speaker vied with each other in praising his services to agriculture in Ireland. The following year, a more distinguished and varied gathering, but equally enthusiastic, assembled in the Council Chamber, UCD, to mark Professor Finlay's retirement.

The 1930 meeting was treated as a very special occasion. Professor George O'Brien presided, and Professor William Magennis delivered the main address. A portrait of Finlay by Leo Whelan RHA was presented to him. Subscriptions had been invited to pay for the portrait. The response was such that it not only covered expenses for the portrait, it also made it possible to establish an endowment for Economics in the College. 'The subscribers', George O'Brien informed the large gathering, 'were drawn from every class in the community – academic and non-academic, Catholic and Protestant, rich and poor'. The gathering itself was drawn from different sectors of the community. The governor-general, James MacNeill, and Mrs MacNeill, attended, as did representatives of the workers from Dungloe.

Professor Magennis was the appropriate choice as speaker, having been a student of Finlay, and then a friend and colleague for more than forty years. As always on such occasions, achievements and praise were to the forefront. He sketched Finlay's career from his time as rector of Belvedere, pointing out that he had never lost his interest in secondary education. He had been chairman of the Board of Intermediate Education when the Provisional government replaced the British regime, and 'few were aware', Magennis declared, 'how many beneficial reforms in Irish educational policy and methods owed their first conception to the creative brain of Fr Finlay'. Going on to university education, the speaker observed:

> It was a fortunate day for the future of higher education in Ireland when, in connection with the new foundation of the Royal University of Ireland, Father Finlay and a few co-workers of his Order undertook that great adventure, the revitalisation of Newman's moribund University College. It was a hazardous enterprise, and the omens were unfavourable, but, happily, they were men cast in a heroic mould.

'In the chair of philosophy', Magennis went on, Fr Finlay had lent 'a fresh impulse and direction' to the subject, imparting to it 'a deeper reality' and 'an ampler scope'. And, he added, 'the higher education of women owed a special debt to him'.

Turning to Finlay's work in the co-operative movement, Magennis considered that his most notable contribution was 'what he had accomplished for the uplift of the farmers'. Then, with a friend's insight into Finlay's outlook and career, he commented:

> He began his crusade of self-help at the precise moment when many of them had become enslaved to the practice of looking to the State for everything as a second Providence. He convinced them, by giving them the experience of it, that in organised co-operative association lay a highway to economic safety.

'The people had faith in him, and so put trust in his ministry of new ideas. Nor was the goal at which his self-help aimed solely material betterment, he saw its psychological value in infusing self-confidence. He developed the worthiest capacities of our farmer community, supplanting sporadic, spasmodic, un-intelligent individual effort by organised collective action. And his scheme of agricultural banks demonstrated the moral value of making character the basis of credit.'[7]

Finlay, in reply, thanked the subscribers, and added that while he appreciated the motives that lay behind the presentation, 'his best reward was the students who had passed through his class-room, and who had distinguished themselves in the service of their country'. He then paid tribute to Sir Horace Plunkett's work in the co-operative movement 'and said he was delighted to see present a representative of the Dungloe workers from Donegal who had rendered a big service to the nation and the country as a whole'. Availing of the occasion to press a point, he added:

> They had taught a lesson to the people which they had a sad need to learn. In an isolated hamlet on the Donegal coast they had established an industry without help from the government, without patronage from capitalists, and by sheer determination and hard work it had become most successful, its wares being sold in different parts of the world.

'The woollen mills at Foxford', he went on, had uplifted the people 'in a squalid and poverty-stricken district' and their success was 'a matter of great satisfaction to him'. The founder was broken in health but still in the convent at Foxford, 'and he would like that a message should be conveyed to her that they at a gathering of this kind appreciated what she had done.' He concluded with a characteristic motif:

> There were many schemes for establishing industry in Ireland, but if the problem was to be solved it would only be by what had made Dungloe and Foxford what they were – hard work and clear thinking.[8]

The writer of the account in the *Universe* added: 'Those who are privileged to be associated with Father Finlay in any of his multifarious works find it hard to believe that he has passed his eightieth year. He still looks very much the same as ever, and he told me the other day that he is still able to enjoy the pleasure of a day's fishing or shooting.'[9]

On the subject of shooting and fishing, as has been suggested earlier, the locations where he was welcome to shoot or fish were multiplied by his numerous contacts throughout the country and his gift for making friends. His grand-nephews, Bill and Tom, recall hearing of some of the more prominent of these places: of Gormanstown Castle, where their grand-uncle was warmly welcomed and about which he told them the legend of the foxes gathering by the house when the death of the owner was imminent; of the King Harmon estate at Rockingham, outside Boyle, County Roscommon; of his friend Tom Esmonde's place in Wexford; of Clonalis, County Roscommon, the home of the O'Conor Don; and of visits to relations the Magans of Kilashee and of Lanesborough, County Longford.

SADNESS AND JOY

Not long after the celebrations of 1930, intimations of mortality came heavily upon him with the deaths of his two close friends, Healy, on 26 March 1931, and Plunkett, just a year later, on 26 March 1932. Finlay may well have recalled with a smile Healy's wry comment to his daughter, Maev, after the death of William O'Brien in February 1928: 'the only residuum of 1880 now are T.P. O'Connor, Sexton and myself. Next please!'[10] The loss of his two friends was added to in 1932 by the unexpected death of his much loved nephew, Thomas Finlay TD. The latter had practised law. At the request of Kevin O'Higgins he agreed, in 1922, to act as district justice in the Longford area. The fact that district justices travelled with an armed escort indicated the dangers of the position in those years of civil strife. Subsequently, he moved from the district court to be assistant secretary of the Department of Justice. After Kevin O'Higgins murder in 1926, Thomas Finlay returned to the bar, and in 1932, while working in Limerick, he contacted typhoid and died. Fr Tom had been close to his nephew's family, and had stayed at their lodge in Mayo. When Thomas died, he felt a responsibility to do all he could for his nephew's two sons, William (Bill) and Tom, aged respectively eleven and ten years. Both, more than sixty years later, have the warmest of memories of the relationship that developed between them. They marvel at how he bridged the gap in generations. They found him encouraging, never didactic, and with a great sense of fun. They looked forward to being with him.[11] Finlay, having more time now that he was retired from University College, took them with him on a variety of fishing and shooting expeditions in different parts of the country. These included a visit to the Magan family in Killashee, and to the Kiernans in Carrick-on-Shannon. The boys were amazed how widely their grand-uncle was known, and how completely at ease he was with people of all rank and class.[12]

In his own religious community at Leeson Street, Fr Tom's fishing and shooting outings were taken for granted. He regularly disappeared for a few days during the Easter vacation, and Good Friday was not complete unless he brought home a salmon for the community. This continued into his eighties, and some conjectured that a faithful gilly in County Wexford or the West of Ireland was really responsible for the reputed catch.[13] Young Bill Finlay, however, was in a position to scotch such speculation. He had been with the old man when he caught salmon; and in 1935, when Finlay was eighty-seven, and they were staying at Kiernans in Carrick-on-Shannon, his grand-nephew was with him on the Shannon as he shot a mallard from the boat.[14] Among the boys' miscellaneous memories of their elderly relation and friend, were his recounting of visits to Maynooth as a young priest, visits on the day the local hunt assembled, when he, by arrangement with his friend, the president of the college, came ostensibly 'for scholastic exercises' but availed of the occasion to school horses; his enjoyment in the novels of P.G. Wodehouse; the fact that he smoked; and the acerbic wit which lingered in their memory concerning the diminutive but vociferous and assertive preacher and writer, Fr Patrick Gannon – 'The smaller the bee, the bigger the buzz'. Another memory took on a special glow in retrospect. The occasion when, on their visit to Leeson Street, Fr Tom brought them to the parlour to view a splendid painting by Hondhurst featuring the kiss of Judas and the arrest of Jesus (later identified as a Caravaggio).[15]

Both boys studied law. Tom was called to the Bar, and after a distinguished career became chief justice. William, too, was called to the Bar and practised there for twenty-four years, for some of which time he was also a law lecturer at University College Dublin. In 1970 he joined the board of the Bank of Ireland of which he became governor. Very appropriately, he was chairman of the Board of Governors of the National Gallery when the Irish Jesuits, in 1993, entrusted the Caravaggio painting to the gallery on continuous loan.

THE LAST YEARS

The mallard shot from a boat in 1935 was Finlay's last mallard. The following year he suffered a stroke. It left his brain and speech unaffected, but he was no longer able to walk. He, who had always been so independent and active, was now dependent on others to push him in his wheel-chair and to take him out for occasional drives. Fortunately, he was able to read and write, and he did both extensively. The house at Leeson Street, however, with its many stairs, was no longer suitable. He moved to Linden Convalescent Home, Stillorgan, County Dublin, where he was made welcome by the Irish Sisters of Charity. There he spent the four years remaining to him; and, despite his life of energy and independence, displayed a patience and acceptance of his condition that impressed his many visitors.[16] These included, of course, members of family and fellow Jesuits. Among the latter was a member of community at Leeson Street, a distinguished historian, Aubrey Gwynn, who recalled: 'there was a great deal of simple piety about Father Tom in his last years. Day by day he was wheeled into the chapel for his morning Mass; and it was seldom indeed that he would allow his nurse to keep him away from the chapel for the daily rosary, which he loved to recite with the other patients every evening'. Another Jesuit visitor was the one to whom Finlay had passed his commitment to the co-operative movement, the very able son of a brilliant father, Edward Coyne, whose father was one of Finlay's earliest and most able students, and subsequently a friend and colleague, W.P. Coyne. Edward was to become president of the IAOS. Others whose visits are remembered, apart from family, and fellow Jesuits, included Lady Fingall, and T.M. Healy's daughter, Elizabeth. He had been particularly helpful to the Healy family in their troubles, now they were kind to him, visiting him and bringing him out for drives into the countryside.[17] He died peacefully on 8 January 1940, having spent the previous two days in almost continuous prayer.[18]

Despite his absence from active life for a number of years, the attendance at his funeral provided a marked tribute to his long life, and a reminder of W.E.H.

Lecky's estimation that he was 'perhaps the most universally respected man in Ireland'.[19] The large attendance was representative of all sections of the community. Four bishops were present, as was Mr Eamon de Valera, wearing the robes of the chancellor of the National University, Mr Little, Minister for Posts and Telegraphs, Mr William Cosgrave TD, representatives of the judiciary and the universities, some 300 clergy, and a general congregation that so crowded the large church that 'a large number of mourners ... were unable to gain admission', and 'remained outside until the obsequies had concluded'.[20]

The daily newspapers chronicled the passing of a great educator and Irishman. Professor George O'Brien, in the *Economic Journal*, edited by J.M. Keynes, March 1940, concluded his obituary somewhat unexpectedly:

> A wonderfully life-like portrait of him is to be found in George Moore's *Hail and Farewell*, where he is depicted as the genial and influential man that he was, accepted and welcomed in many mutually exclusive circles. Father Finlay was unquestionably one of the outstanding personalities of modern Ireland, and his loss will be mourned far outside the narrow circles of the academic world.[21]

Several accounts of Finlay's career paid tribute to him as, above all, an educator: recalling his work in Jesuit colleges and his university teaching in three different subjects, and how he motivated generations of young men and women to high standards of public service; his role as commissioner of intermediate education for many years; the active part he took in the establishment and early administration of the new system of technical education at the beginning of the twentieth century; his editorship of 'The School and College Series' of books for pupils and students; and how, with Horace Plunkett, he inspired and guided the men who created the Department of Agriculture. In a wider field of instruction, he was for many years a prominent member of the Senate of the National University of Ireland and of the governing body of University College, was a trustee of the National Library of Ireland, 1907, and chairman of the trustees from 1909 to 1938, was a member of the Royal Irish Academy, and in 1913 was appointed president of the Jesuit owned University Hall. His unstinting work for the co-operative movement might also be placed under 'education'. One writer, who knew him well, claimed that 'Father Finlay was especially interested in the co-operative movement because of its educational value, and of its effect upon the character of the people who carried out its teaching'.[22] At a deeper level, as noted in an earlier chapter, the motivating factor appears to have been to provide a service to benefit others, especially the less well-off. His is 'the story of a remarkable living Irishman', Plunkett wrote, 'who, for a full half century, laboured disinterestedly for the moral, social, and economic uplifting of the poor.'[23] Intertwined with all that was his work as priest: the sought-after preacher and retreat-director, the confidant of numerous religious and clergy. And then, he was also an author, founder or co-founder of six journals and editor of three, and a founding member of the National Literary Society of Ireland. Little wonder that George O'Brien, in an appreciation in *Studies*, March 1940, observed that 'to write about him is like writing about a number of persons rather than a single man',[24] or that, many years later, a historian, familiar with his career, would speak of him as 'pre-eminently the Renaissance man of the Irish Renaissance'.[25]

With a figure of such ability, with so many contacts and friends in all sectors of society, the absence of personal papers is a matter for regret. George O'Brien had pressed him to write his memoirs, and had urged young William Finlay to persuade his grand-uncle to do so. The old man's rather lame comment was: 'At my age I'm not sure what I heard in confidence and what not.'[26] The reality seemed to be that he had no desire for posthumous renown. 'The desire for posthumous renown', he had stated in his pamphlet *The Name of Jesus*, 'has never been a mark of minds that were wise.'[27] The nearest he came to a comment on his own long life was a remark to one of the grand-nephews – 'Looking back at this age, I can assure you I have never regretted my vocation'.[28]

In the light of Finlay's long devotion to, and belief in, the co-operative movement, and his capacity to make friends amongst people of all faiths or none, it is fitting to leave the final reflections to H.F. Norman, assistant secretary of the IAOS, a litterateur, and a theosophist.

> 'Father Tom' ... stressed in his addresses, the importance of 'quantity' and 'quality' in agricultural production at a time when the advocacy of combining efficient with sufficient production was novel if not revolutionary. His economics never obscured belief in technical hazes or abstruse niceties, but ever sought and found the key to the swift and unexpected progress of the Irish co-operative movement in what he called 'the magic of commonsense' ... He combined a consistent idealism balanced by a clear realisation of stark actuality.[29]

The idealism and hope for co-operation continued to the end. In his final year he wrote to Norman:

> I am in full accord with the co-operative commonwealth as the only feasible solution of the class problem, and believe that eventually humanity will be driven, after many mistakes in other directions, to accept this way out of its difficulties.[30]

And linking Finlay's contribution to Plunkett and his movement, Norman's reflections were penetrating:

> It is almost certain that the millions of pounds sterling which flowed from co-operative sources ... into hundreds of thousands of farmers' pockets over several years, guided thereto by Plunkett's genius, would have been damned or directed elsewhere if Father Finlay, recognising and pro-

claiming Plunkett's integrity and unselfish patriotism, had not, out of like qualities within himself, extended an influence on Plunkett's behalf, which his clerical position and unequivocal nationalism made it impossible for mischievous or misguided middlemen and partisans to withstand or misrepresent.[31]

It must be added finally that factors other than his clerical position and nationalism were basic to his success in the face of opposition. These, most notably, were his distinctive personality, partly moulded in his family circle and circumstances, which was marked by quiet self-assurance and calm courage – 'one mustn't pay any attention to criticism', he had told George Moore – and was bolstered, in the overall unity of the person, by buoyancy and a robust constitution, an indefinable aura of 'presence', the capacity to relate to and communicate with all kinds of people, and, of course, a powerful practical intelligence.

Notes

1 THE YEARS OF PREPARATION

1 *Irish Province News* (IPN), 1940, obituary by Aubrey Gwynn SJ.
2 Family account. Interviews with Chief Justice Tom Finlay and William Finlay, grand-nephews of Fr Finlay.
3 Ibid.
4 Annual Letters of the Society of Sacred Heart, obituary of Annie Finlay, RFCJ, third part, 1933–5, pp 747–59.
5 Annual Letters, obituary of Margaret Finlay, who died in 1936.
6 Ibid., obituary of Annie Finlay.
7 IPN; as n. 1.
8 *Anglo-Celt*, 13 Jan. 1940, obituary.
9 Family account as recalled by Judge Tom Finlay.
10 Ibid.
11 IPN; as n. 1.
12 Friedrick Wilhelm Raiffeisen, 1818–88, a German civil servant, credited with the foundation and philosophy of the Credit Union movement. See reference also on pp 93–4.
13 IPN; as n. 1.
14 A record of Finlay's writings are in Richard J. Hayes (ed.), *Sources for the history of Irish civilization: articles in Irish periodicals*, pp 310–11.

2 UNIVERSITY PROFESSOR AND RECTOR OF BELVEDERE COLLEGE

1 T.J. Morrissey, *Towards a national university* (Dublin, 1983), p. 65.
2 Letters from Finlay to Fr Beckx, Belvedere archives, courtesy of Fr Paul Andrews SJ, former rector of Belvedere College.
3 Jesuit Fathers (eds), *A page of Irish history: the story of University College, Dublin, 1883–1909* (Dublin, 1930), p. 383.
4 Finlay–Beckx, 8 Jan. 1884.
5 Obituary by Fr Aubrey Gwynn in *IPN*, 1940.
6 The *Lyceum* was aimed at a university and reflective readership, and was the forerunner of *Studies*. The *Messenger of the Sacred Heart* brought popular, but balanced spirituality to a wide readership and became the most widely read magazine in the country.
7 Finlay–Fr General, Anton Anterledy, 10 June 1888, copy in Belvedere archives.
8 Ibid., 15 July 1888
9 MacNeill papers, Finlay letters, MS 10,881, National Library of Ireland.
10 Ibid.
11 Ibid., Finlay–MacNeill, April/May 1906, and 29 Aug. 1906.
12 Ibid.

3 AT UNIVERSITY COLLEGE

1 T.J. Morrissey, *Towards a national university*, pp 98–9.
2 Delany–Emly, 12 Dec. 1884, Monsell MS NLI.
3 Morrissey, op. cit., pp 98–9.
4 Delany–Emly, 1885, no other date, Irish Jesuit Archives (IJA).
5 Morrissey, op. cit., pp 110–11. 6 Ibid., p. 140. 7 Ibid., pp 131–3.
8 Ibid., p. 141. 9 Ibid., p. 140.
10 C.P. Curran, *Under the receeding wave* (Dublin, 1970), pp 80–1.
11 Jesuit Fathers. *Page of Irish history*, pp 574–5.
12 Aubrey Gwynn SJ, 'The Jesuits and University College' in M. Tierney (ed.), *Struggle with fortune: a centenary miscellany for Catholic University of Ireland 1854, University College Dublin 1954* (Dublin, 1954), pp 31–2.
13 William Dawson in James Meenan (ed.), *A centenary history of the Literary and Historical Society of University College Dublin, 1855–1955* (Tralee, 1955), p. 47.
14 Curran, op. cit., p. 75.
15 J. Meenan. *George O'Brien* (Dublin, 1980), p. 143.
16 Foley–Delany, Nov. 1897, IJA; cit. in *Towards a national university*, p. 145.
17 *Page of Irish history*, pp 412–3.
18 Ibid., section on 'Entrance of women students' prepared with the assistance of Mary Hayden MA, pp 452–5.
19 Ibid., p. 456. 20 *Towards a national university*, p. 216.
21 *Page of Irish history*, p. 471. 22 *Lantern*, Christmas 1916, vol. 2, no. 1.
23 Meenan, *George O'Brien*, pp 157–8.
24 Meenan, *Cent. Hist. of the L. and H. Society*, pp 35, 201. 25 Ibid., p. 38.
26 Ibid., pp 46–7. 27 Ibid., pp 38–9. 28 Ibid., Patrick Little's account, pp 90–1.
29 Ibid., p. 116. 30 Ibid., p. 33. 31 Ibid., p. 40.
32 Ibid., p. 84. 33 Ibid., pp 50–1. 34 Ibid., p. 47.
35 Ibid., pp 52–3. 36 Ibid., p. 47.

4 FINLAY AND LITERATURE

1 *Page of Irish history*, pp 290–1; *Under the receding waves*, pp 72–3.
2 *Page of Irish history*, pp 316–17.
3 Marcus Bourke, *John O'Leary* (Tralee, 1967), p. 191.
4 Ibid., pp 230–1. 5 James Meenan, *George O'Brien*, p. 119.
6 McGreevy–Finlay, 7 Nov. 1924. IJA J 9/32 (1).
7 Meenan, *George O'Brien*, pp 117–19.
8 *Hail and Farewell* (3 vols, 1911–13), ed. R.A. Cave (Gerrards Cross, Bucks., and Washington, 1985), p. 324.
9 Ibid., pp 338–43; inverted commas have been added to the quotations from Moore to facilitate reading.
10 Ibid., p. 353. 11 Ibid., p. 366. 12 Ibid. p. 587.
13 W.G. Fallon in *Cent. hist. of the L. and H.*, p. 98. 14 Ibid., p. 98.

5 THE EDITOR OF JOURNALS

1 *Page of Irish history*, p. 295. 2 *Under the receding wave*, p. 76.
3 T. Clyde, *Irish literary magazines*, p. 124.
4 W. Magennis, 'A disciple's sketch of Fr T. Finlay', *Belvederian*, 9 (summer 1931), pp 19ff.

5 *Lyceum* (Nov. 1892), p. 25. It was a simplistic presentation. At least one bishop, Dr E.T. O'Dwyer, Limerick, did not see the Parnell situation as necessitating episcopal intervention.
6 *Page of Irish history*, p. 296.   7 Washbourne publication, 1899.
8 *Lyceum* (Feb. 1890), pp 140–2.   9 Jesuit consultors' minute book, IJA.
10 Ibid.
11 Delany papers, IJA; quoted in *Towards a national university*, pp 153ff. and see p. 395, fn. 129.
12 See *Hail and farewell* earlier; also quoted by George O'Brien in 'Fr Thomas A. Finlay, SJ', *Studies* (Mar. 1940), p. 37.
13 *Lyceum*, 'University of Ireland (Royal)' (Sept. 1887), p. 5.
14 T.J. Morrissey, *William J. Walsh, archbishop of Dublin, 1841–1921*, pp 34–9; and *Towards a national university*, pp 89–97.
15 *Towards a national university*, p. 133.   16 Oct. 1890, p. 26.
17 *Lyceum* (Sept. 1891–Sept. 1892).   18 Ibid. (July 1891), p. 239.
19 Ibid. (July 1893), p. 218.   20 Ibid. (Sept. 1893), p. 255.
21 *Page of Irish history*, p. 298.   22 Ibid., p. 299.
23 Ibid., pp 300–1.
24 Ibid., pp 303–4, quoting Fr John Ryan, Professor of Early Irish History.
25 *Centenary Hist. of L and H*, pp 133–4.
26 *New Ireland Review* (March 1904), 'Ireland and free trade', no. 2, p. 3.
27 Ibid., 3rd article, p. 73.   28 Clyde, *Irish lit. magazines*, p. 125.
29 Also in *Page of Irish History*, pp 310–11.
30 Quote from M. Packe, *John Stuart Mill* (London, 1954), p. 406; see, too, James Meenan, *George O'Brien*, p. 165.
31 'Father Finlay SJ and Socialism' in *James Connolly: selected political writing*, ed. Owen Dudley Edwards and Bernard Ransom (London, 1973), pp 201–5.

6 SOCIO-POLITICAL AMBIENCE, 1890–1908

1 Wm. Magennis, 'A disciple's sketch of Father T. Finlay' in the *Belvederian*, 9 (summer 1931), pp 19, 20.
2 *Page of Irish history*, p. 505.
3 Irish Jesuit Archives. Also *Towards a national university*, pp 29–32.
4 Magennis, op. cit.   5 London, 1958, p. 94.
6 Quoted in C.P. Curran. *The receding wave*, p. 101.
7 This third proposal was to be the one favoured by a majority of the Robertson Commission, 1903. The 'National University of Ireland' prefigured the name chosen in the 1908 University Act.
8 *Towards a national university*, p. 133.
9 Walsh–Logue, 2 March 1896. Armagh diocesan archives, Logue correspondence in Toner transcripts.
10 *Towards a national university*, pp 151–2.   11 Ibid., p. 216.
12 Delany–Redmond, 16 May 1908. Delany papers, IJA.
13 Redmond–Delany, 19 May, ibid.   14 Talbot–Delany, 20 July, ibid.
15 Birrell–Delany, 4 Aug. 1906, ibid.   16 *Towards a national university*, p. 166.
17 Ibid.   18 C.P. Curran, op. cit., p. 76.

7 THE EARLY YEARS OF CO-OPERATION

1 'Sir Horace Plunkett on Professor Finlay's career as social reformer' in *Page of Irish history*, p. 247.
2 Ibid. 3 Ibid., p. 248. 4 Ibid., p. 249.
5 Plunkett's diary, Plunkett Foundation Oxford, courtesy Ms Kate Targett.
6 *Page of Irish history*, p. 249. 7 Ibid., p. 250.
8 Patrick Bolger, *The Irish co-operative movement: its history and development*, p. 72.
9 Ibid., p. 74. 10 Ibid., p. 75. 11 Ibid., p. 70.
12 Ibid., pp 75–6. 13 Ibid., p. 75.
14 R.A. Anderson, *With Horace Plunkett in Ireland* (London, 1935), p. 71.
15 *Page of Irish history*, pp 250–1. 16 Anderson, op. cit. pp 69–70.
17 Ibid., and Plunkett in *Page of Irish history*, pp 251–2.
18 Plunkett, as n. 1, p. 251.
19 H.F. Norman papers, MS 8824 (3), NLI; also in *Year Book of Irish Agricultural Co-operative Society*, 1941.
20 *Page of Irish history*, p. 252. 21 Ibid., p. 253. 22 Anderson, pp 68–9.
23 Ferdinand Lassalle, leader of the German Social Democrats and a rival of Marx.
24 *Lyceum*, 15 March 1892, 'Co-operation in Ireland', pp 126–30.

8 THE RECESS COMMITTEE

1 Horace Plunkett, *The evolution of Ireland's agricultural policy: a retrospect and a prospect* (London 1925) p. 8, quoted in Trevor West, *Horace Plunkett* (Washington, 1986), p. 42.
2 Patrick Bolger, *Irish co-operative movement*, pp 77–9.
3 Plunkett's diary 4 Minute book of the Recess Committee, MS 4532, NLI.
5 Bolger, p. 80. 6 Minute book. 7 Ibid. 8 Bolger, p. 80.
9 *Report of the Recess Committee* on the establishment of a Department of Agriculture and Industries for Ireland (Dublin, 1896), quoted in Bolger, p. 81.
10 *Freeman's Journal*, 4 Aug. 1896, quoted in T. West, op.cit., p. 47.
11 Gill–Gladstone, 25 Aug. 1896, in T.P. Gill papers, Ms 13,509 (5), NLI.
12 Bolger, op. cit., pp 84–5. 13 Ibid., pp 85–6.
14 'Sir Horace Plunkett on Professor Finlay's career' in *Page of Irish history*, p. 254.
15 Liam Kennedy, 'The early response of the Irish Catholic clergy to the co-operative movement', *Irish Historical Studies* 21 (1977–8), p. 59.
16 Ibid., p. 68, fn. 40.
17 Ibid., p. 69, fn. 42, cit. in *Record of Maynooth Union*, 1897–8, p. 33.
18 Ibid., pp 61–2. 19 Ibid., p. 61.
20 'Father Thomas Finlay: an Irish co-operative pioneer', by H.F. Norman, in *Year Book of Agricultural Co-operation*, 1941, and reprinted in pamphlet form – see Horace Plunkett Papers, containing H.F. Norman papers, MS 8824(3), pp 5–6, NLI.
21 *Irish Homestead*, 4, no. 157.
22 'Ourselves' in *Irish Homestead*, 16 Nov. 1901, quoted in Nicholas Allen, *George Russell (Æ) and the New Ireland, 1905–30* (Dublin, 2003), p. 28.
23 H.F. Norman, op. cit., p. 4. 24 Trevor West, op. cit., p. 49.
25 *With Horace Plunkett in Ireland*, pp 149–50.
26 F.S.L. Lyons, *Ireland since the Famine*, pp 213–14, referring to R.B. McDowell, *The Irish administration, 1801–1914*, pp 224–9. 'The business of agriculture and technical education was taken seriously, and in time ten separate institutions were brought under its control, including the Royal College of Science, the Albert College (of agriculture) and the forestry

centre at Parnell's old home, Avondale; in addition, it maintained a staff of peripatetic lecturers (138 of them by 1914) giving itinerant instruction in agriculture, horticulture, poultry breeding, and butter manufacture. It was no less active in other directions – devising experimental schemes for the improvement of livestock and crops, making agricultural loans, encouraging afforestation, wrestling with problems of animal disease, stimulating fisheries, and collecting and publishing a vast amount of information on many different aspects of Irish economic life.'

27 E. Sheerin–Eoin MacNeill, 2 July 1906. MacNeill papers, MS 10,881, file on 'industry', NLI.
28 MacNeill papers, ibid., report of the 'Industrial Committee', NLI.   29 Ibid.

9 VICE-PRESIDENT OF IAOS

1 *Page of Irish history*, p. 253
2 Anderson, op. cit., pp 68–9. Already, in November 1897, the impact he made on the third annual general conference was such that his speech was reproduced as a pamphlet entitled *Co-operation and the saving of the Celt* (a reprint from *Irish Homestead*, 1898).
3 R.F. Foster, *Modern Ireland, 1600–1972* (London, 1988), p. 426.
4 IAOS, Reports of annual general meetings, 1901, pp 126–7
5 R.F. Foster, *W.B. Yeats: a life, 1865–1914* (Oxford, 1998), pp 311, 589 n. 33. But note that a report of Finlay severely criticising Yeats as 'dramatist, poet and orator', at a dinner at the end of December 1903, during the American tour, is to be found in *Collected letters of W.B. Yeats* (vol. 3, p. 537, n. 539, and vol. 2, 379, note). It is based on letters from John Quinn, Yeats's American agent, to Yeats and Æ, letters that, in turn, are based on an account given to Quinn by someone who was at the dinner. One wonders if an American listener (not for the first time) took literally what was really ironic wit on Finlay's part. Finlay may, or may not, have had little sympathy with Yeats's spiritualism and Celtic twilight, but it is very difficult to envisage the co-founder with Yeats of the National Literary Society of Ireland and a key supporter of his *Countess Cathleen* seriously dismissing Yeats as a dramatist, poet and orator, or, indeed, to take Æ seriously when he told Quinn that Finlay 'hated Yeats' for his 'mysticism'!   6 Bolger, op. cit., p. 96.
7 Ibid., pp 98–100, p. 99, n. 24.   8 Ibid., pp 103, 106.
9 J. Connolly, 'Labour and co-operation in Ireland' in *The reconquest of Ireland* (Dublin, 1972), p. 58.
10 *Irish Independent*, 1 Sept. 1913.   11 Bolger, p. 102.
12 IAOS, Report of vice–president's address, Appendix E, pp 53–61, AGM 1913.
13 Bolger, p. 106.   14 Ibid., p. 107.
15 IAOS, Report of 1914 AGM, Appendix E, pp 70–5.
16 Ibid., Report of 1915, pp 45–8.   17 Ibid., Report of 1916, pp 54–8.
18 T.M. Healy. *Letters and leaders*, vol. 2, p. 582.
19 Diary in Plunkett Foundation, Oxford, courtesy Ms Jillian Harris and Ms Kate Targett.
20 T.M. Healy–Maurice Healy, 2 June 1917, quoted in Healy, op. cit., pp 582, 599.
21 IAOS, Report for 1917, Appendix D, pp 52–3.
22 John A. Ryan, 'The democratic transformation of industry', *Studies* (Sept. 1920), p. 395.
23 Ibid., p. 393.   24 IAOS, Report for 1919, Appendix C, pp 30–2.
25 See T. M. Kettle's introduction to the English edition of Paul-Dubois', *Contemporary Ireland* (Dublin & New York, 1908).
26 Ibid., Report for 1921, pp 49–50.   27 Ibid., 1922, pp 45–50.
28 Quoted in Bolger, p. 147.

10 THE PRIEST AND PREACHER

1 *Anglo-Celt*, Sat. 13 Jan. 1940, commemoration after Finlay's death.
2 Ibid. 3 Ibid. 4 'Duties to our enemies', IJA, JP/28 (16).
5 *The Name of Jesus*, (Dublin, 1958 edition re-print), pp 1–23.
6 Ibid.
7 *The drunkard in Ireland*: an address by Rev. T.A. Finlay SJ (Dublin, 1907), p. 2.
8 Ibid., p. 13. 9 Ibid., p. 15. 10 Ibid., pp 16–17.
11 *Anglo-Celt*, 13 Jan. 1940. 12 Ibid.

11 A RANGE OF FRIENDS AND SERVICES

1 West, *Horace Plunkett*, pp 97–100.
2 *Seventy years young: memoirs of Elizabeth countess of Fingall*, pp 226–7.
3 Ibid., pp 227–8
4 The house in Merrion Square is still the headquarters of the IAOS, now re-styled the Irish Co-operative Organisation Society (ICOS).
5 Meenan, *George O'Brien*, pp 79–80.
6 'The jovial Jesuit' in *Fruits of a century: an illustrated centenary history, 1894–1994*, pp 18–19.
7 Finlay's pamphlet on Providence Woollen Mills, p. 7.
8 *Seventy years young*, p. 229. 9 Finlay's pamphlet, p. 21.
10 Ibid., p. 28, and see p. 23. 11 Ibid., p. 23.
12 *Seventy years young*, p. 228. 13 *Anglo-Celt*, 13 Jan. 1940.
14 *Province News*, pp 429–30. 15 Finlay's pamphlet, p. 25.
16 IAOS Annual Report, 1910, p. 45.
17 Aileen Heverin, *ICA: the Irish Countrywomen's Association, a history 1910–2000*, pp 23–5; and Bolger, op. cit., pp 104–5.
18 Plunkett–Monteagle, 16 March 1911, Monteagle papers, MS 13414, NLI. On the need to wait until the United Irishwomen were 'firmly established', see Monteagle–Plunkett, 20 March 1911, idem.
19 Plunkett–Monteagle, 21 March 1911. 20 Ibid., 29 March 1911.
21 IAOS Annual Report, 1898, quoted in Bolger, p. 301.
22 Bolger, p. 301. 23 IJA, J 9/5 (2).
24 Verbal information from Judge Tom Finlay, grand-nephew of Fr Tom.
25 IJA, J. 9/5 (1). 26 IJA, J. 9/8. 27 IJA, J. 9/11 (1).
28 IJA, Food Supply Society Ltd. J. 9/7 (2).
29 IJA, J. 9/25 (1). Hospitals Commission. Public Hospitals Act 1933. Letter of A.F. Cooney, secretary, to Finlay, 21 Dec. 1934, on provision of hospital care for children in Dublin. J 9/26 (1) contains a memorandum of the Irish Medical Guild of St Luke and SS Cosmas and Damien on the proposed reorganisation of the Irish hospitals.
30 J. Stafford Johnson–Finlay, 19 Jan. 1935, IJA, J. 9/3 (7)
31 Pamela Jones, 'The age of Caravaggio', *Studies* (spring 1997), pp 36–7. For an account of the re-discovery of the painting see Sergio Benedetti. *Caravaggio: the master revealed* (Dublin, National Gallery of Ireland, 1993). Also Brian Fallon, 'Controversial in his lifetime, Caravaggio remains so after his death', *Irish Times*, 16 April 1993; and Jonathan Harr, 'A hunch, an obsession, a Caravaggio', *New York Times Magazine*, 25 Dec. 1994.
32 *My story*, p. 138. 33 Ibid., p. 139. 34 Ibid., pp 141–2. 35 Ibid., p. 152.
36 Ibid., p. 161. 37 Ibid., pp 162–3. 38 Ibid., p. 160. 39 Ibid., p. 163.
40 *Anglo-Celt*, 13 Jan. 1940. The co-operative industry in the parish of Templecrone was a 'vigorous and successful knitting industry' under Patrick Gallagher as manager – see W.L. Micks, *History of the Congested Districts Board* (Dublin 1925), pp 82–3.

41 *Irish Jesuit Province News*, 1940, pp 429f.
42 Birrell–Finlay, 5 March 1915, IJA, J. 9/3 (5); and Birrell–Finlay, 21 Feb. 1915, J. 9/3 (4).
43 Plunkett–Finlay, 10 April 1928, Plunkett Foundation, Oxford, Finl.-4. Courtesy Ms Jillian Harris.
44 Finlay–Plunkett, 14 June 1928, idem, Finl.-5.
45 Plunkett–Finlay, 17 Jan. 1928, idem, Finl.-6.
46 Plunkett–Finlay, 10 Jan. 1932, idem. Italics in text.
47 *Page of Irish history*, p. 249.
48 Comment made on 2 March 1892. Healy–Sullivan papers, P 6/A/38. UCD Archives.
49 'Tim Healy' by Maev V. Sullivan in Healy–Sullivan Papers, UCD Archives, P 6/E/3, p. 20.
50 Ibid., p. 21.   51 Ibid., p. 208b.
52 Healy–Finlay, 19 Dec. 1930. IJA J 9/3 (6). 'M'onam thu'– an expression of affection, endearment in Irish, literally 'You are my soul'.
53 'Tim Healy' account by Maev V. Sullivan, P 6/E/3, pp 213–14.

12 THE FINAL DECADES

1 *Universe* correspondent, 2 Jan. 1931.   2 Ibid.
3 IPN, 1940, p. 428.   4 *Man of no property*, vol. 2, p. 41.
5 Horace Plunkett papaers, containing H.F. Norman papers, MS 8824 (3), NLI. The quotations used by Norman are attributed to Karl Walter's *Co-operation and Charles Gide*.
6 Although Keynes had published the *The economic consequences of the peace* in 1919, and during the 1920s and 1930s became a leading critic of the established economic theory, he did not achieve widespread attention until after the publication, in 1936, of *The general theory of employment, interest and money*.
7 *Irish Independent*, 20 Dec. 1930; *Universe*, 2 Jan. 1931.
8 Ibid.   9 Ibid.
10 Healy–Sullivan papers, Account of Tim Healy, p. 627, P 6/A/78, Archives at UCD.
11 Recollections of Tom and Bill Finlay, 2002.
12 Ibid.   13 IPN, p. 430.   14 Interview with Bill Finlay, 4 March 2002.
15 Ibid.   16 IPN, ibid.
17 Fr Gwynn's account is in IPN 1940, p. 426; other information from interviews with Tom and Bill Finlay.
18 IPN, ibid.   19 Quoted in West, *Horace Plunkett*, p. 24.
20 *Anglo-Celt*, 13 Jan. 1940. The four bishops were: Dr Lyons, bishop of Kilmore; Dr Sheehan, titular archbishop of Germia; Dr Mac Sherry, titular archbishop of Amaura; and Dr Wall, bishop of Thasos, who presided at the obsequies.
21 *Economic Journal* (March 1940), p. 159.   22 *Anglo-Celt*, 13 Jan. 1940.
23 In *Page of Irish history*, pp 246–7.
24 'Father Thomas A. Finlay SJ', *Studies* (March 1940), pp 28ff.
25 Owen Dudley Edwards, 'Belvedere in history' in J. Bowman & R. O'Donoghue (eds), *Portraits: Belvedere College, 1832–1982*, p. 15.
26 Bill Finlay, 3/3/2002.   27 Pamphlet, p. 1.
28 Bill Finlay, ibid.
29 H.F. Norman. 'Father Thomas Finlay: an Irish co-operative pioneer' in *Year Book of Agricultural Co-operation*, 1941, and in pamphlet form in Horace Plunkett papers, containing H.F. Norman's papers, MS 8824 (3), pp 5 and 8 in pamphlet.
30 Ibid., p. 9   31 Ibid., p. 10.

Sources

MANUSCRIPT SOURCES

Irish Jesuit Archives
    Thomas A. Finlay file
    William Delany papers
    Province Consultors' Minute Book, 1890 and 1896
Belvedere College Archives
    Copy of Finlay's letters to Jesuit Generals Beckx and Anterledy, courtesy Paul Andrews SJ
National Library of Ireland
    Bryce papers, MS 11,016
    T.P. Gill papers, MS 13,509
    John MacNeill papers, MS 10,881 ('Finlay Letters' and 'Industry')
    Monsell papers, MS 8318
    Monteagle papers, MS 13,414
    Horace Plunkett papers, including H.F. Norman's papers, MS 8824
    Minute Book of the Recess Committee, MS 4532.
Armagh Diocesan Archives
    Cardinal Logue correspondence in Tanner Transcripts.
Dublin Diocesan Archives
    Archbishop William Walsh papers.
University College Dublin Archives
    Healy–Sullivan papers.
Irish Cooperative Organisation Society
    Congress Reports.
Plunkett Foundation, Oxford
    Plunkett's diary and letters re. Finlay, courtesy Ms Jillian Harris and Ms Kate Targett

INTERVIEWS

With grand-nephews of Fr Finlay, namely, Tom and William Finlay

PRIMARY PUBLISHED SOURCES

Anderson, R.A., *With Horace Plunkett in Ireland* (London, 1935)
Curran, C.P., *Under the receding wave* (Dublin, 1970)
Finlay, T.A., *The chances of war* (Dublin, 1877)
—, address as vice-president of IAOS in the Annual Reports
—, pamphlets: *Foxford and the Providence Woollen Mills* (Dublin, 1932); *The name of Jesus* (Dublin, 1958 reprint); *The drunkard in Ireland* (Dublin, 1907)
—, List of his articles in R.J. Hayes (ed.) *Sources for the history of Irish civilization: articles in Irish periodicals*, vol. 2 (Boston, 19709), pp 310–12

Gallagher, Patrick, *My story by Paddy the Cope* (London, 1939)
Irish Jesuit Province News, 1940
Jesuit Fathers (eds), *A page of Irish history: the story of University College, Dublin, 1883–1909* (Dublin, 1930)
The Lyceum
The New Ireland Review
The Irish Homestead

NEWSPAPERS AND PERIODICALS

Anglo-Celt	*Irish Independent*	*New Ireland Review*
The Belvederian	*Irish Times*	*Studies*
Economic Journal	*The Lantern*	*The Universe*
Freeman's Journal	*The Leader*	*Year Book of Agricultural Co-Operation*
Irish Homestead	*Lyceum*	

SECONDARY SOURCES

Allen, Nicholas, *George Russell (Æ) and the New Ireland, 1905–30* (Dublin, 2003)
Andrews, C.S., *Man of no property*, vol. 2 (Dublin 1982)
Benedetti, Sergio, *Caravaggio, the master revealed* (Dublin, 1993)
Bolger, Patrick, *The Irish co-operative movement: its history and development* (Dublin, 1977)
Bourke, Marcus, *John O'Leary: a study in Irish separatism* (Tralee, 1967)
Bowman, J. & O'Donoghue, R., *Portraits: Belvedere College, 1832–1982* (Dublin, 1985)
Callanan, Frank, *T.M. Healy* (Cork, 1996)
Clyde, T., *Irish literary magazines* (Dublin, 2003)
Connolly, James, 'Labour and co-operation in Ireland' in *The reconquest of Ireland* (Dublin, 1972 ed.)
Digby, Margaret, *Horace Plunkett: an Anglo-American Irishman* (Oxford, 1949)
Dubois, P., *Contemporary Ireland* (Dublin and New York, 1908)
Edwards, Owen Dudley, 'Belvedere in history' in Bowman and O'Donoghue (eds), *Portraits*
& Ransom, B., 'Father Finlay SJ and Socialism' in *James Connolly's selected political writings* (London, 1973)
Fallon, Brian, 'Controversial in his lifetime. Caravaggio remains so after his death', *Irish Times*, 16 April 1993
Fingall, Elizabeth, *Seventy years young: memoirs of Elizabeth countess of Fingall* (Dublin, 1991 ed.)
Forster, R.F., *Modern Ireland, 1600–1972* (London, 1988)
—, *W.B. Yeats: a life, 1865–1914* (Oxford, 1998)
Gwynn, Aubrey, SJ, 'The Jesuits and University College' in M. Tierney (ed.), *Struggle with fortune*
—, obituary of Thomas A. Finlay in *Irish Province News*, 1940
Harr, Jonathan, 'A hunch, an obsession, a caravaggio' in *New York Times Magazine*, 25 Dec. 1994
Healy, T.M., *Letters and leaders of my day*, 2 vols (London, 1928)
Heverin, Aileen, *ICA: the Irish Countrywomen's Association, a history, 1910–2000* (Dublin, 2000)
Jones, Pamella, 'The age of Caravaggio' in *Studies* (spring 1997)
Kennedy, Liam, 'The early response of the Irish Catholic clergy to the co-operative movement' in *Irish Historical Studies*, 21 (1977–8)

Kettle, T.M., Introduction to P. Dubois, *Contemporary Ireland*
Lyons, F.S.L., *Ireland since the Famine* (Glasgow, 1973 ed.)
MacMahon, J.A., 'Catholic clergy and the social question, 1891–1916' in *Studies* (winter 1981)
Magennis, William, 'A disciple's sketch of Father T. Finlay' in *Belvederian*, 9 (summer 1931)
Meenan, James, *George O'Brien* (Dublin, 1980)
— (ed.), *A centenary history of the Literary and Historical Society of University College Dublin, 1855–1955* (Tralee, 1954)
Micks, W.L., *History of the Congested Districts Board* (Dublin, 1925)
Moore, George, *Hail and farewell* (Gerrads Cross, Bucks, 1965).
Morrissey, Thomas J., *Towards a national university: William Delany SJ, 1835–1924* (Dublin, 1983)
—, *William J. Walsh, archbishop of Dublin, 1841–1921* (Dublin, 2000)
— (ed. and introduction), *The social teaching of James Connolly* by Lambert McKenna SJ (Dublin, 1991)
Nolan, W., Ronayne, G. and Dunleavy, M., *Donegal: history & society* (Dublin, 1995)
Norman, H.F., 'Father Thomas Finlay: an Irish co-operative pioneer' in *Year Book of Agricultural Co-operation*, 1941
O'Donnell, Peadar, *The gates flew open* (London, 1932)
Packe, M., *John Stuart Mill* (London, 1954)
Plunkett, Horace, 'Sir Horace Plunkett on Professor Finlay's career as social reformer' in Jesuit Fathers, *A page of Irish history*, pp 246ff
Tierney, M., *Struggle with fortune: a centenary miscellany for Catholic University of Ireland, 1854, University, College Dublin 1954* (Dublin, 1954)
West, Trevor, *Horace Plunkett: co-operation and politics* (Washington, 1986)

Index

Aberdeen, Lady, 134
Aherlow, Glen of, 79
Alexander, Major John, 80
Allingham, William, 52
Anderledy, Anton, superior general of Jesuits, 45
Anderson, R.A., 78, 80, 82, 94, 96, 99, 119, 128, 134, 136, 142
Andrews, C.S (Todd), 145
Andrews, Rev. Paul, 10
Andrews, Thomas, 88, 90
Anglo-Celt, newspaper, Cavan, 13, 146
Anglo-Irish Treaty, 118
Anti-Treating League, 125-7
Anti-Treaty forces, 146
Ardagh, Co. Limerick, 80
Armstrong, K., 10
Arnold, Mathew, 26, 34, 52
Arnold, Thomas, 26, 34
Arnott, Lady, 134
Arnott, Sir John, 88, 90
Ashbourne, Lord, 91
Austria, 88, 90

Baconian theory (re works of Shakespeare), 34
Bagehot, Walter, 27
Balfour, Arthur, 52
Balfour, Gerald W., 89-91, 128
Balzac, Honoré de, 39
Barbour, Harold, 119, 137
Barry, Rev. Dr William, 28, 34, 36, 56
Bavaria, 88
Beckx, Rev. Pieter, superior general of the Jesuits, 18, 22
Belfast, 80
Belgium, 88, 100, 101
Belvedere College, 18-21, 147
Bernard Morrogh, Sr Agnes (Foxford), 129-31, 133
Birrell, Augustine, MP, chief secretary of Ireland, 60-1, 140

Blackrock College, 46,
Board of Intermediate Education, 147
Boers, Boer War, 56
Boyne, battle of the, 80
Bosnia and Turkish rule, 23
Browne, Rev. Thomas, Jesuit provincial, 21, 46
Browne & Nolan, publishers, 22
Bryant, Mrs Sophie, 60
Byrne, James, 80

Cambridge University, 28
Campbell, Rev. Edward Fitzharding (chaplain to Orange Order), 130, 137
Caravaggio (Michelangelo da Marisi), 9, 136, 150
Carroll (O'Carroll), Rev. John, 26, 43, 46
Carnegie Library, 42
Carrick-on-Shannon, 149
Casement, Sir Roger, 128
Casey, Dr, mathematician, 26
Castletownroche, Co. Cork, 80, 139
Catholic Ireland, 51
Catholic University, 18, 24, 55, 58
Cavan, town of, 13, 146
Celbridge, Co. Kildare, 80
Celtic Ireland, 51
Central Savings Committee, 145
Chesterton, G.K., 128
Chinese workers, USA, 49
Clarke, Rev. Gerard, 10
Clery, Arthur, 32, 42, 51, 61
Cloncurry, Lord, 79
Coblenz, 93
Collins, Michael, 128
Coiste Gnotha, 97
Congested Districts Board, 131
Conmy, John, bp. of Kildare, 123
Connolly, James, 9, 53-4, 57, 108-10
Coolgreaney, Co. Wexford, 134
Corcoran, Rev. Timothy, professor, 143
Cosgrave, William, TD, 151

Countess Cathleen, 34, 36, 56–7
Cox, Arthur, 32
Coyne, Rev. Edward, president IAOS, 150
Coyne, W.P., 26, 34, 43, 45, 51–2, 61, 150
Craigavon, Lord, 119
Co-op agency, case for, 85–6
Crescent College, Limerick, 15
Cullen, Rev. James, 21
Curran, C.P, 26–7, 43–4, 61
Curtis, Rev. Robert, 43

Dane, Richard, MP, 88
Danish co-op movement, 87
Dante, 124
Darlington, Rev. Joseph, professor, 26, 34
Davitt, Michael, 49, 91
Dawson, Charles, 32
Dawson, William, 27, 31–2, 42
Dease, Col. Gerald R, 80
Delany, Rev. Dr William, president of UCD, 18, 24–5, 27–9, 31, 56–7, 59–61
Denmark, 88, 100
Dept Agriculture (& Technical Instruction), 55, 86, 91, 97–8, 103, 105, 151
de Valera, Eamon, TD, 151
de Vere, Aubrey, 34
Digby, Margaret, 95
Dillon, John, MP, 32, 55, 57, 90, 91, 107, 128
Dillon, Kathleen, 17
Dion Bouton, motor car, 128
Dixon, Sir Daniel, 90
Dominican College, Eccles St., Dublin, 29
Doneraile, 80, 83
Donovan, Robert, 43, 45, 61
Doochary, Co. Donegal, 139
Dostoievsky, 44
Dowden, Edward, 52
Dublin Castle, 139
Dublin Food Supply Society, 135
Dublin, slums in, 77
Dublin University (TCD), 28
Dufferin, Lord, 58
Duffy, Charles Gavan, 52
Duke, H.E., chief secretary, 115
Dumas, the younger, 34
Dungloe, Co. Donegal, 133, 137–8, 140, 148.

Economic Journal, 151
Education Endowments Bill, 25,
Emly, Lord (William Monsell), 25
English Co-op. Wholesale Society, 101
Erne river, navigation works, 13
Esmonde, Sir Thomas, 133, 137, 148
Eucharistic Congress (1932), 141
Ewart, Sir William, 90.

Falkiner, C. Litton, 80, 89
Fallons, publishers, 22
Fenians, 32
Fenian tradition, 6
Fermanagh, co-op possibilities, 104
Ferguson, Samuel, poet, 52
Ferry, Jules, French government minister, 17
Field, William, MP, 88
Fingal, countess of: *see* Plunkett, Elizabeth.
Finlay, Annie, sister of Fr. Tom, 13, 14
Finlay, Eileen, niece of, 13
Finlay, John, brother of, 13
Finlay, Margaret, sister of, 13, 14
Finlay, Maria (née Magan) mother of, 13, 14
Finlay, Mary, sister of, 13
Finlay, Rev. Peter, brother of, 13, 14, 19, 28, 37–8, 44–5, 55
Finlay, Rev. Thomas Aloysius: summary, 9–10; birth & family, 13–15; early education, 14; early years in Jesuits, 15–16; novel *The Chances of War*, 16–17; other early writing and ordination, 17; professor of philosophy, 19; rector of Belvedere College, achievements and criticism, 19–22; 'deplorable blunder' as professor of philosophy, 24–5; experiencing 'vigilant hostility', 25; prefect of studies, 26; defends scholastic philosophy, 27; influence on students, 27; as preacher and person, 28; work for women students, 28–30; the professor, 30; revives the L & H society, 30–3; and literature, 34–42: George Moore, 35–41, D.P. Moran, 41–2, wit and humour, 34–5; *Lyceum*, 43–51; subjects and problems, banned from writing, 44–5, on Freemasons, 47–8, the Jews in Ireland, 48–51; *New Ireland Review*, 51–4, topics considered 51–3, views on

INDEX

socialism, response of James Connolly, 53–4; socio-political ambience, 55–62: Irish Ireland movement, 55–7, university question and suspicions of the archbishop and of politicians, 57–62. Irish Co-operative Movement. Early years, 77–86: friendship with Plunkett, 77–8; gift of humour and of 'popular exposition of the co-operative idea', 80–1; 'unrivalled knowledge of human nature', 82. Role in Recess Committee, 87–98: guides the propagandist work, 91–2; influence with the clergy, 93; Raiffeisen model, 93–4; *Irish Homestead*, 94–5. Speeches as vice-president, 99–119: their quality and impact, 99–104; on 'Co-operative Commonwealth', 108–110; war years, 112–17, importance of organisation and preparation for post-war years, opposes National Convention, 113–15; acting chairman, 116; his faith in the co-op movement as the way forward in the post-war world, 116–17; troubled years (1919–22), 117–19. Priest and preacher, 123–7; friends and services, 128–44: friends, including Rev. Campbell of Orange Order, George O'Brien etc, resourceful, 'Mr Fixit', influence in government Commission on National Education, in various royal commissions, trustee of National Library, involvement in the Foxford mills, 128–33; work with United Irishwomen (later ICA), 133f, Women's National Health Association, 134, Dublin Food Supply Society, 135; Mrs Lea Wilson and gift of a Caravaggio, 136; Paddy the Cope story, 137–40; letters of Birrell and Horace Plunkett, 140f; friendship with T.M Healy, 142–4. Final Decades: criticism by Todd Andrews, 145–6; recognition and honours, 146–8; shooting and fishing, 148–9; last years, 150–2; tributes and assessment, 151–3.
Finlay, Thomas A, nephew, 13
Finlay, Thomas, A, grand-nephew, chief justice, 10, 148–50
Finlay, William, parent of Fr Tom, 13
Finlay, William, brother of Fr Tom, chairman of Cavan Co Council, 13,15

Finlay, William, grand-nephew, 10, 148–50
Field, William, MP, 88
Fintown, 139
Fitzgibbon, Lord Justice, 25
Flanders, 116
Foley, Patrick, bp. of Kildare & Leighlin, 28
Foster, Roy, professor, 106
Foynes, Co. Limerick, 78
Foxford mills, Co. Mayo, 129–33, 148
Foxrock station, 128
France, 78, 83, 88, 100
Freeman's Journal, 37, 58–9, 90, 95–6
Freemasons, 48

Gaelic Athletic Association, 55
Gaelic League, 36, 55–6, 97, 134
Gallagher, Patrick (the Cope), 127, 134, 137–9, 140
Gannon, Rev. Patrick, 150
Gardiner, Dr and Mrs, 140
Garibaldi, invasion of Rome, 15
George, Henry, 44
George, Lloyd, 114–15
German Catholic Party, 49
German agricultural industry, 78, 83, 94, 100, 101
Ghent, 82
Gibbons, James Cardinal, 44
Gide, Charles, economist, 145–6
Gills, of Dublin, publishers, 23
Gill, T.P, 41, 88–91, 97
Gladstone, William Ewart, 90
Glasnevin cemetery, 144
Gogol, Russian writer, 44
Goldsmith, Oliver, 34, 52
Gonne, Maud, 9, 34
Gore Booth, Eva, 52
Gormanstown Castle, 148
Gregorian University, Rome, 15
Griffith, Arthur, 56, 97
Gweedore, Co Donegal, 23
Gwynn, Rev. Aubrey, professor, 27, 140, 150

Hackett, Felix, professor, 32–3, 61
Haeckel's philosophy, 52
Hague, Vasey, 51–2
Hail and Farewell (George Moore), 35ff
Hamlet, 34

Harp (1908), 54
Harrington, T.C., MP, 88
Harris, Ms Jillian, 10
Hazelton, R., 97
Healy, T.M., MP, 55, 57, 107, 140, 142–4, 149
Healy, Mrs Erina (née Sullivan), 143
Healy, Erina (Sr Bernard), daughter, 143–4
Healy, Elizabeth, daughter, 143, 150
Healy, Joseph, son, 143
Healy, Maev, daughter, 143, 149,
Healy, Maurice, brother, 31
Healy, Paul, son, 143–4
Healy, Timothy, son, 143
Hogan, P.T., 51
Hogan, Rev. Edmund, professor, 26
Holland, dairy industry, 88, 110
Home improvement scheme, 134
Home Rule, 42, 56, 87–8, 115
Home Rule Party (Irish Party), 41, 54, 55–7, 60, 61
Homestead Law, North America, 23
Honthorst, Dutch artist, 136, 150
Hopkins, Gerard Manley, 32
Hungary, 88
Hyde, Dr Douglas, 22, 34, 41, 55, 97, 134

Ignatius Loyola, 125
Inchiquin, Lord, 16
Irish College, Rome, 96
Irish Co-op Agency, 79
Irish Co-operative Agricultural Organisation Society (IAOS), 9, 10, 43, 54, 62, 79, 90, 97–9, 103–9 (and emigration 104), 110–15, 117–19, 133, 141, 150
Irish Ecclesiastical Record, 22, 25
Irish Free State, 118, 145
Irish Homestead, 9, 43, 94–97, 100, 137
Irish Industries League, 134
Irish Messenger (Messenger of the Sacred Heart), 9, 21
Irish Monthly, 9, 15, 17, 22, 34
Irish Parliamentary Party (*see* Home Rule Party)
Irish Sisters of Charity, 129–30, 150
Irregular forces, 140,
Italy, 93, 100

Jesuit community, Leeson St, Dublin, 136, 149, 150

Jews in Ireland, 48–50
Johnson, Dr J. Stafford, 136
Joyce, James, 26, 32
Joyce, Stanislaus, 57

Kane, Rev. R.P., grand master, 90
Kennedy, Charles, 131
Kennedy, Hugh, 32, 61
Kenny, Rev. Timothy, Jesuit provincial, 45
Kettle, T.M., 29, 31–2, 34, 51, 60, 61.
Keynes, John M, 145–6, 151
Kieffer, Rev., 26
Kiernan family, 149
Kilkee, Co Clare, 134
Killeen Castle, Dunsany, Co Meath, 141
Kilmore, Co. Cavan, hedge-school, 14
Kilmore, diocese of, 14
Kilteragh (Plunkett's house), 35, 128
King Harmon estate (Rockingham), 148
Klein, Marshal, Napoleon's general, 26
Klein, Rev. Martial L., 26

Lanesborough, Co. Roscommon, 13, 15
Lanigan, Rev. Stephen M, 17
Lassalle, Ferdinand, 82
La Touche, Christopher Digges, 80, 127, 136
Lawless, Emily, 133
Leader, 41, 56
Lecky, W.E.H., professor, 151
Leech, H Brougham, professor, 88–9
Lee, Sir Thomas, 88, 90,
Leighlinbridge, Co Carlow, 125
Leo XIII, pope, 47
Lett, Mrs Harold, 133
Liberals (party) 57
Limerick, dairy industry, 78–9, 83, 85
literary institute, 17
siege of, 16
Linden convalescent home, 150
Little, Frank, 51
Little, Patrick, 31, Minister of Post and Telegraphs, 151
Logue, Cardinal Michael, 41, 56, 58, 92
Londonderry, Lord, 128
London University, 18, 28
Loreto convent, Dalkey, 88
Lough Rea, 13
Lowell, Laurence (Harvard), 128

INDEX

Lyceum, 9, 21–2, 27, 34, 42–3, 45–7, 50, 51, 55–8, 61, 82, 94,
  Club, 20

McCarthy, Charles (Wisconson Univ.), 128
McCarthy, Justin, MP, 88
McCoy, R.F., 88
McDonald, Rev. Walter, Maynooth, 25
McGilligan, Michael, 31
McGlynn, Malachy, 10
McHrath, Rev., Clonliffe College, 25
McGreevy, Thomas, 35
MacNeill, Eoin, 22, 51, 97
MacNeill, Hugh, 22,
MacNeill, James, governor general, 147
MacNeill, Mrs James, 147
Magan, Maria, mother of Fr Tom, 13, 14
Magan family of Kilashee and Lanesborough, 148–9
Magennis, William, of UCD, 26–7, 32, 34, 43, 45–6, 51–2, 57–9, 61, 136, 146–7
Mahaffy, John P., TCD, 32
Mallac, Père, 26
Mangan, Timothy, 31
Mangan James Clarence, 52
Manning, Cardinal Henry Edward, 47
Maria-Laach, German house of studies, 15
Martin, Rev. Luis, Jesuit superior general, 59
Maynooth College, 41, 53, 149
Maynooth College Union, 53
Marx, Karl, 54, 82
Mayo, Lady, 129, 134
Mayo, Lord, 88, 90
Meredith, George, 34
Meredith, James, 51–2
Mill, John Stuart, 53
Milner, Lord, 128
Miltown Park, Jesuit house of studies, 20
Messenger of the Sacred Heart see *Irish Messenger*
Molloy, Monsignor Dr Gerard, 25, 32, 88, 90
Moloney, Frances Lady, 135
Monaghan, co-op possibilities, 104
Monteagle T., Lord (Spring Rice), 78–9, 88, 90, 106, 134
Montgomery, J K, 95
Moore, Count Arthur (Moorefield, Co. Tipp.), 79, 88, 91

Moore, George, 34–6, 38, 41, 45, 52, 127, 151, 153
Moran, D.P., 41, 52, 54, 56, 97
Mulhall, Marian, 52
Mulhall, Michael, 88
Mullingar, 129
Murnaghan, James, 33
Murphy, Rev. Alfred, 45
Murphy, Rev. Denis, 26, 43
Murphy, William Martin, 115
Musgrave, Sir James (Jamie), Belfast, 80, 88, 90

Napoleon, 124
National Convention, 114–15
National Farmers Union, 141
National Gallery of Ireland, 150
National Library of Ireland, 140, 145
National Literary Society of Ireland, 9, 34, 152
National University of Ireland, 58, 151,
Nationist, 60, 61
Newcastlewest, Co Limerick, 79
New Ireland Review, 9, 22, 27, 34, 42–3, 45–6, 50–3, 55, 57–9
Newman, Cardinal John Henry, 17, 18, 24, 55, 59, 147
Neville, Monsignor Henry, 18
Norman, H.F., 81, 93, 95, 136, 141, 152
North of Ireland administration, 118

O'Brien, Dermod, 135
O'Brien, Edward William, 79
O'Brien, Francis Cruise, 31, 42, 145
O'Brien, George, 28, 30, 31, 35, 51, 53, 129, 130, 136, 146, 151–2
O'Brien, Mrs, 135
O'Brien, William, MP, 149
O'Carroll, Rev. John J., see Carroll
O'Conor Don, 88, 90, 148
O'Connor, T.P., MP, 149
O'Donnell, Patrick, bp. of Raphoe, 78–9, 92
O'Donnell, Peadar, 138
O'Donoghue, Rev. Fergus, 10
O'Donoghue, Taidgh, 40
O'Dwyer, Edward Thomas, bp. of Limerick, 17, 78, 92, 96
O'Gorman, Mrs, 43
O'Hanlon family, 132

O'Hanlon, Edward, 146
O'Hanlon, John F., 146
O'Hanlon, Margaret, wife of William Finlay, 13
O'Hartegan, Rev. Mathew, 16
O' Higgins, Kevin, TD, 35, 143, 149
O'Leary, John, 'old Fenian', 9, 32, 34, 127
O'Neill, Eoin Rua, 16, 17
O'Neill, Rev. George, professor, 34,
O'Neill, Hugh Dubh, 16
O'Neill, Moira, 52
Oranmore, Co. Galway, 79
O'Riordan, Monsignor Michael, 96
Ormond, duke of, 16
Our Christian Heritage, 44–5
Oxford, Plunkett House, 10
Oxford University, 28

Parnell, Charles Stuart, 44, 55
Parnell, John, MP, 88
Parnellites, 55, 81
Pascal, Blaise, 34
Pater, Walter, 34
Pearse, Padraic, 29, 32, 60
Pilkington, Mrs Ellice, 133–4
Plan of Campaign, 14
Plunkett, Elizabeth (Daisy), countess of Fingal, 128–9, 132, 134, 150
Plunkett, Horace, 9, 16, 35, 52–3, 55, 57, and Irish Co-op Movement: 77–9, 80, 81, 83, 87–9, 90–3, 95–7, 99, 103, 106–8, 112, 114, 116, 117, 119, 128–9, 131, 133–4, 136–8, 140–1, 142, 148–9.
Plunkett House, Merrion Sq. Dublin, 129, 133
Polin, Abbé, 29
Pombal, Marquis de, 17
Pope, Alexander, 91
Preston, General Thomas, 16
Providence Mills, Foxford, 132, *see* Foxford mills
Prussia, 93
Prussian government's agricultural policy, 15

Queen's University Colleges, 18, 24
Queen's University, 27
Quigley, Patricia, 10
Quinn, John (USA), 106

Raiffeison, co-op credit societies, 15, 93–4
Recess Committee, 86, 88–91, 94, 96
Report, 89–91, 96
Reddington, Christopher Talbot, 79
Redmond, John, MP, 32, 57, 60, 61, 80, 115, 128
Reichstag, anti-semitic party, 49
Religious Songs of Connacht, 51–2
Renaissance man, 9, 152
Rerum Novarum, papal encyclical, 47
Review of Reviews, 50
Ricardo, David, 23
Rinuccini, Giovanni B., papal nuncio, 16
Robinson, Lennox, 35
Roche, Rev. George R., 135
Ronan, Rev. William, Mungret College, 19
Ross, Mr Justice, 88, 90
Rossetti, Christina, 96
Royal Dublin Society, 96
Royal Industries Association, 134
Royal Irish Academy, 151
Royal University of Ireland, 18, 24–5, 28, 46, 57–9, 60, 90, 145, 147
Russell, George W. (AE), 32, 36, 40, 52, 97, 106, 128, 133
Russell, Rev. Mathew, 15
Russell, Thomas Wallace, 107
Ryan, Rev. John, professor (Cath. Univ. America), 116

St Acheul, near Amiens, 15
Sacred Heart Sisters, congregation of, 13, 14
St. Augustine College, Cavan, 14
St Beuno's, Jesuit theologate, Wales, 16, 17
St Mary's University College, 30
St Patrick's College, Cavan, 14
St Stanislaus College, Tullabeg, 18
Sarajewo, 23
Scandinavian dairies, 85
Scotland, Finlay Presbyterian grandparents in, 13, 14
Sexton, Thomas, MP, 80, 88, 149
Shannon, river, 13, 16
Shaw, G.B., 35, 128
Sheehy, David, 10
Sheehan, Canon, 52
Sheerin, Eugene, 97
Sinclair, Thomas, 88, 90

Skeffington, Francis Sheehy, 32
Smith, Adam, 52
Smith, J.C. (Caledon Woollen Mills), 131, 134
Socrates, 124
Sources for the history of Irish civilisation, 23
Spiritual Exercises of St Ignatius Loyola, 37–8
Spring Rice, Thomas, *see* Monteagle, Lord
Stanwell, Charles, 52
Stead, W.H., 50
Stoeckl, Albert, 15, 26
Studies, 9, 27, 143
Sullivan, John Marcus, 33, 61
Sutton, William, 34
Sweetman, John, 97
Swift, Jonathan, 52
Switzerland, 88, 93
Synge, John Millington, 34, 41.

Tablet, 25
Talbot, Edmund, MP, 61
Targett, Kate, 10
Templecrone Co-operative, 134, 140
Temple Street, college in, 18
Tennyson, Alfred Lord, 34
Tisdale, Mr, 106
Tisserand, Monsignor E., 76
Todi, Jacopone da, 34
Tuite, Rev. James, Jesuit provincial, 18
Turgenev, 44
Turkish rule, 23
Tyrell, John T., 10
Tyrone, co-op development, 104

Ulster agricultural organisation, 119
Unionist electors, 97
United Irishmen, 56
United Irishwomen (later ICA), 133–4, 139
University College Dublin, 9, 15, 18, 19, 22, 24–5, 28–9, 39, 42, 46, 52, 55–7, 59, 61–2, 119, 143, 146–7, 149, 150, 151
University Hall, 151
Universe, 146, 148

Vatican Council, First, 15
Voltaire, 41

Walsh, William, abp of Dublin, 25, 30, 41, 46, 54, 56–8, 60
Wealth of Nations, 52
Wells, H.G., 128
Whelan, Leo, RHA, 146
Whitelock, A. (pseudonym for Finlay), 16
Whitman, Walt, 34
Wibberley, Thomas, 128
Wicklow & Wexford railway line, 20
Wilson, Mrs Dr Lea, 136
Wilson, Mrs Marie P., 135–6
Woodehouse, P.G., 149
Women's National Health Association, 134
Woodlock, Bartholomew, bp of Ardagh and Clonmacnoise, 25
Woods, Rev. Brendan, 10
Wurtemberg, 88

Yeats, W.B., 9, 34–5, 52, 10